Booth Who?

A biography of Booth Gardner

Washington's charismatic 19th governor

by John C. Hughes

THE WASHINGTON STATE
HERITAGE CENTER

LEGACY PROJECT

First Edition
Copyright © 2010
Washington State Legacy Project
Office of the Secretary of State
All rights reserved.
ISBN 978-1-889320-21-2

Front cover photo Washington State Archives
Book Design by Kathryn E. Campbell

Printed in the United States of America
by Gorham Printing, Centralia, Washington

"Booth Who?" is one in a series of biographies and oral histories published by the Washington State Legacy Project. Other Washington history-makers profiled by the project include Congresswoman Jennifer Dunn; former first lady Nancy Evans; astronaut Bonnie J. Dunbar; Bremerton civil rights activist Lillian Walker; former Chief Justice Robert F. Utter; former Justice Charles Z. Smith; trailblazing political reporter Adele Ferguson; Federal Judge Carolyn Dimmick and Nirvana co-founder Krist Novoselic. For further information, go to The Legacy Project Web site: http://www.sos.wa.gov/legacyproject/

Washington
Secretary of State
SAM REED

For my grandchildren and Booth's

CONTENTS

Who's who
(In order of appearance)

Robert Moore, Governor Booth Gardner's great-great-great grandfather. He arrived in the Oregon Country from Illinois in 1840 and played a key role in its emergence as a territory.

Manville S. Booth, the governor's great-grandfather. He was elected King County auditor in 1874.

Laurence S. Booth, the governor's grandfather. He helped save the King County Courthouse in the great Seattle fire of 1889 and became president of the Washington Title Insurance Co.

Evelyn Booth Gardner Clapp, the governor's mother; a former model, she became a noted socialite in Tacoma and Seattle.

Bryson Ross "Brick" Gardner, the governor's father; sales manager for the Tacoma Cadillac dealer.

William Booth Gardner, born August 21, 1936; Washington's 19th governor.

Gail Gardner, the governor's sister. (Gardner's daughter is named in her honor.)

Norton Clapp, president of the Weyerhaeuser Company and the governor's powerful stepfather.

Mildred "Millie" Blethen Gardner, the governor's stepmother.

Joan Blethen, the governor's stepsister. They bonded in a household punctuated by dysfunction.

Isaac Thomas, the African American man who befriended young Booth Gardner and coached the neighborhood football team.

Stephen Merrill, the childhood friend who accompanied Booth and his mother on a fateful ski trip in 1951.

Laird Harris, Booth's policy adviser when he was governor and good friend.

Lou Booth, the governor's beloved aunt, with whom he lived while attending the University of Washington.

Emory Bundy, student body president at the UW (1957-58) when Booth was first vice president.

Katie Dolan, a tireless activist for the disabled whom Booth first met on the playfields of Seattle's Central Area.

O.L. Mitchell, a Seattle Central Area volunteer who inspired Booth.

Al Rosellini, 15th governor of the State of Washington (1957-1965). He had a summer home near the Gardner family getaway on Vashon Island.

Jean Forstrom Gardner, Booth's first wife and mother to Doug and Gail Gardner.

Larry Faulk, the Republican state senator Booth defeated in 1970 in a race for the Legislature, then again in 1981 for Pierce County executive.

Greg Barlow, Booth's swashbuckling chief of staff when he became Pierce County executive. Also a friend of Faulk.

Henry M. "Scoop" Jackson, Washington's legendary U.S. senator, who campaigned for Booth.

Jim McDermott, a state senator from Seattle and future congressman; Booth's rival for the 1984 Democratic nomination for governor.

John Spellman, Washington's 18th governor (1981-1985), who lost to Gardner in 1984 after a hard-luck term.

Adele Ferguson, the feisty capitol correspondent for *The Bremerton Sun*. Her 1982 column introduced Booth to the rest of the state.

Ron Dotzauer, Booth's freewheeling 1984 campaign manager.

Steve Excell, Spellman's 1984 campaign manager, fighting an uphill battle.

Richard W. Larsen, *The Seattle Times* political writer who dubbed Booth "Prince Faintheart."

Pete Taggares, the potato-grower who bankrolled Booth's 1984 campaign in the early going.

Denny Heck, a hard-charging state representative from Vancouver. An early supporter of Gardner, he was the governor's second-term chief of staff.

Jim Kneeland, Gardner's first press secretary and a genius at staging photo-ops.

Dean Foster, Gardner's first chief of staff and key legislative liaison.

Orin Smith, Gardner's first director of the Office of Financial Management and a future CEO of Starbucks.

Rosalie Gittings, Booth's indispensable personal assistant when he was governor.

Mary Faulk, who headed three major agencies for Gardner. After her divorce from Larry Faulk, Booth's old rival, she married Chase Riveland, Booth's director of corrections.

A.N. "Bud" Shinpoch, a hard-nosed liberal legislator who became director of the Department of Revenue, then attempted to "de-layer" the Department of Social & Health Services.

Richard A. Davis, whom Booth named director of Labor & Industries.

Joe Dear, Davis' whiz kid assistant, later the agency's director.

Isiah Turner, named to head the Department of Employment Security. The Gardner administration's leading African American, Turner departed in a scandal.

Dan Grimm, the bright young chairman of the House Ways & Means Committee.

Dixy Lee Ray, Washington's controversial 17th governor. (1977-1981)

Amos Reed, Riveland's predecessor as head of Corrections. Gardner pushed him out.

Dan McDonald, the affable but tenacious Republican floor leader in the State Senate.

Dick Thompson, who first headed the Department of Community Development; later Gardner's governmental operations director.

Norm Maleng, the highly regarded King County Prosecutor who sought the GOP nomination for governor in 1988.

Bob Williams, the "gadfly" Republican legislator from Longview who defeated Maleng, only to be crushed by Gardner.

Chris Gregoire, the future two-term governor Gardner named director of the Department of Ecology.

Mike Murphy, a Grays Harbor County commissioner who was one of Gardner's earliest supporters. Booth urged him to apply for the job of Wildlife director.

Curt Smitch, the Gardner staffer who got the job Murphy wanted.

Charles Z. Smith, Gardner's first Washington Supreme Court appointee. The widely respected former prosecutor, judge and law professor was the court's first ethnic minority.

Joe King, the lanky speaker of the House. He liked Booth but questioned his political moxie.

Ralph Munro, Washington's ebullient secretary of state and co-chairman of the 1989 Centennial with First Lady Jean Gardner.

Cynthia Robin Perkins, the young woman Booth met in Geneva and fell in love with. They married in 2001 after his divorce from Jean, and divorced in 2008.

Dan Evans, the three-term Republican governor who teamed up with Gardner to promote a funding plan to boost higher education.

Dr. Tom Preston, an "aid-in-dying" activist who was a stalwart of the Death with Dignity campaign.

Daniel Bergner, the writer whose 2007 profile of Gardner in *The New York Times Magazine* created a stir.

Doug Gardner, the governor's born-again Christian son.

Gail Gardner, the governor's daughter; now his personal assistant.

Arline Hinckley, the social worker who was one of Death with Dignity's leading voices.

Duane French, the initiative's most eloquent foe.

Chris Carlson, the poster-child for the opponents. He was still alive and well some five years after he was told he had only six months.

BOOTH WHO?

If you go to see Booth Gardner, never arrive empty handed. You stop first at Frisko Freeze, a classic 1950's drive-in just a few blocks from his condo in Tacoma. Order him a Doubleburger—"no cheese, lots of mustard"—and a medium Coke; $5.25 worth of gourmet fast food. If it's a drizzly day, noontime customers huddle under the eaves as they wait, savoring the aromas wafting from inside: Patties sizzling on an old short-order grill; french fries burbling in their baskets; mustard and relish being slathered on buns. One day in the winter of 2009, a writer on an important errand encountered a burly young man in a Seattle Mariners jacket. They struck up a conversation about baseball and burgers:

"You know who really likes Frisko Freeze?" the young man said.

"No. Who?"

"The governor."

"Chris Gregoire?"

"No! *Booth Gardner.*"

It's been a long time since he was Washington's governor, but everyone still knows his name. In 1983, however, when he decided to challenge a sitting governor, he was little known outside Pierce County where he grew up. His brain trust put "Booth Who?" on a button and it became the catchiest campaign slogan in state history. He was handily elected

```
      FRISKO  FREEZE
       1201 DIVISION ST
         TACOMA, WA.
        (253)272-4800
DATE      12/22/2009
 1  D BURGER T1               TUE
 1  M COKE T1              $3.30
    TAX1 AMT               $1.50
    TOTAL                  $0.45
    CASH                   $5.25
        * E 0123 *         $5.25
NO.101223 REG 01 R.J.
                       TIME 12:00
```

twice and could have had a third term—maybe more—or a seat in the U.S. Senate. In terms of sheer popularity, his only rival to date is the late Henry M. "Scoop" Jackson, who served in Congress for 42 years. From his first campaign, an upset victory for the State Senate in 1970, to his last, a 2008 landslide that saw Washington become the second state in the nation to allow "Death with Dignity," Booth Gardner has been a relentlessly analyzed collection of contradictions.

Actually, it all began much earlier. Exceptionally bright, Booth was also puckishly charming and an excellent athlete. He quickly became a big man on campus when he enrolled at the University of Washington in 1954. Curiously, he didn't quite fit at the frat house and soon moved in with his aunt and uncle. His beloved Aunt Lou promptly sent him to the Parks Department for a part-time job because he was underfoot. First assigned to Yesler Terrace, a housing project, he began filling in at the other playfields in Seattle's largely African American Central Area. To the surprise of many, especially the handful of people who knew he was from a wealthy family, the new white guy was a huge hit with the black kids. There was something about him—his boyish smile, the way he looked you in the eye and listened so intently. His squeaky voice was even engaging.

The Central Area was an epiphany: "I realized I could make a difference in people's lives." Coaching and supervising led to tutoring and impromptu field trips. Booth often brought a carload of kids home to Aunt Lou's for mac and cheese. If a kid didn't have football shoes, Booth bought them, along with a lot of bats, balls and jerseys. When he heard that Ernie Rose's athletic equipment store was for sale in the wake of the owner's death, he decided to buy it. One of the salesmen, Stan Dray, was running the business for Rose's widow. When Booth's lawyer contacted him, Dray insisted on meeting the prospective buyer. A fresh-faced college kid walked in. Dray was flabbergasted—more so when Booth casually wrote a check for the down payment. Dray called the bank to make sure it wouldn't bounce. The banker just laughed. "Jeeze, Stan, you could add a couple more zeroes and we'd still honor it!"

"The kids would all pile into my yellow Chevy station wagon with big fins and off we'd go to some part of the city to play a game," Booth remembers. "If some kid had an appointment at the dentist, I'd take him to that. Prejudice just went right over my head. Then when we started traveling to games and getting outside the Central Area, my education accelerated. While all my peers were at the U-Dub taking sociology I was out in the community learning it. And I still think to this day that I had a better education. I learned about disabled people. I learned about the underprivileged. I settled down in school and started to work hard because I realized I couldn't get to my goal if I didn't get out of college. I wanted to make a difference."

His goal was to become governor.

Booth as a student body officer at the UW in 1958. *Tyee yearbook*, 1958, pg. 33.

~~~

He has an MBA from Harvard and was president of a huge company. He is confident and insecure; wealthy and unpretentious; generous and tight-fisted; at turns self-effacing and self-absorbed. He likes to be liked and loves attention, yet he has "trouble getting close to people." All those paradoxes and more. While he was busy being a coach and award-winning mentor, he was a workaholic, absentee father to his own son and daughter. Public life took its toll on his family.

No public figure in Washington State history has been written about so intensely for so long. Other politicians and the press corps had never seen his like. They couldn't resist playing armchair shrink. "Basic psychology is one of my subroutines," Arnold Schwarzenegger says in *Terminator 3* when someone asks how a cyborg can size up humans so easily.

Dubbing him "Prince Faintheart," one columnist said Gardner was a governor who would rather schmooze through photo-ops with school kids than play hardball with the Legislature. A lawmaker called him "The Cabbage Patch Governor." Others, however, saw him as "a phenom" and "a visionary." He was inspiring, exasperating and endlessly fascinating, all at once. He is a Democrat who easily could have been a Republican; rated one of the top three governors in America in 1991 and mentioned as vice-presidential material.

Who Booth Gardner is *is* complicated. There are days now when even he isn't sure. Like a million other Americans, notably Michael J. Fox and Muhammad Ali, he is fighting Parkinson's. It's a nasty disease that deprives the brain of dopamine, the chemical that coordinates your muscles. Parkinson's can give you tremors and make you feel slow as a slug and stiff as a board. Depression is a frequent side effect. When he first realized something was wrong, Booth says he felt like The Tin Man in *The Wizard of Oz*.

Two deep-brain surgeries gave him a reprieve but Parkinson's is stealthy. It finds new ways to short-circuit neurotransmitters. Nearly 20 years on, it has taken the sparkle from his eyes and given his wonderfully expressive face a mask-like countenance. He is intensely competitive—absolutely

Booth hugs Margaret Rogers, a member of the Bellevue Drill Team. Dale Blindheim
© *The News Tribune* (Tacoma, WA) 1986. Reprinted with permission.

hates to lose. He accepts, however, that this is one battle he's not going to win, so he tries to make the most of every day and "stay useful." In 2000, he helped found the Booth Gardner Parkinson's Care Center at Kirkland, which offers specialists, physical therapy and many other forms of assistance to patients and family members.

Parkinson's is the last challenge in a life filled with exultant highs and tragic lows. An avid baseball fan since childhood, he calls the lows "curve balls." They've been coming his way for as long as he can remember. "Oliver Twist was a piker compared to Booth," says Mari Clack of Spokane, who first met him when they were teenagers in Seattle. "He overcame so much in childhood" but still has bouts of depression and guilt "that really weigh on him," Clack adds.

⌣

He carries the names of two of the state's most enterprising pioneer families, the Booths and Gardners. When he was 4½, his parents' society marriage collapsed all over the front page. His mother, Evelyn Booth Gardner, a beautiful socialite, divorced his father to marry Norton Clapp, a powerful scion of the Weyerhaeuser Company. Bryson R. "Brick" Gardner, Booth's father, was a wild-hare redhead with a weakness for alcohol and Cadillacs. Booth's younger sister went with Evelyn to live among the Clapps, but Brick finagled custody of Booth and took out his bitterness on the sensitive boy. Booth seldom saw his mother and sister. When he was 14, there was a tragedy and Booth inherited a fortune. Money can't buy you happiness or mend an insecure boy's broken heart, but when Clapp told the teenager he'd always be there for him, Booth felt empowered. Governor Al Rosellini had a summer home not far from the Gardner getaway on Vashon Island. Booth saw him arrive in a National Guard helicopter one Friday night and decided that would be the best job there ever was.

Be careful what you wish for. Gardner campaigned for governor boasting that he was "the real manager" the state needed. He quickly discovered, however, that being governor wasn't like running a business or being

Booth at 10 in 1946. *Laird Norton Company Archives.*

Pierce County executive. A governor has 147 legislators to contend with and hundreds of constituencies. He always said he wished he could have just applied for the job.

He enjoyed a recovering economy except at the beginning and the end. Nevertheless, he always fretted about the size of the state's reserves and was never willing to give the teachers everything they wanted. (A frugal millionaire, Booth refused to have new stationery printed until they'd used up the leftovers from the last administration.) The increasingly militant Washington Education Association declared that the self-proclaimed "Education Governor" deserved a dunce cap.

Perspectives change with time. History never stands still. Washington's teachers, college faculty in particular, made major gains on Gardner's watch.

William Gerberding, who was president of the University of Washington during the Gardner years, says, "Booth was easily the best friend the UW had." Harry Carthum, a widely respected educator from Aberdeen who was in the trenches during the WEA's first strikes, says that "If you grade on a curve, he gets an A."

Veteran state employees will tell you Gardner was the governor they saw the most, popping up unannounced to stroll through an office or to have lunch with a road crew. Booth always said his "MBWA"—Managing by Walking Around—was more valuable than his MBA from Harvard. Gary Lowe, the lobbyist for the Association of Washington Counties during the Gardner era, marveled that Booth "could step in dog shit and splatter it on the Queen and have her say, 'Thank you very much and I enjoyed my visit to Olympia.' "

Most of the reporters who couldn't get over how much he liked to be liked will tell you how much they like him. "Give my best to Booth," they all say.

His former staffers and cabinet members have regular reunions. They're extremely proud to have been part of his team. That includes Governor

"Hi! I work for the state!" says Booth, greeting Tim Miller when the Puyallup resident stopped for gas at a filling station in Puyallup. Geff Hinds © *The News Tribune* (Tacoma, WA) 1988. Reprinted with permission.

Chris Gregoire. She was a young assistant attorney general working on a landmark pay-equity settlement when Booth spotted her as someone special. He'd call and say, "Hey, how are you doing, kid?" The first time it happened, she recognized his voice but was incredulous. "*Governor?*" And he said, "Yeah. I'm heading your way. Let's get a cheeseburger." "It was amazingly disarming," Gregoire says. "But that was Booth."

At home and nationally, when he became president of the National Governors Association, Gardner campaigned for health care reform. "Health care is a right," he insisted in the 1980s. The Basic Health Care program he launched in 1987 to assist the "working poor" was the first of its kind in the nation. He also played a leading role in the push for standards-based education. Later, however, when the Washington Assessment of Student Learning—the controversial WASL—emerged as the litmus test for high school graduation, Booth insisted that there had to be alternatives. If he had learned only one thing in his 40 years of working with minorities and other disadvantaged kids, Gardner said, it was that one size doesn't fit all "and every kid counts." When he championed early-childhood education and "First Steps" programs for needy kids, his mantra was "You can pay me now or you can pay me later—and later will cost a lot more."

～

Gardner appointed the first ethnic minority to the Washington State Supreme Court, the sagacious Charles Z. Smith, and a number of other judges who went on to have distinguished careers. Gerberding notes that Booth also took great care in picking high-quality college regents and trustees. He strived to promote women and minorities and championed gay rights. He banned smoking in state workplaces. Indian tribes hailed him for a landmark accord that recognized their sovereignty. He helped usher in modern growth management and environmental regulations to rein in sprawl, clean up waterways and protect farms, wetlands and wildlife. In timber towns he is remembered as someone who worked tirelessly to assist workers displaced by the spotted owl set-asides when big-city environmentalists didn't give a hoot.

Gardner readily admits, though, that his checkered record of working with the Legislature, especially in his first term, thwarted major portions of his agenda and frustrated him to no end. All that infighting and horse-trading— "*I hated it!*" Booth says. "It was so distasteful to me. I almost wish I could do it all over again. It was a missed opportunity. I should have been better at it."

That MBA of his became so much red meat for his political opponents and disappointed pundits. Jim Dolliver, a Washington Supreme Court justice who had been chief of staff to three-term Governor Dan Evans, had this assessment of Gardner in a 1999 oral history: "Booth was a

Booth contemplates a question during an editorial board meeting in 1991. *Kathy Quigg © The Daily World, Aberdeen.*

charming young man who got along with everyone just fine. He came to the governor's office with some legislative experience, and I admired some of his ideas. He might have been a great governor, but he was not willing or able to risk any of his personal political capital to achieve greatness. He just sort of sat there, being nice to everybody, never making anybody angry. For two terms. He was very lucky."

The fact is, Gardner's gumption on key issues—tax reform and standards-based education, to name two—made a lot of people angry, notably the Washington Education Association and leading lawmakers in his own party. Washington State has a "beltway" of its own, and some Olympia insiders and other old hands maintain that Gardner was a mediocre governor. Adele Ferguson, whose *Bremerton Sun* political column was syndicated statewide, feels more hoodwinked than most. She introduced him to a statewide audience in 1982 and said he was *the* man to watch. When the honeymoon ended, she spent most of the next seven years declaring with snarky vengeance that he was a charlatan.

Dan Evans disagrees. Not long after Booth took office in 1985—exactly 20 years after Evans—he came to Washington, D.C. and asked to see him. Appointed to the U.S. Senate by Governor John Spellman two years earlier when Scoop Jackson died, Evans had campaigned for Spellman, only to see him turned out of office by Booth after one hard-luck term. "I was a little wary about this guy who had just defeated my good friend but when he walked in with that quirky little smile, we immediately connected," Evans recalls. "Our interest in education and the environment created a bond, and we worked hard on a bicoastal partnership to help Washington State succeed. We began a friendship that lasts to this day. I watched with amazement and some envy Booth's ease with people. He could communicate with kings and kindergartners, popes and politicians on equal terms." In 2003, the two former governors teamed up to secure more funding for higher education. "Neither of us was in political office," Evans notes. "We had no campaign money or staff. We didn't know many of the current legislators, but we knew there was a crisis. We visited the state treasurer and received his blessing on our proposal to tweak the state's capital debt limit." Lacking a lobbying staff, they were slowed by gimpy knees and Parkinson's—a pair of "old punks," Gardner quipped—but they deftly worked both sides of the aisle. The Legislature enacted the Gardner-Evans Plan, which authorized $750 million in general obligation bonds to fund new buildings and improve facilities on college campuses statewide over the next six years.

~~⌐

Booth likes grades. Tossing out Adele's F, a measured assessment, 17 years on, is a C+ at worst, a B at best. Sid Snyder, who worked his way up from elevator operator to Senate majority leader, observed governors and would-be governors up close for half a century. A street outside the Capitol bears his name. "Booth started slow," Snyder says, "but he grew into a good governor—and he worked hard at it. During session there's always two or three events a night—a reception for the nurses' association, a banquet for the accountants, the loggers, you name it. In the beginning, Booth was going to every one of them he could. I saw him everywhere. But he wasn't up at the head table; he was out in the crowd, talking to people. I told him, 'Booth, you're going to kill yourself.' And he said, 'Isn't this what I'm supposed to be doing?' He really cared. I give the guy a B."

Booth believes that's what he deserves. It's just that he'd hoped to be great—"like Al Rosellini and Dan Evans." What would it have taken to get an A? "This will sound strange," he says, "but I didn't think it was worth the price to go for an A." After six years he was burned out from 16-hour days. In retrospect, he realizes he was also showing the early symptoms of Parkinson's.

When his whole body of work in public life is examined—from the Central Area in 1958 to "Death with Dignity" 50 years later—Gardner's accomplishments snap into focus. He could have been a Palm Springs playboy. He chose civic involvement. Facing the ultimate curve ball, a debilitating illness, he chose to try to inspire and help other victims of Parkinson's.

Laird Harris, Booth's policy adviser during his first term and friend of 28 years, says the answer to "Who is Booth?" is remarkably complex. "He is a survivor of a traumatic childhood but never immobilized by it. He cares deeply about people he does not know, particularly the underprivileged, but is often emotionally distant from people he knows and loves. He is fiercely independent, wanting to be his own man, but he was helped along at critical times by a powerful and demanding stepfather. He suffers from Attention Deficit Disorder, but his eight years as governor were marked by a consistent focus on his lifelong passion for education. He is a noted pinchpenny in his own affairs, but an easy mark for friends who need help. He wanted to be governor and ride in helicopters, but when he got there he wanted to drive his car alone and hated the trappings of the office. He was 'Prince Faintheart' at times but also a national leader among his peer governors on education, health care and trade issues. I remember his response to a question about how he could stay so calm. He said he was like a duck, calm and graceful to the naked eye but paddling like hell beneath the water. I think this is part of him, too."

CHAPTER ONE:

Booth's roots

He looks more like a Booth than a Gardner, but both branches of the family tree are substantial. A sixth-generation Northwesterner, Booth Gardner has illustrious ancestors who arrived a half century before Washington statehood in 1889. It's often noted that he is an heir to the Weyerhaeuser fortune through his stepfather, the formidable Norton Clapp. But Gardner is descended from a long line of prominent self-made businessmen who were also pioneer politicians, newspapermen, sportsmen and boosters. His great-uncle was once part-owner of the *Seattle Post-Intelligencer* and dubbed Washington "The Evergreen State." The women in the family were strong and smart. His great-grandmother walked most of the way from Missouri to Oregon—2,000 miles—and his grandmother was a suffragist.

The Booths and Gardners, like the Nortons and Clapps, were of Scottish, Irish and English stock. They married into the Allen, Bryson, Cathcart, Clark, Crawford, Roe, Knowles, Manville and Moore families. Members of those clans arrived in the colonies early in the 17th Century, settling in New York, Pennsylvania and Virginia. Several served in the Revolutionary War. Others came first to Canada.

Ronald C. Crawford, Booth's great-grandfather, who arrived in Oregon in 1847 at the age of 20, served in Washington's Territorial Legislature. *The Rise and Progress of an American State.*

In the spring of 1843, when Oregon settlers gathered on a field near a grain warehouse in the Willamette Valley at a place called Champoeg (*sham-POO-ee*), Booth Gardner's ancestors cast key votes that led to the creation of the Oregon Territory. Ten years later, the portion north of the Columbia became Washington Territory.

Robert Moore, the future governor's great-great-great-grandfather, arrived in the Pacific Northwest in 1840 from Peoria, Illinois. He was 59. A corpulent Scotsman, Moore was "irascible, opinionated and eccentric" but unwaveringly honest. He had been a major in the Pennsylvania militia during the War of 1812 and a legislator in Missouri before catching "Oregon fever." His granddaughter, Elizabeth Jane Moore—Booth Gardner's great-grandmother—was 10 years old when she came to Oregon in 1847 with her father, James Marshall Moore.

Gardner's great-grandfather, Ronald C. Crawford, then 20, was also among the pioneers who made the six-month trek from Missouri that year. A skilled horseman, Crawford was one of the party's scouts. By 1847, the Oregon Trail—actually a series of routes—was well traveled. The first "Great Migration" was in 1843 when some 800 men, women and children in 110 wagons left Missouri with thousands of animals—oxen, horses, mules, and cattle. The newcomers tipped the balance of power in the Willamette Valley to the Americans. Robert Moore's experience in the Missouri Legislature in 1830 proved invaluable. A committee he headed produced a remarkable document that was "in essence Oregon's first written constitution."

⌣⌐

Ronald C. Crawford was a carpenter whose skills were immediately in demand in Oregon. However, when gold was discovered in California in 1848 the 22-year-old saddled up and joined the mass exodus south. Panning the rivers near Sacramento from sunup to sundown, he struck it rich, extracting $100 to $250 worth of gold a day. Many of the "49ers" came home with $30,000 to $40,000 and promptly squandered their fortunes on orgies of "profligacy and waste." Crawford was a frugal family man. He returned to Oregon City in 1852, married 16-year-old Elizabeth Jane Moore, Booth Gardner's great-grandmother, and started farming. Carpentry began as a side business but soon led to a successful contracting partnership. The years to come found Crawford and his growing family in Tumwater where he manufactured furniture. In 1870 he took up a homestead in the Lincoln Creek area along the Chehalis River in Lewis County. Booth Gardner's grandmother, Nelle, the sixth of the Crawfords' seven children, was born there in 1876. Her father was elected to the Territorial Legislature from Lewis County and served in the House of Representatives during the Fifth Biennial Session, 1875-77. The Assembly, as it was then known, called for a constitutional convention and petitioned for statehood. The legislators were paid $4 a day during session.

Nelle's brother, Ronald Marcus Crawford, was the court crier at the King County Courthouse in the 1880s. He became friends with the county auditor, Manville S. Booth.

⌣⌐

The Booths, industrious Irish Catholics, came to Washington Territory before the Gardners—perhaps to escape ethnic and religious prejudice, only to see their name besmirched by guilt by association with an assassin.

Manville Booth, a farmer, arrived in 1861 from Battle Creek, Michigan. He established a farm and cattle ranch near the sawmill town of Port Discovery between Sequim and Port Townsend. Two years later he sent for his English-born wife, Mary Roe Booth, and three young children, including Booth Gardner's grandfather, Laurence Stephen Booth, who was 2. Reunited, the young family settled in on the homestead. In 1865, however, when news of President Lincoln's assassination by Confederate sympathizer John Wilkes Booth reached the Olympic Peninsula, "a severe prejudice arose" against Manville Booth in the small community even though he explained repeatedly that he was no relation to the loathsome killer. Booth moved his family to Port Ludlow, then to Port Townsend, where he proved to be so upstanding that the fallout dissipated. Booth prospered in both cattle ranching and real estate, also doing business in Seattle. He moved his family there in 1872.

Personable and public-spirited, Manville Booth was elected King County Auditor in 1874 and served until 1881. He opted to become a real estate broker rather than seek another term. "He was a rather dashing figure...and a great lover of horses." In one Fourth of July race that old-timers talked about for decades, Booth rode to victory his favorite steed, *General Grant*, but lost his high silk hat in the process. Mrs. Booth was one of Seattle's most active charity volunteers. Their son entered the University of Washington in 1873 when he was 12 years old. The governor's grandfather was extremely bright, but the feat was not as prodigious as you might think. Seattle pioneer Arthur Denny, the speaker of the House, pushed construction of a territorial university in Seattle long before there was a ready supply of high school graduates eager for

Laurence S. Booth, the governor's grandfather, as a young businessman in Seattle. *University of Washington Libraries, Special Collections, UW21791.*

higher education. The university in Laurence Booth's day was a shoestring operation largely resigned to teaching grades six through 12.

Young Booth joined his father in the Auditor's Office in 1875 at the age of 14. By 1879 he was a deputy auditor and remained with the office for 12 years, buying and selling land on the side. In 1887, Booth and Edwin S. Briscoe launched an abstract and title business, purchasing "the first set of books for the King County land titles ever compiled." Booth had joined the Washington National Guard in 1884 and rose through the ranks to commander of Company B of the First Regiment. An excellent athlete, he was a member of Seattle's first amateur baseball team, the Alkis. His most famous exploit found him on the front lines of Seattle's baptism by fire.

It hadn't rained in weeks and Seattle was savoring a storybook spring. The business district was bustling. Some 27,000 newcomers had arrived in the past decade, boosting the population to nearly 31,000. One was John E. Back, 24, a stubby Swede who left the old country in 1887, made his way to Seattle a year later and found a job in a cabinet shop along the waterfront. John was a good worker but by most accounts not very bright.

It was June 6, 1889, and things turned bad around half past 2. "I cut some balls of glue and put them in the glue pot on the stove," the carpenter told a *Post-Intelligencer* reporter the next day in his broken English. "I put in some shaving where there was little fire, and then went to work about 25 feet away, near the front door. After a while, somebody said, 'Look at the glue!'" The pot had boiled over, spewing flaming globs onto the floor. "Then I run and took the pot of water to smother the fire." A co-worker shouted "No!" But it was too late. "When I throw the water on," Back said, "the glue flew all over the shop into the shavings and everything take fire."

"Everything take fire" neatly sums up the next 11 hours. The floor was covered with weeks of wood shavings marinating in turpentine. The water became an accelerant. In an instant, the whole windowless basement shop was ablaze and filled with dense smoke. Back and four fellow workers ran for their lives. Upstairs in the Pontius Building, a dentist, a logger with a tooth-ache, a shoe salesman with a prospective customer and a soothsayer with a curious client also fled as the flames burst through the floor and ceilings.

Passersby spotted the smoke almost immediately and sent a runner to the Fire Department. Men and boys pulled a hose cart from a nearby station. Minutes later, the city's first steam pumper arrived, drawn by a team of galloping horses, their "hoofs drumming hard on the dry planked street ...black smoke pouring from the polished brass stack."

"The burning glue and leather threw off so much smoke that the firemen had trouble finding the heart of the flames," Murray Morgan recounts in *Skid Road*, his classic history of early-day Seattle. "They shot water hope-fully onto the outer walls of the two-story wood building and onto the roof until someone pried off the clapboards at street level: the basement was a furnace. The firemen poured water into the basement but it was too late: the fire was out of control." Wood-frame buildings, including the real estate office owned by Booth Gardner's great-uncle, were consumed block by block. Then the wind kicked up, spreading the embers. "By 4 o'clock, most residents realized that downtown Seattle was doomed. The fire had crossed Second Avenue and was heading up to Third. Smoke could be seen in Tacoma, and the roar of the fire heard for miles."

What Booth Gardner's grandfather did that day made him a legend in his own time. Laurence Booth, like his father, had always been public-spirited. He joined Hook & Ladder Company No. 1 of the fledgling Seattle Volunteer Fire Department in 1883. Having literally grown up as a keeper of county records, the 28-year-old headed for the Courthouse as the fire advanced. A three-story wood-frame building, its claim to something ap-proximating frontier grandeur was an awkward tower and crenellated trim along an overhanging roof. The building was wedged between Jefferson and Yesler along Third Street. Alongside was a smaller building occupied by the county auditor, treasurer and sheriff. The spire-topped bell tower of Trinity Episcopal Church across the street was ablaze, "sending sparks and flaming shingles onto the roofs of the county buildings."

Judge Cornelius H. Hanford was presiding over a murder trial. Although bells were clanging and people outside could be heard shouting and running, he balked at halting the proceedings, fearing a mistrial if the jury was not sequestered. Then smoke poured in and a witness being cross-examined was obviously distracted. The jury was fidgeting, too. Some of its members were merchants who "suspected that everything they owned was being burned up by the fire or blown up by the firefighters, and they were right." Hanford adjourned the court, admonishing the jurors not to discuss the case with anyone or read the papers. They scrambled for the door but "before they could get out of the room" he and the court crier, Ronald M. Crawford, drafted some of them to try to save the Courthouse.

Outside, Booth and other firemen were struggling to get enough water pressure to soak the smoking roof, which was being bombarded by cinders. "Clerks were hastily bundling records into baskets and sacks and carrying them up the hill," Morgan wrote. The jailers, meantime, herded their shackled prisoners out of harm's way. "We got a ladder from somewhere," the judge told reporters, "but it was too short to reach the eaves of the building. It was long enough, however, so that if some of us held it perpendicular, an agile fellow could reach from the top end to the roof and pull himself up."

Larry Booth was that agile fellow, and a brave one, too. In a scene that resembled a circus stunt, two men steadied the ladder as best they could as he stood tippy-toe on the top rung, stretched to grasp the overhanging eaves and pulled himself up and over onto the roof. Judge Hanford, Crawford and others on the ground formed a bucket brigade from a faucet to the flagstaff. "We used the halyards on the flagstaff to haul buckets of water up to him," the judge said. "He dashed the water on the roof" and poured water down the sides of the building. The Courthouse was saved. Booth's feat inspired other bucket brigades and several homes were also spared.

The last flames were extinguished around 3 a.m. When the sun rose on June 7, 1889, Seattle was 29 square blocks of smoldering rubble. Miraculously, no lives were lost—except for an estimated one million rats. As was the case

King County Courthouse in 1885. *University of Washington Libraries, Special Collections, A. Curtis 25167.*

with many other blooming Western towns of the era, Seattle's great fire was also a blessing in disguise. New building codes were adopted, mandating brick construction in the central business district. A professional fire department was established, together with a municipal water supply system.

Laurence Booth's children and grandchildren often asked him to tell the story of the day Seattle burned, especially the part about climbing onto the Courthouse roof. His father-in-law and brother-in-law told it too. On April 12, 1893, Booth married Nelle Crawford, the court crier's fetching 17-year-old sister. Ronald C. Crawford, the father of the bride, was much impressed with young Booth—so much so that he swallowed deep and smiled thinly when his friends asked how the only surviving charter member of the first Masonic lodge on the West Coast could countenance the marriage of his daughter to a staunch Roman Catholic.

~⁓

Booth Gardner's maternal grandparents picked a bad year to be married. The "Panic of '93" was the worst depression America had seen. The title company survived, but Laurence Booth took some lumps in real estate.

As a teenage deputy county auditor, he had closely following realty transactions. In 1880, he bought 340 acres in a parcel that lapped into Snohomish County. He paid $1,200 down and took out a mortgage for the remaining $1,200. When the economy went sour in '93, he lost all but the 40 acres in Snohomish County. After that bumpy start, Booth rarely suffered a setback and carefully diversified. (He sold the last nine acres in 1925 for $9,000—nearly $110,000 in today's money—but groused in a 1936 interview that the King County land he lost "was at Richmond Beach and where the Golf Club property now is.")

Booth's grandfather, Laurence S. Booth, around 1900. *University of Washington Libraries, Special Collections, UW2686.*

The title business Booth and Briscoe launched in 1887 morphed and merged into the Washington Title Insurance Company around the turn of the century. Booth became vice president and treasurer, then president of the largest title company in the Northwest. Seattle had grown from 43,000 people in 1890 to 237,000 in 1910.

Booth Gardner's mother, Evelyn Beatrice Booth, was born on November 28, 1911, in Seattle, the beautiful baby in a family of five children. Her father was 50. He moved his family into a stately new Tudor Revival home at 1664 Federal Ave. In 2009, it was on the market for $2.8 million.

The governor's maternal grandparents were enthusiastic supporters of Bertha Knight Landes, the formidable Seattle clubwoman whose election as mayor in 1926 marked the first time a woman had been named to lead a major American city.

Like his future son-in-law, Norton Clapp, Laurence Booth was an avid supporter of the Boy Scouts of America, having served as president of the Seattle scout council. His wife campaigned for equal rights for women. She was active in clubwork, church and community activities, including the Seattle Historical Society, the Daughters of the Pioneers of Washington and the Catholic Childhood Association. The Booths lived long and eventful lives. Both succumbed at the age of 92—Laurence Booth in 1953 and Nelle Booth in 1968. They had 14 grandchildren and 45 great-grandchildren.

~⁓

The Gardners, Protestant Scots who took up plumbing, were much less colorful than the Booths. If they ever struck it rich in the gold fields or doused courthouse fires there were no reporters around—or in the family. That said, they were an upstanding, industrious family and not without a sense of adventure. The future governor's paternal great-grandfather, William Gardner, was born at Castlegate, Scotland, "and in young manhood crossed the Atlantic to Canada," where he became a carpenter and builder. Elizabeth Bryson, Booth Gardner's paternal great-grandmother, was born in Canada to Scottish immigrants. After her husband died in Montreal, Elizabeth came to Tacoma to live with their son, William Jr. She died at the age of 86 in 1912.

The governor's paternal grandfather was born in Montreal in 1852 and apparently had the equivalent of an eighth-grade education. In 1874 when he turned 22, "he determined to try his fortune elsewhere" and made his way to San Francisco where he learned the plumbing trade. A tall man with dark, wavy hair and a dashing mustache, he departed for Portland four years later and stayed for nine years, working as a plumber and heating contractor with steadily increasing success. When he moved to Tacoma in 1887 he founded William Gardner & Co. The firm installed the first heating plants on the Northwest coast, from Portland to British Columbia, equipping the new city halls at Tacoma and Seattle as well as schools all over the west side of the Cascades. In 1898 Gardner launched a wholesale plumbing and supply business that became one of the largest in the Northwest, with a branch in Portland. He also acquired other commercial properties in Pierce County and resolved to start a family.

In 1900, at the age of 48, William Gardner married the governor's grandmother, the beautiful Ada May Cathcart, who was 20 years younger. The daughter of a shoemaker, she was born in 1871 in Ontario, Canada. William and Ada Gardner had three children—Ruth, William and Bryson Ross Gardner, Booth's father, who was born on August 18, 1905.

William Gardner & Co. was sold to the Crane Company in 1906. The governor's grandfather retired. He tended to his investments, calling himself a "capitalist." He was a Republican, "supporting the party since becoming a naturalized American citizen," but not much of a joiner. He never ran for office or headed anyone's campaign committee. Built in 1901, the Gardner home at 1415 N. 5th St. in Tacoma was spaciously upper-middle class, certainly nothing ritzy. Grandpa was, in short, a conservative old Scot, but he'd done very well indeed. He loved his summer home on Vashon Island. His wife died in 1929 at the age of 57, some six years before the birth of her grandson. Gardner outlived his

Above: William Gardner, Booth's paternal grandfather, in the 1880s, around the time he moved to Tacoma. *Gardner family album.*
Below: Ada May Cathcart Gardner, Booth's beautiful grandmother. She was 20 years younger than her husband. *Gardner family album.*

much younger spouse by nearly nine years and posed proudly with William Booth Gardner on the youngster's first birthday in 1937. He died a year later at the age of 86, perhaps secretly hoping that his namesake would be a more substantial chip off the old block than his raffish son.

Booth on his first birthday, August 21, 1937, with his father, "Brick," and Grandfather Gardner. *Gardner family album.*

CHAPTER TWO:

The curve ball

At the fashionably late hour of 9 o'clock on the evening of June 1, 1933, Evelyn Beatrice Booth, chastely elegant in an ivory satin gown with a high neckline and medium-length train, entered the living room of her parents' Seattle home on the arm of her proud father. The groom, Bryson R. Gardner, awaited her at "an improvised altar of white blossoms." She carried three calla lilies, "their golden stamens being the only bit of color about this exquisite white wedding ensemble." Virginia Boren, the popular society columnist for *The Seattle Times*, gave her readers all this and more in minute detail the next day under a banner headline: BOOTH-GARDNER NUPTIALS HELD AT BRIDE'S HOME

Evelyn was thrilled when the columnist asked if she could attend the wedding, and happier yet when the paper followed up with a photo and another story that Sunday, hailing it as "one of the loveliest weddings of the year." The guest list was "limited to members of the bride's and bridegroom's families and a circle of intimate friends who had watched the couple grow from childhood into womanhood and manhood." They were all enchanted by the flower girl—Beverly Booth of Wenatchee, the bride's niece—"an exquisite wee figure" in ruffled organdy. "With a reverent hush falling over

Evelyn Booth on her wedding day. Madeleine Sheahan, right, was the maid of honor. Evelyn's niece, Beverly Booth, was the flower girl. *McBride & Anderson Studio/ The Seattle Times.*

the assembled guests," the Rev. Theodore Ryan conducted the rites. Mr. Fred Lynch sang "Ah, Sweet Mystery of Life," accompanied by Miss Frances Kelly, a cousin of the bride. "At the reception which followed, Mrs. William Gardner of Tacoma, sister-in-law of the bridegroom, poured."

Like a Shirley Temple movie, society page readers surely found Boren's write-ups—classics in the genre of 1930s journalistic gentility—a pleasant respite from the real world down by the tracks. A couple of miles from the 5,000-square-foot Booth home on Capitol Hill and a few blocks south of Pioneer Square, some 600 refugees from the Great Depression had erected a shantytown they dubbed "Hooverville," a sarcastic nod to Franklin D. Roosevelt's hapless predecessor. FDR had taken office in March, reassuring Americans that "The only thing we have to fear is fear itself." The national unemployment rate was just short of 25 percent.

In keeping with a society page custom that lasted into the 1960s, the 27-year-old groom didn't get his picture in the paper. An athletic six-footer, with a receding hairline and aristocratic nose, Brick Gardner bore a resemblance to F. Scott Fitzgerald, the celebrated Jazz Age author. That was apt in another way. Both were alcoholics. Every summer weekend, Brick was the life of the party at "uninhibited" dances at the clubhouse near the Gardner family summer home on Vashon Island. Carloads of his fraternity brothers and pretty girls took the Friday night ferry. Brick Gardner was witty in an edgy way, dressed well and drove fast. After receiving a B.A. in business administration from the University of Washington in 1928, he had been a salesman for Standard Oil Co. in Long Beach, Calif., Tacoma and New York.

Although the Gardners were respected upper-middle-class Tacoma pioneers, the Booths were a rung up the social ladder. Seattle society wrinkled its nose at Tacoma. A graduate of Seattle's Forest Ridge Convent School, 21-year-old Evelyn Booth had attended Trinity College in Washington, D.C. Her regally assured pose for the wedding photographer looked like a page from *Harper's Bazaar*. Blond, slender and ambitious, she aspired to a modeling career, followed by a couple of kids and life as a socialite, the title bestowed upon her by the press in the years to come.

She was the girl of Brick's dreams. However, she was a practicing Roman Catholic and he was an indifferent Presbyterian. The Booths had their doubts about a "mixed marriage," as they used to say, but Brick promised their children would be raised in the church. The union was duly blessed by Father Ryan, the first Seattle native to be ordained a priest. He had the ecclesiastical attaboy of a monsignor's title and was a celebrity in the Catholic community.

The newlyweds "motored to California and from there will go on to New York, being at home after July 1 at Bronxville," *The Times* reported. Evelyn had been accepted by the famous Powers modeling and acting school in New York, with her father likely paying the tuition. She was a quick study, and landed some modeling jobs. Brick worked for the oil company at least part-time. On one occasion, he was dunned by a bill collector. When they returned to Tacoma three years later, he had a job with Pennsylvania Salt Manufacturing Co. and Evelyn was pregnant.

⌒

Washington's 19th governor was born at Tacoma General Hospital at 2:35 p.m. on Friday, August 21, 1936. For reasons no one can recall or fathom, they named him *Frederick* Booth Gardner. The first photo in his

Evelyn brings Booth home from the hospital in 1936. *Gardner family album.*

Brick and 10-month-old Booth at Burton Cove on Vashon Island. The Gardner family has had a vacation home there since the 1890s. *Gardner family album.*

baby book shows him arriving home from the hospital in his mother's arms. Evelyn captioned the photo "Frederick Booth…" A few days later, however, they had his birth certificate changed. "Frederick" is crossed out and "William" written in, obviously a nod to his grandfather. There were lots of Williams in the family, but no Fredericks to be found. Even the governor doesn't know what that was all about. One thing is for sure: No one ever called him William, Will, Billy or Bill. He was always Booth. His childhood friend, Stephen Merrill, tells a wonderful story about Booth's genteel name. When they were in ninth grade at Clover Park Junior High, "we had a substitute teacher one day and had some sort of an assignment to keep us busy. We all had our heads down. It was very quiet. Booth was sitting right in front of me. He gets up and goes to sharpen his pencil, and when he sits back down he immediately jumps and says, 'Ouch! Ouch!' like he'd sat on a tack. The substitute teacher looks right at me, but I hadn't done anything and had an innocent look. So she looks at Booth and says, '*What's your name?*' He pops right up like a little soldier and says, 'Bryson William Edward Norman Gordon Ross Booth Gardner the fourth!' The whole class just roared."

Everyone liked Booth, according to Merrill and their pal Jim Griffin, because he was funny and nice, not because he seemed to be well off. "He never put anyone down and he went out of his way to make his classmates feel good about themselves," Griffin says. A lot of kids at that school were from well-to-do families. Many of them—like Merrill and Griffin, whose dad was one of Brick's drinking buddies—knew that *Ozzie & Harriet* and *Father Knows Best* were fairy tales. "Behind those stone fences, down those long, forested driveways" and inside those handsome homes there were dysfunctional adults and children suffering from the fallout.

A great story-teller, Gardner has a repertoire of homilies he can tweak to fit his audience. He's passionate about education. Talking with young people never failed to recharge his batteries. He loved coaching a championship girls' soccer team and probably would have been happiest as the director of a youth club or superintendent of a medium-size school district. In 2007, he told a rapt group of high school students and social studies teachers his "How-I-Got-Here" story: "I've got to start by telling you about my relationship to God: In 1936 He took me to two adults in the north end of Tacoma, dropped me off and said, 'I'm a busy man....I'm giving you a

Booth around the age of four.
Gardner family album.

set of skills, and depending on how you do with those skill sets I'll take you back when it's your time to come back. But I want you also to remember that along the way you're going to come across people in need. Don't ever ask for anything in return, just help 'em. Just step out there and do what you can for them. Don't acknowledge. Don't wait for anything. Just do it.' The other thing He said—and this is my line—is 'Watch out for the curve ball.' By that I mean that every family I know has had tragedy—something that's happened in the course of bringing up kids, something with their wife or husband. Some way shape or form there's a tragedy in there. And what He said very simply is 'I'm going to measure you on how you deal with adversity.' Everybody can make good decisions without pressure on them, but when pressure's on 'em it becomes a different ball game. So I've lived my life that way. Now in fairness to all of you, I'm an 80 percenter. That's a passing grade. What it means is that I'll talk about 80 percent of what I've done to any of you but I'll never talk about the other 20 percent. But it's a passing grade and I think I'll get to where He wants me to go."

That story is a metaphor for practically his entire life. Booth Gardner has been dealing with curve balls since he was two years old.

Booth's sister, Gail, was born in 1937. She suffered from epilepsy, which put more strain on a marriage that was already on the rocks. Under stress, Brick upped his intake of cocktails. They were living way beyond their means. Evelyn was used to comfort "but motivated by power," according to Booth, while Brick was just plain materialistic.

Since his sister was only a year younger, Booth didn't understand what was wrong with her until he was much older. "In those days they didn't know how to treat epilepsy very well. She was sick all the time. I never got close to her. I just disliked her because she got all of the attention. I'd do things to torment her and then I'd get in trouble. So I spent the first four years of my life being told, 'Stay away, you're always

Booth and Gail Gardner in 1948.
Laird Norton Company Archives.

Eveyln wears overalls to the Halloween Barn Dance at the Tacoma Country Club in 1937. *Photo from Richards Studio Collection Series, Tacoma Times, Tacoma Public Library.*

trouble.' I remember just saying to myself, 'You're no good.' Then, even though I was just a little kid, I thought, 'Well, that's not right.' I became determined to someday prove my father wrong."

Brick had moved up to sales manager for Pennsalt Chemicals. The Gardner name meant something in Tacoma society, and Evelyn's charm, style and Seattle pedigree made her a popular figure. On her a pair of bib overalls looked chic as she posed with some cornstalks for a photo in *The Tacoma Times* to publicize the 1937 Halloween Barn Dance at the Country Club. Evelyn was elected to the executive board of the Tacoma Junior League in 1939, posing with the likes of Helen (Mrs. J.P.) Weyerhaeuser in the garden at Camille Pessemier's home. The Gardners were an upwardly mobile couple with a downwardly spiraling marriage. Evelyn intimated to friends that life at home was getting unbearable.

She might have met Norton Clapp at the Barn Dance. Six-four, 230 pounds and already a multi-millionaire at 31, Clapp was an imposing man. Although not handsome, he was personable and masculine in a way that was simultaneously rumpled and refined. He liked his Scotch on the rocks but he had the self-discipline to never get drunk. He exuded confidence. Women found all that very attractive.

Norton Clapp, like Booth Gardner, carried an important family name. His maternal grandfather, Matthew G. Norton, was a pioneer lumberman in Winona, Minnesota. In 1855, together with his brother James and their cousin, William Laird, Matthew Norton founded the Laird Norton Company. In 1900, they were key investors as Frederick Weyerhaeuser saw a fortune in vast stands of great-girthed Douglas fir and moved into Washington State.

Clapp "was born atop a mound of wealth, which he then turned into a mountain," writer Nick Gallo observed in the 1980s. Clapp began buying stocks in 1927 when he enrolled in law school in Chicago. "The stock market was beginning to go wild," he recalled years later. "I decided I'd like to buy some. I used to go to Winona on the Milwaukee Railroad in big, comfortable, orange cars. I liked them. So I decided to buy some Milwaukee stock." He kept the certificates in a safe deposit box. After graduating in June of 1929, he and his bride, Mary Davis, a minister's daughter, were packing to head home to Pasadena. Clapp decided against carrying the valuable certificates. He told his broker to sell and reaped a nice profit. Then the market crashed "and I became a hero because I didn't know how to ship it west.

So that's how I started my career." Clapp was not only very smart—conservative, but rarely to a fault—he was lucky, at least when it came to making money. Clapp's life was also punctuated with sadness. His mother, a noted philanthropist, died in an automobile crash when he was 13 and there were many more curve balls to come. Clapp strived to follow his mother's example of caring and sharing, often recalling how as a child he had accompanied her to deliver baskets of food to the poor. "I learned early on that there could be hardships and disappointments in life. And that it behooved me to be nice to the less fortunate."

Norton Clapp towers over the Pierce County school superintendent, Louise S. Taylor, as they show off their Jubilee hats for Tacoma's Golden Jubilee Celebration in 1939. *Richards Studio Collection, Series D8529-8, Tacoma Public Library.*

Clapp founded the Medina Foundation, one of the Northwest's leading philanthropies.

About the time the Clapps met Brick and Evelyn Gardner, Norton had become corporate secretary of the Weyerhaeuser Company. The Clapps were also busy developing the landmark Lakewood Center in suburban Tacoma, the first shopping center west of the Mississippi. An avid Boy Scout in his youth, Norton was the scoutmaster of Tacoma's Troop 37. Scouting was one of his favorite causes for nearly 80 years. It taught boys to be "physically strong, mentally awake and morally straight."

Clapp invariably got what he wanted. He fell in love with another man's wife and that was that. Although the Gardner marriage was already imploding, and Clapp saw little to like about Brick, two spouses were about to be jettisoned and children divvied up, including the Clapps' year-old son and Booth and Gail Gardner.

~

The Gardner and Clapp divorces were front-page news in the *Tacoma News Tribune* in 1941. Evelyn Booth had moved to Coeur d'Alene two months earlier, preparatory to seeking a divorce under Idaho's more expeditious laws. The decree was granted on Jan. 14 on grounds of "extreme cruelty." Evelyn told the judge that Brick's job kept him "away from home a great deal and that when home he refused to participate…in the usual social affairs customary to their station." She said he had "a jealous disposition" and "continuously nagged and unjustly charged her with neglect of the home duties and has accused her of having no affection for him." The newspaper described the Gardners as "prominent members of Tacoma's younger set," adding that Evelyn had "taken an active part in Little Theater dramatics," while Brick was "active in business and club circles." Evelyn was granted custody of their two children, Gail, 3, and Booth, 4½. "She receives permanent custody of Booth until he is 6, when custody will go to his father," the newspaper reported. "A trust fund provides for permanent maintenance of the children." Evelyn also was to receive a thousand dollars in cash "and various other property."

The rest of the story was revealed on the next day's front page under a Missoula dateline: "Norton Clapp, secretary of the Weyerhaeuser Timber company and prominent Tacoma civic leader, was married here today to Mrs. Evelyn B. Gardner, Tacoma socialite, in the chambers of Montana Supreme Court Justice Leif Erickson, who is a cousin of Mr. Clapp. Mrs. Edwin Booth of Wenatchee, sister-in-law of the bride, was the only attendant." The ceremony was witnessed by "several intimate friends of the couple." Clapp, the paper added, had received a final decree of divorce from his wife Mary in Tacoma two days earlier. "After an extended trip," the couple planned to make their residence in Tacoma's tony Interlaaken district. For the time being, Booth and his sister went to Wenatchee to stay with their Aunt Lou and Uncle Ed. "That boy cried and cried on the train," she recalled years later. "He just kept sobbing, 'I want to go home to C Street (in Tacoma).' " Brick was also "crushed" by the divorce. "He never got over her," Booth says.

Clapp had more expensive attorneys, but Brick was not without connections of his own. He had a friend who was a judge in Pierce County and managed to retain custody of his son. Gail Gardner went to live with her mother, her stepfather and Clapp's sons from his first marriage. Mary Clapp moved back to California where she and Norton had grown up. She placed on the market the "picturesque Colonial mansion" she and Clapp had built "at an original cost of $130,000. It featured "five acres of natural and landscaped beauty with 333 feet of the finest frontage on exclusive Gravelly Lake—one of the most beautiful estates in the Northwest." The asking price was $35,000, "one of the most tremendous bargains ever offered," the Realtor said in large newspaper ad.

⌁

With the outbreak of World War II, Norton Clapp and Brick Gardner joined the Navy as officers. Booth got the news abruptly when he was 5. "My father woke me up at 6 o'clock in the morning, standing at my bedside in

Brick as a naval officer at the outbreak of World War II. *Photo courtesy Joan Blethen.*

full uniform. That surprised me, but I was even more surprised when he told me that the Navy was shipping him out that day and that I would be spending time with my mother while he was gone." Booth moved in with Clapps that afternoon. Norton was stationed in Seattle with the Convoy & Routing Office. Brick went off to the South Pacific.

Clapp's sons from his first marriage viewed Booth as an interloper. Boys will be boys, and he says they often made his life "miserable." He was "No. 5 at the end of the pecking order" and sensitive, so they teased him. He was finicky about food, but learned to be a fast eater to get his share, a habit he could never break. In adulthood, he came to realize that he also had Attention Deficit Disorder, but no one knew much about ADD back then—just that he was fidgety, talkative and, little wonder, insecure. He was also a beautiful little boy with a luminous smile and intense hazel eyes. Everyone realized he was unusually bright.

Booth was in awe of Norton Clapp. "He was a super guy, but he didn't know how to be around young kids because his own father was such an autocrat," Booth says. "He was so strict that he didn't know how to loosen up…and that was difficult."

Before he shipped out, Brick met an attractive divorcee, Mildred McMahon Blethen, the second of Frank A. Blethen Sr.'s five wives. Blethen was a scion of *The Seattle Times* family and president of the company by the 1940s. Their spunky daughter, Joan, was a fifth grader when her mother started dating Brick Gardner. She was dubious. Brick was witty, but there was something disquietingly "elusive" and "clumsy" about him. Still, he looked sharp in his dress whites, she recalls.

Brick wrote Millie practically every day. One letter featured the news that Ernie Pyle, the celebrated war correspondent, was his shipmate and they'd really hit it off. Injured when a kamikaze pilot slammed into his ship, Brick was sent to a naval hospital in Honolulu to recuperate and fell in love with the islands. By 1944, he was back in Seattle. Brick and Millie quickly became the life of every party in town. "I think she thought he had money and he thought she had mon-

Norton Clapp as a naval officer in 1944. *Laird Norton Company Archives.*

ey," Joan Blethen surmises with a smile. "I was sort of her sidekick. She had a number of boyfriends, and she'd say, 'Now, I like this fellow because he's a good dancer. And I like this one because he's *very* smart. And I like this one because he's handsome.' Then Brick came along and apparently he embodied all of those characteristics because away they went. She just ran off and married him."

Lt. Cmdr. Gardner and the ex-Mrs. Blethen were married on May 26, 1944, in Tacoma. He was 38, she 35. Joan was 11, Booth, 7. Both had been thrown another curve ball. Reclaimed by his father, Booth now had a stepmother and a stepsister. Joan, likewise, was uprooted and tossed in with two strange males. "We had to leave my wonderful school that I had been in for seven years and move to Tacoma," she recalls. "And as we're driving along, Brick said, 'OK, we're almost there. There it is—right over there. See? Gosh, the roof is falling in but we're going to be able to fix that.' And he thought that was hilarious. I was just like, 'Ugh.' " It was in fact a "very nice house" on fashionable Gravelly Lake Drive south of Tacoma. Brick was now the Cadillac sales manager at Tacoma Auto Sales Co. A Cadillac, as Bob Dylan once observed, is "a good car to drive after

Brick and Millie on their honeymoon.
Photo courtesy Joan Blethen.

a war." Brick sold a lot of Cadillacs, but not enough to support a lifestyle that featured household help. Booth says it's possible that his father inherited some money from his parents. However, it was common knowledge in Tacoma society that Brick received a settlement or stipend from Clapp to not make trouble over the divorce. Brick acknowledged it to Millie, according to Joan. Several others corroborate the story, adding that Brick apparently threatened an alienation-of-affection lawsuit. The whispering made Brick's mercurial nature worse. Clearly embarrassed for his father, Booth doesn't want to talk about it.

⌒

Joan Blethen's first vivid memory of her new stepbrother was that "he was just sitting there, across the dinner table from me, declaring, 'I don't eat on-dions! And I don't eat peas!' I don't eat this, and I don't eat that. I thought he was a spoiled brat. And I thought, '*Wow*, I could never have gotten away with that. Someone ought to slap the crap out of you!' For the next couple of years, I knew to just kind of leave him alone." His passion was baseball. "He played baseball all the time," painstakingly recording statistics on all the Major League teams and players. In the spring and summertime, they'd all go to the Gardner getaway on Vashon Island. "Booth would do his statistics or he'd be focused on something, but never in a group activity," Joan recalls. "I used to try to drag him in, but he wouldn't go for it. He'd get very mad at me." As Booth grew older, however, "he got more gregarious. He was doing well in school, and he did well in track, and he just sort of came out of it....He came out a very serious, very hard-working young man who was also charming."

Along the way, they became best friends. Booth needed an insightful big sister and she had grown protective of him, loathing Brick's relentless put-downs. They had another thing in common: Both of their parents were alcoholics. "He drank downtown, and she drank in the afternoon with the Gin Rummy or whatever crowd, and they were both tight by the time they got together in the evening," Joan remembers. Weekends were one big party in the Lakes District. The war was over, life was good. Walter Hatch, who covered the state capitol for *The Seattle Times* in the 1980s, interviewed many people who knew Brick Gardner during the post-war years for a profile of the governor. They told him that "every night was like a Friday night on fraternity row," with Brick Gardner in the thick of it—a free-spirited "overgrown child with a mean and destructive streak. Dressed in a silk suit and seated behind the wheel of a silver Cadillac, he played the part of a wealthy rogue—even while he ridiculed the rich."

Booze transformed Brick Gardner into a Jekyll and Hyde character— "funny and warm one minute and then just downright ornery the next," a friend re-called. Booth invariably ended up on the receiving end of his sarcastic digs: Brick made the kid feel as if he was wimpy, inept and unlikely to ever amount to much. Many who knew the family at that time believe Booth became Brick's emotional punching bag because Evelyn had left him for "a rich guy." Booth says Brick rarely let him see his mother, his sister or his half-brothers, Bill and Steve, the two sons Evelyn had with Norton Clapp. One time when he returned from a visit to the Clapps in their posh Lake Washington neighborhood, Joan recalls Brick sarcastically

Booth around 12. *Gardner family album.*

inquiring, "What did the Chinese cook fix for you over there at Medina?"

Millie, a good-hearted person, was also getting fed up with Brick's bitterness. She felt sorry for Booth and always treated him well. "Brick was just *mean*," Joan Blethen says. "He had all that alcoholism and depression and everything to live with"—maybe even post-traumatic stress from the war, she adds, knowing what we now know about the disorder. "But he was terrible....Came home, sat in his chair and went to dinner, went to bed. We'd be upstairs in our rooms and he would shout at us, 'Turn off your radios up there! Booth, Joan, turn off those radios!' We might not even be playing them." One night, the adults were having a party. "Pennsylvania 6-5000," the popular Glenn Miller tune, was the last record on the turntable. It was playing over and over. Joan tells what happened next: "There's the sound of a telephone ringing in the middle of the tune— '*Ring*, Pennsylvania 6-5000!' Brick would run to the bottom of the stairs and shout, 'Booth, I told you, *stop that!* Get off those phones! I'm going to come up there!' " That's how soused he was. Needling "was his method of communication. He never cut Booth any slack whatsoever," Joan says. "We were always up there in our bedrooms. Booth would be shooting baskets behind the door, or practicing ping-pong in the basement so that anytime he lured in a competitor he could beat the socks off of them. I mean, he was *so* competitive at such a young age. Our parents would be fighting downstairs and we'd sort of meet at the top of the stairs and see if we thought everything was going to be all right or not. We bonded over those kinds of fears and looking out for one another."

"The only whole person in the household," Joan says, was the part-time handyman, Isaac Thomas. A kindly young African American, Thomas was in the Army at Fort Lewis. His wife Dorothy did the cooking and other domestic chores. Thomas doted on Booth and Joan. He drove her to skating lessons "and would come in to applaud as I tried to learn various tricky stunts." Thomas quickly realized Booth desperately needed a nurturing grown-up. He called him "Big Shot"—not because the boy was haughty, but because he lacked confidence. He taught him to play the saxophone

Coach Isaac Thomas, standing far left, with his sandlot football team. Booth Gardner
is at right, behind the quarterback wearing a dark shirt. Steve Merrill is at center.
Ted Griffin, Jim's brother, is at far right. *Photo by Lee Merrill.*

and offered to coach the ragtag neighborhood football team. "Thomas
came up and watched us one game," Booth recalls. "We were all sitting
around after getting beat again and he came over and said, 'Do you guys
want help?' And every kid on the team looked at him. There was silence,
and finally we said, 'Yeah.' So he started coaching us and we did well. He
treated us like human beings. We learned a lot from Thomas. The thing
was, I didn't know blacks were supposedly bad. I didn't know they were
mistreated. I didn't know they were secondary citizens. I didn't know any
of that. It was just Thomas and Dorothy. They were great. I kidded with
them all the time. He was firm with me because I was not the greatest kid
in those days. He kind of settled me down. So when I got to the Central
Area to volunteer when I was in college I wasn't afraid of being around
blacks, but I didn't know the other side of the equation—how tough life
was for them. That's where I learned that, but it all started with Thomas."
Stephen Merrill, another member of that sandlot team, remembers, "We
always called him 'Thomas'—just 'Thomas.' We all looked up to him." Their
pal Jim Griffin seconds the motion. "All the neighborhood kids idealized
him. He was a great organizer and coach…and he gave Booth some stability." Thomas "brought Booth through some very bad times," Joan Blethen
says. When Booth was feeling blue, Thomas would yell up the stairs, "OK,

big shot, let's go!" "He saw something was amiss" in the Gardner home, she says, and did what he could to help. "I'd love to find him. He was so wonderful to us." Booth has tried to find him, too.

⟋⟍

Merrill and Booth played baseball together at recess all through fifth and sixth grade and became good friends in junior high. "I lived on Interlaaken Drive, less than two minutes away from his house on my bike," Merrill remembers. "Booth created games of all kinds. We played 'basketball,' tossing rolled-up socks into the floor lamp from which we'd removed the shade. He was always into games. In the basement rec room, which had a well-polished wood floor, we played floor hockey, sliding around in our stocking feet. Booth didn't have a life lived in the middle of the house. He created a life for himself in his bedroom and in the basement. I would go over on Sunday mornings and find Brick and Millie drinking. …It was only when I was older that I realized the enormity of the imprint on Booth from living isolated in his own home." He was lucky to have Joan and Thomas. "I was a little afraid of Brick, especially when he'd been drinking—not physically afraid, but wary of his sarcastic (barbs)," Merrill says. "Booth had ways of coping, or getting things. We'd be playing up in his room and without warning he'd say, 'Just a minute.' Running down the stairs, he'd shout to Brick in the study, 'Steve wants a Coke. Can he have one?' Booth, of course, wanted the Coke."

Some of the most fun they ever had, Merrill says, was when they'd horse around with Jim Griffin and his brother Ted. Their dad owned a fuel company and had a stable of antique cars. "On Sundays and holidays Ed would take us for rides. I remember a Duesenberg and a great old fire engine." Jim Griffin says his dad was a jokester who used to deploy the fire engine to drain his friends' swimming pools when they left town. The Griffins also had a tennis court—a *lighted* tennis court. "Even then we thought that was cool," Merrill says, recalling that Booth was an athletic southpaw. He kept dislocating his shoulders but didn't let that hold him back. "He became an expert at slipping the shoulder bone back in the socket and usually completed the game, no matter how great the pain," Griffin says.

Merrill recalls a day when he was ahead of Booth "by a good margin in the set but he ended up beating me. 'You just beat yourself.' he said. It seemed like a very profound comment at the time. It was the first time I was aware that it was my mistakes that lost the set instead of my opponent's better play. Booth is competitive," physically and emotionally, Merrill emphasizes, "and if you listened carefully he could teach you things about focusing your energies." He managed to be simultaneously intense "and warm and playful."

Nick Handy, now Washington State's director of elections, had a regular tennis game with Booth when he was with the Department of Natural Resources and Gardner was governor. "He loved to play tennis and was a very accomplished player," says Handy, whose Wenatchee High School team won the state tennis title in 1966. Handy also played tennis in college, so he knows talent when he sees it. "Booth was mentally very tough and you always knew when the points really counted that you were going to have to really fight for it. But he was also always very good natured about the match, win or lose. He really enjoyed bantering with everyone from the desk clerk to the folks working around the courts. I think he really liked these little forays into the world of real people where he was very comfortable. Everybody liked Booth. Although he and I had great matches," Handy adds, "they were nothing compared to his matches with a guy named Cipriano Araiza, known as 'Cip.' I thought it was great that the governor of the state was slipping away from work to play tennis with a blue-collar Hispanic truck driver with a heavy accent. Booth was great with both of my kids, too. They were taking lessons and developing their games. He would always talk with them. Years later, when I would run into Booth at various events, he would always ask first about the kids and what they were up to. I loved that he cared about my family."

Booth was chosen class president in the eighth grade—his first try for elective office. He loved it. Merrill maintains that part of Booth's charisma is temperament and some is in the stars. A retired college professor, Merrill is also an astrologer. He says he wasn't the least bit surprised when Booth had an epiphany while working with underprivileged kids as a college student. Not only did he have an unhappy childhood, "he's a Leo…and (working with kids) is very compatible with his energy. Leos like attention and they need attention. They can take that attention and turn into positive energy. It's like actors talking about their relationships with an audience. When the audience is with them they do better. Leos are at home on stage.…The feedback is instantaneous. Energy goes out and immediately finds its mark, and for a Leo, that is heaven. I wasn't surprised either that Booth was able to run for governor and make it, even as a relative unknown."

Joan Blethen wasn't surprised either. After Millie and Brick divorced, she and Booth stayed close and remain so a half century later. They never refer to one another as stepbrother or stepsister. It's "my sister Joan" and "my brother Booth."

Norton Clapp endured heartache of his own during Booth's bumpy years with Brick. His ex-wife, Mary, who had remarried early in 1945, was killed in an auto accident that July near Oxnard, Calif., together with their 10-year-old son, Ralph Davis Clapp. Ralph and his brothers, Matthew, 11, and James, 14, lived with their father and stepmother in Seattle, while their brother Roger, 5, lived with his mother and stepfather in California. The three older Clapp boys had been visiting their mother and brother. They were all in the car driven by Mary, 34, when another motorist swerved across the center line and hit them head on. Matthew and Roger Clapp were critically injured but survived, as did James, who was less seriously hurt. Roger was left disabled by the accident and would succumb to cancer at the age of 24. Evelyn Booth Clapp told reporters that her husband had caught the first plane to California to be with his sons.

The former Mrs. Clapp "was carrying $35,000 in currency on her person," according to The Associated Press account of the crash. It could be just a coincidence, but that was the asking price for the "picturesque Colonial mansion" the Clapps occupied in Tacoma during happier days.

Clapp's relationship with his ex-wife's widower, naval aviator David Joyce, quickly became litigious. A court case that percolated into the open 20 years later revealed that Norton Clapp had made a payment to Joyce to settle his claims that Clapp had defrauded his ex-wife out of most of their community property when they divorced in 1941. "As sole legatee and executor" of his wife's estate, Joyce claimed to be owed "not less than $14,705,839.71 and perhaps as much as $26,000,000." He settled for $125,000. Clapp later sued Uncle Sam for an income tax refund, asserting that he had expended more than $300,000 on attorney's fees between 1947 and 1950 before Joyce agreed to the settlement. Clapp's attorneys argued that the entire $425,000 should have been deductible from his gross income for tax purposes. The U.S. Court of Claims dismissed the petition. It was a rare loss for Norton Clapp.

CHAPTER THREE:

Alone in the world

It was March of 1951. Booth Gardner was 14. "Out of the blue," his mother called. "You've got spring vacation coming up and I'm going to talk to your dad and take you skiing," Evelyn said. "By the way, since we haven't seen each other very much, bring a friend." Brick grudgingly consented, and Booth invited his buddy Steve Merrill, who had been with them on a trip to Sun Valley the previous year. This time it was a shorter outing to Mt. Hood in Oregon.

"It was snowing hard when we got there on Saturday," Booth recalls, "We were supposed to leave on Sunday, but it snowed so much we couldn't get out and we ended up staying 'till Tuesday. I had more fun than I ever had with anybody," he says, voice quavering with emotion nearly 60 years later. "The snow was too deep to ski, but there was a bowling alley nearby and we spent a lot of time there. It was the happiest time of my life. She was glib—witty and fun. All the help there loved her."

"His mom was a wonderfully easy person to be with," Merrill says. "We had a lot of fun. One night, Booth and I were jumping on the two twin beds, back and forth. Booth landed on my bed and it broke. When he confessed to his mother, he made a point of telling her that it was the bed I slept in; he left out the part that he had jumped onto my bed from his."

Evelyn enjoyed being around the lively boys, but she was also anxious to get back to Seattle. Her hobby was raising orchids, and a big show in Santa Barbara was only a week away. The Beall Company had a large greenhouse on Vashon Island, Booth recalls, "and they were after her to go down to the show. They said, 'You've got a winner. You ought to be there.' " That Friday, Evelyn got word that her orchid was the sweepstakes winner. She caught a flight for San Francisco and picked up Booth's sister, who was attending Sacred Heart Convent School in the Bay Area.

Eveleyn Clapp with one of her prize orchids in 1951. *Gardner family album.*

Southwest Airways Flight 7, a twin-engine Douglas DC-3, departed Santa Maria at 8:16 p.m. on April 6, 1951, on what should have been a 20-minute hop to Santa Barbara. "Two minutes later, it made routine radio contact. That was the last word." When it failed to arrive, a search was immediately initiated. Norton Clapp, who was in Portland on business, flew immediately to Santa Barbara and called Brick when he sized up the situation from search headquarters.

Still in his bathrobe, Brick shook Booth awake around 6 a.m. Saturday. "What's wrong?" Booth asked, sitting bolt upright. "Your mother and sister have been in a plane crash and it doesn't look good," Brick sobbed. Booth was stunned. "I thought the world had come to an end because I had finally spent time with her. *Really* liked her. Anticipated the future, and suddenly she's gone. I spent the rest of the day hoping against hope. Then we got the news that they were gone." There was little that his stepmother could say to comfort them. The marriage was in the process of unraveling, so the moment was especially difficult. Joan was away on a spring break trip of her own.

Coast Guard and Air Force planes joined "scores of civilians" in the search. Around 10:30 a.m. the pilots spotted smoke rising from scattered rubble on the northern slope of Refugio Pass some 14 miles northwest of Santa Barbara. They directed ground searchers to the remains of the plane. The flight crew of three and all 19 passengers, including Evelyn Booth Gardner Clapp, 39, and Gail Gardner, 13, died when the airliner pancaked into the rugged terrain at an altitude of 2,740 feet. It bounced several times, broke into pieces and burst into flames. The flight crew, for unknown reasons, had failed to maintain the minimum nighttime altitude of 4,000 feet over the Santa Ynez Mountains. *The Seattle Daily Times,* the *Post-Intelligencer* and *The Tacoma News Tribune* gave the story banner headlines. **Mrs. Norton Clapp Killed In Air Crash**, the *TNT* reported. It printed a two-column portrait of Evelyn, calling her a well-known Tacoma and Seattle socialite. A sidebar headlined "Tragedy in Clapp Family Third in Seven Years" noted the death of Norton's ex-wife and 10-year-old son in the 1945 auto accident, adding that in 1944, his half-brother, James Norton Clapp, was killed when a tractor overturned while he was mowing grass on his 1,240-acre ranch at Chino, Calif. The *P-I* story featured a photo of Evelyn with an orchid a Seattle grower had named in her honor.

Norton, Brick and Booth were all grieving. Norton had lost the love of his life and a stepdaughter he had grown to adore; Brick, still conflicted over the divorce, was also mourning a daughter he had rarely seen since she was 3. Booth's loss was probably the most profound. "That event had a greater effect on me than anything else in my life, before or after," he says. "I felt alone in the world and that I was somehow responsible for all of this." The mother he had rediscovered was dead, together with the sister he never really knew, the one he had "tormented" when they were pre-

Mrs. Clapp On Plane

(Continued From Page One)

circling at about 200 feet, 10 to 12 miles south of the pass.

A search plane left immediately from San Francisco airport, and two Navy and Coast Guard planes cruised the Pacific off the Gaviota Pass area.

Fog Hampers Search

The lost plane left San Francisco at 5:45 bound for Los Angeles. The passengers, including 10 servicemen, were en route to Santa Barbara, Oxnard and Los Angeles.

The passenger liner ordinarily follows the coastline and could have fallen into the ocean, unseen in the fog.

Asa Brown, who lives on the Rutherford ranch 12 miles south of Gaviota, saw and heard a plane about 8 o'clock last night. He said he assumed it was the Southwest Airways plane because he hears it every night.

Last night, however, Brown said, the southbound plane for some unexplained reason turned and headed in a northerly direction toward Santa Ynez peak. The 4,292-foot-high mountain is the tallest in that region.

Jeanette Loustalot, Las Cruces, reported hearing a roaring sound like that of a low-flying plane about 8:30 p. m., but it faded out suddenly.

Sheriff's deputies said the terrain around Gaviota Pass is slashed with deep canyons. A plane crashing into one of these might be impossible to find by air or ground, they said.

Others Aboard Plane

Others aboard, identified by Southwest Airways and from other sources, included:

John Burgan, assistant editor of

Socialite Missing—Mrs. Norton Clapp, well known in Seattle and Tacoma social circles, was on a Southwest Airways plane missing in a flight between Santa Maria and Santa Barbara Friday night. A daughter of Mrs. Clapp, Gail Gardner, 13, also was on the missing plane.

A clipping from *The Tacoma News Tribune*.

schoolers. When he had a daughter of his own he named her Gail. Booth was never really comfortable with the sizable trust-fund inheritance he received when he turned 25. However, it did allow him to follow Norton Clapp's example and "try to help others."

Steve Merrill recalls that his dad, Lee, went over to offer his condolences to Brick. After they'd talked for a while, Brick said, "Well, Booth will never have to work again."

Ironically, the funeral notice in the *P-I* on April 10 included the standard boilerplate: "Please omit flowers." It was either a misprint or an oversight. In any case, no one paid any attention. "Flowers banked the walls" and "the orchids with which Mrs. Clapp had won prizes" graced the altar of the Church of the Sacred Heart in Bellevue, which was packed with mourners. Monsignor Theodore Ryan, who had married Brick and Evelyn in 1933, was on hand. The Mass was followed by private interment.

"It was my first funeral," Merrill says. "I remember seeing the two urns with their ashes. I wasn't sitting with the family, so I did not see Booth until after when we went to someone's house on the edge of Broadmore golf course. Booth and I went and played golf—like a couple of orphans. The adults just sort of let us out and thought it good if we played golf, so we did. Of course, it is difficult to deal with death, but the adults were no help at all."

Merrill says he was raised to always write thank-you letters—"I think we called them 'bread-and-butter' letters in those days." After the ski trip, "I wrote one to Evelyn right away and mailed it. I wondered if she'd got it" before leaving for Santa Barbara. "Norton told my parents she had."

CHAPTER FOUR:

Running away

About three weeks after the funerals, Norton Clapp had his secretary summon his stepson. "Norton would like to see you," she said. Booth dressed up and nervously presented himself. They made awkward small talk for a few minutes. "Now," said Clapp, clearing his throat, one of his tics, "I want to tell you why you're here: Your mother was far and away the best wife a man could ever have, and because she meant so much to me I'm saying the following to you: If you ever get in trouble, call me."

"That had the effect of taking a big anchor and moving it out deeper," Booth says. "I knew I could go in the deep water now because I had a way out. I had a savior. And that's when I started really thinking big." It wasn't so much a matter of money. He didn't fully grasp that he was going to be a millionaire, thanks to his mother's will and the trust fund. It was that he could count on someone who was somebody—someone who always kept his promises.

This revelation made it easier to handle three more curve balls Brick was about to toss his way, one right after the other. The first lacked velocity: He and Millie were getting a divorce. The next two were zingers: He had tuberculosis and he was sending Booth to boarding school. Brick told his

Teenage Booth. *Laird Norton Company Archives.*

son he was heading to a sanatorium for treatment. Some say that was a smokescreen for an attempt to kick his addiction to alcohol, but Joan Blethen says Brick really had TB. In fact, she contracted it from him.

"Look," Brick told Booth, "school is going to be starting. I can't take care of you myself. I've arranged for you to go to school on the East Coast." Emboldened, Booth's response was "No way in hell!" "You have to do it," Brick said, adding that Vermont Academy was a top prep school. He tried to sweeten the deal by noting that Jim Griffin, Booth's pal from next door, was going there and the skiing was great. "Well, let's explore alternatives," Booth countered, only to strike out. "So I got on the train and went back. I kept score all the way—where we stopped, how much things cost, every detail. I talked to all the porters on the train. Not being a grown-up I could check out conversations and not threaten people. I plotted an escape. I got off at Springfield (Massachusetts) and took another train out to Saxtons River near Bellows Falls in Vermont, where the school was."

It was the fall of 1951. Booth, just turned 15, dutifully enrolled for his sophomore year in the bucolic new setting. "I hung around for a month. Then, on a full-moonlit night, I ran away." He walked to town and caught the train to Boston. In September, he'd struck up a conversation with the father of a boy from Providence, Rhode Island, so he decided to head there. He got a job waiting tables at a restaurant and found a place to stay. "I was on my own for about five weeks. I called the school and I called my dad. I told him, 'Here's what I've done. But I'll negotiate with you.' He said, 'If you stay there I promise you can come back next year.' So it was a deal. I went back to school. My world had been turned upside down, but I learned I was in control of my life, and that I could make it."

Laird Harris, Booth's friend and former policy aide from his years as governor, was listening intently in 2009 when he related how he'd run away all those years ago—a story few have ever heard. "Most people who run away know what they *don't* want but have little idea of what the answer is," Harris observed. "You knew and you were 'running to' the solution." Booth nodded. The memory of his declaration of independence was still vivid.

As things turned out, his year at Vermont Academy was a welcome break from the upheavals back home. Although he was a year older, he was assigned to a freshman dorm—actually a seven-bedroom house— with Griffin and 12 other ninth-graders, likely because he and Jim were friends and the administration was nervous about him taking off again. Griffin, who years later ended up being a key fund-raiser for all of Booth's political campaigns, has fond memories of that year in Vermont. "I lived on the third floor with a roommate and Booth had a single room on the

Skiing in Vermont. Booth second from left. *Gardner family album.*

Booth at a weekend party during his year at Vermont Academy. *Photo courtesy Jim Griffin.*

second floor," he recalls. "But Booth and I were often together in the evening until 'lights out.'" One of Booth's parlor tricks was to remove the arms from his spindle-back desk chair and play "Taps" on the radiator like a drummer. The sound vibrated off every room's radiator, Griffin says. "When he heard Mr. Lucy, our 'master,' sneaking up the creaking stairs and tiptoeing down the hall listening at each door, Booth quickly put the arms of the chair back in place. He was never caught. It's a good example of his mischievous sense of humor. However, during our childhood and throughout adulthood, I never saw Booth use his humor at anyone's expense."

Come June, they both headed home to the Northwest. Booth was going to board with family friends and attend the Lakeside School in Seattle, while Griffin—who bounced around after his own parents' divorce—returned to Clover Park High School. That winter, Mildred Blethen Gardner was granted a divorce from Brick. She received a 1950 Pontiac; a checking account in her name in the amount of $14,164.71; a savings account of about $5,000 and a judgment against him in the sum of $15,000.

～

Brick Gardner's TB symptoms abated, his drinking tapered off and he moved to Hawaii. He seemed to have plenty of money. In the summer of '53, Brick was so upbeat that he invited Booth, former stepdaughter Joan and one of Booth's Lakeside School classmates, Norman "Bud" Branchflower Jr., to visit him in Honolulu. Brick told Joan he wanted her and Booth to remain brother and sister, apparently oblivious to the fact that they didn't need any encouragement. Joan was still wary of Brick,

Bud Branchflower, Joan Blethen and Booth in Hawaii, 1953. *Photo courtesy Joan Blethen.*

but the teens had a wonderful time, posing at Trader Vic's and splashing through the surf at Waikiki. In Joan's scrapbook photos, Booth looks like the All-American boy. Brick was angling to purchase a controlling interest in a Honolulu radio station, KHON, and started taking classes toward a master's degree at the University of Hawaii.

That fall, Booth began his senior year at the Lakeside School. His injuries kept crimping his athletic aspirations, but he gutted it out and was a star on the track team. He was popular and happy. A flirt, all the girls thought he was cute. The guys saw him as a leader and the teachers knew he had "real potential." He wasn't a straight-A student, "but we were impressed by his ability to assess a problem quickly," Branchflower says. "He was very savvy."

"Booth and I were the best of friends during our high school years," says Branchflower, whose father was an oral surgeon. "Lakeside was a great school. The classes were small and the instruction was fabulous. We played basketball together. But his bad shoulder kept flopping out on him. It's because of that that I'm not a doctor today. I was premed at Princeton. When I was home in Seattle one summer, Booth had a major operation on his shoulder. They let me go in and watch and I passed out four times. Obviously I wasn't cut out to be a doctor. They practically used a crowbar on his shoulder."

Entering their senior year, another friend, Bobby Stewart, decided to run for student body vice president, Branchflower recalls. "I offered to be his campaign manager. Then a week later, Booth decided he wanted to run. I had a real dilemma since we were such good friends. I kept my word and was campaign manager for Bobby, but at election time I voted for Booth and he won by one vote, so he probably has me to blame for launching his political career."

Booth enrolled at the University of Washington in September of 1954 and pledged Phi Delta Theta. When his new brothers decided it would be a hoot to hide his featherless non-allergenic pillow, he quickly concluded that frat boy horseplay was not his style. He moved in with his Uncle Edwin and Aunt

Booth as vice president of the Lakeside School during a meeting of the student senate in 1954.
Photo courtesy the Lakeside School.

Lou Booth on Capitol Hill. Aunt Lou booted him in the backside every now and then, just for drill. Better than anyone she understood how dysfunctional his upbringing had been, but she wasn't cutting him much slack. For one thing, she couldn't understand why an 18-year-old college freshman would rather live with his aunt and uncle than on Greek Row. She sent him to a psychologist. After a couple of sessions, Booth burst into the house one day, declaring, "Hey, guess what, Aunt Lou? The doctor says I'm better off staying with you and Uncle Edwin."

"I was driving her nuts," Booth says, smiling at the memory of her hands-on-hips exasperation. "I'd thrown my arm out doing summer ball, so I couldn't pitch any more and I wasn't involved in many outside activities at the U. I was just hanging around the house...or when

Emory Bundy, left, and Booth at the UW in 1957. Bundy was student body president, Gardner first vice president. *Tyee yearbook, 1958, pg. 99.*

I'd go out I'd never tell her where I was going. She never pulled punches. That's why I liked her so much. She was pivotal in my life." She suggested that he apply for an after-school job with the Seattle Parks Department. "So I went down to the Parks Department and had an interview and got a job. I found out later that she was personal friends with the head of the Parks Department and she had it greased for me." It was vintage Aunt Lou.

Booth loved working with the black kids, and they loved him. Emory Bundy, the student body president at the UW in 1957-58, was initially oblivious to the fact that Booth was "spending a prodigious amount of time" in the Central Area. After Booth was elected first vice president, "I was meeting with him and the other two ASUW officers every week," Bundy says, "and I had no idea what he was up to. He was just doing all that work—organizing programs, bankrolling activities—without tooting his horn. Years later, when I learned about it, I was all the more impressed. I was very keen on civil rights work while I was at the university, and Booth was well aware of that. But without saying anything to me or anyone else, he was out there working with minority kids and kids with disabilities. I realized he never did anything self-serving."

Cecile Evans, whose future husband, Reese Lindquist, was one of Booth's fraternity brothers, was active in student government. "Booth had a wonderful ability to connect with people," she says, recalling driving with him to a campus leaders' retreat on Whidbey Island. At dinner that night, Cecile's own ability to connect with people prompted him to talk about his childhood. "I had no idea what he'd been through. In later years, I learned a lot more, but I got a good inkling that night, and I thought to myself, 'Oh my, this is not easy stuff.' Then when Reese told me he'd found out that Booth was working with kids in the Central Area" it all added up.

One of Booth Gardner's playground football teams included a scrawny kid named Jimi Hendrix, who became one of the most mesmerizing guitarists in the history of Rock 'n' Roll. Jimi, amazingly, was self-taught, learning the guitar by listening to B.B. King and Chuck Berry. When Booth met him, the boy's home life, to use the phrase loosely, was chaos. "Jimi roamed the neighborhood at all hours of the day and night with little supervision," Hendrix biographer Charles R. Cross writes. "Many in the Central District came to know him as they would a stray dog who wanders from house to house."

"I went to pick him up one day and the house was dark," Booth recalls. "The city had turned the power off. Someone said, 'Jimi's upstairs if you want to see him.' Here I am. I'm just a kid myself. I don't know what's going on in the world. He was lying on his bed with a broom, playing a song to himself in his head and humming. He was alone in the dark, wearing several layers of clothing because it was so cold. He was a brilliant kid.

Wonderful kid. He liked me. So I'm sitting there on the edge of the bed saying to myself, 'Geez, I wonder if he's eating?' After the practices I'd take him out to eat. Jimi wanted to play sports, but he was a *terrible* football player. I never put him in the game. So finally one day toward the end of the season some of the other kids came up and said, 'Put Jimi in.' I said, 'I'll do it on the condition that you guys'—my two stars—'you guys play tackle and guard.' They go, 'OK.' They were all pumped up for it. Jimi carried the ball and gained some nice yardage. That was fun for us all."

Booth fondly remembers another game one drizzly Saturday in mid-October. His team was playing a team from Laurelhurst, an upscale Seattle neighborhood. "Our kids were dressed in a combination of street clothes and uniforms. It was about 40 degrees and raining hard." They were do-ing their warm-ups when the opposing team arrived in a chartered bus, wearing spiffy uniforms, complete with hand warmers and slickers. "It was the mismatch of the season," he says, "but something happened that day that was little short of a miracle. I noticed the determined look on my

Booth, center, with the UW's high school relations committee. *Tyee yearbook*, 1955, pg. 103.

kids' faces. We scored twice so fast that it took the other team off guard."
Laurelhurst eventually rallied to tie the score and Booth's kids spent most
of the rest of the game on defense, with the enemy deep in their territory.
The score was still deadlocked when time expired. They left the field feeling
like winners in more ways than one.

The idealistic college student met "all kinds of people who needed help.
They came from neighborhoods where incarceration, drugs, aggression,
dysfunctional family structures and single-parent homes were the norm,"
Booth says. "I saw kids with severe disabilities and met their brave and
frustrated parents. I saw things that were very different from my own
upbringing. Even though I thought I'd been pretty much hammered as a
kid, they had it a lot worse. I did what I could to make life a little better for
them and to create as many opportunities as I could, in my limited way."

One day when Booth was coaching a baseball game at Broadway
Playfield, a striking woman named Katie Dolan showed up with her autistic son, Patrick, who was around 7. He was in a wheelchair in the wake of
the latest in a series of mishaps. The boy was non-verbal but Booth found
a way to include him in the game. "I had him hold the baseballs when we
were taking batting practice. I'd walk over and take one ball at a time from
him." Katie was impressed and they struck up a friendship.

Kathleen Houlahan Dolan, 33 when she and Booth became friends
and allies, had a degree in drama from the University of Washington.
"As audacious and driven as she was beautiful and charming," Katie had
worked as an actress and model and hosted KIRO-TV's popular "Women's
World" program. When Patrick was diagnosed with autism and became
a hyperactive wild child, she thought she would lose her mind. She went
to see a psychiatrist. "I suppose it helped me," she said years later, "but it
didn't help Patrick," who had stopped eating and talking. Dolan channeled
all her drive and chutzpah into improving the lives of children with disabilities and assisting their families.

A wonderful thing happened during a game between Broadway and
Mountlake Terrace. The Mountlake pitcher motioned to Katie to bring

Patrick to the plate. "Standing about halfway between the pitcher's mound and home plate, he pitched underhand," Booth recalls, "and to everybody's surprise Patrick hit the ball—although it went straight back to the pitcher." The pitcher threw it over the first baseman's head. "Next thing I knew, Katie was running down the baseline, pushing Patrick's wheelchair. All the kids shouted at her to 'run, run, run!' Katie and Patrick turned and headed for second base" as the right fielder retrieved the ball and took his time getting it back to the pitcher, who lobbed it over the third baseman's head. Katie and Patrick barreled into home plate and scored a run. Everyone cheered. It all happened so spontaneously, Booth says. "It was great."

In the years to come, Gardner encouraged the Seattle Parks Department to develop programs suited to kids like Patrick Dolan, and Katie started networking with other formidable moms.

⌒

During his junior year at the University, Booth encountered O.L. Mitchell, a standout football player at Whitworth College in Spokane who was also working summers for the Parks Department. He'd been an all-city football player at Seattle's Franklin High. Mitchell "had more character than anybody I had met up to this time," Booth says. "My own tendency was to cut corners when I found a corner that could be cut, but Mitch went straight over the center. He played by the rules." The slender white guy and the black linebacker went nose to nose in "a huge argument" at Yesler Terrace. In those days, "getting a practice field was nearly impossible," Booth says. The coach had to go down to the Parks Department office and fill out paperwork. But Booth convinced the ladies there that he was a twin and finagled two practice fields a week by impersonating himself. "Mitch figured out what I was doing and confronted me." They ended up good friends and 1963 teamed up with another dedicated volunteer, John Little, to launch the Central Area Youth Association, which provides athletic programs year-round.

Joe Staton, who became executive director of the association in 2002, met Gardner around 1962 when he was a 14-year-old playing Pony League baseball in the Central Area. Booth always told his kids that if they applied themselves—practiced hard, played fair, did their homework, set an example for others—they would all be big leaguers. That came true literally for Staton, who went on to play first base with the Detroit Tigers. His Garfield High School classmate, Bill North, was another of Booth's kids. North became the American League's base-stealing champ and won two World Series rings with the Oakland A's.

"I'm sure Booth took a lot of flak for chauffeuring black kids all over town in his car during that era," Staton says. "I'm also sure it never bothered him. He was always bucking the tide. He always stood up for the rights of his kids. He taught us how to play the game and be young men. He emphasized discipline and order and always made sure his players had the proper equipment and looked sharp. That was our trademark." Gardner coached baseball, soccer and football, Staton adds, but above all he was a mentor. "When Booth teamed up with O.L. Mitchell, that changed everything for him and the Central Area. They were both men of high integrity and they were dedicated to the welfare of African American kids. They had rules and expectations—from the shining of your shoes to the pressing of your uniform; cleaning your room—the whole picture, not just playing ball."

Booth made a lot of lasting friends on the playfields of Seattle. It was there that one of his mantras as governor—"You can pay me now or you can pay me later"—first came to mind. Poverty and poor education beget more poverty, broken homes, fatherless children, joblessness, hopelessness, violence and crime. Booth believes the United Negro College Fund's slogan sums it all up: "A mind is a terrible thing to waste." Working with the Central Area kids as a college student "was one of the best times of my life, as well as one of the worst," Booth says. "I was getting a hands-on education while the bulk of my peers were getting a book education. I learned that people liked me. I could relate to them, and then they'd trust me. And then I could help—I could make a difference in their lives. But there was so much to be done."

CHAPTER FIVE:

Al's Helicopter

What his former aides call "The Helicopter Story" is another of Booth's evergreens—a yarn for any occasion, from Anacortes to Zillah. It goes like this: "Al Rosellini was our next-door neighbor at our summer place on Vashon Island, and when I was about 15 years old my dad sent me to the store one day. As I was walking back home, here comes this helicopter. I stopped and watched it hover down. The tide was out, and they landed on the beach. Out gets Al and walks up to his house. And I'm standing there thinking, 'Well, I like that.' So I went and found my dad and said, 'What's John's dad do for a living?' My dad said, 'What do you want to know for?' I said, 'Because that's what I'm going to do someday.' I wanted to ride in that helicopter! My dad said, 'He's the governor.' When people ask me why I wanted to be governor I tell them that story. I had a goal early in life."

Sometimes he's returning from baseball practice, and sometimes you'd think he was only in grade school. There's always a spoonful of confabulation. When Al Rosellini was elected governor and started coming to the beach in a National Guard helicopter it was the spring of 1957. Booth Gardner was a 20-year-old junior at the University of Washington, not an awestruck lad heading home from the store with a Popsicle and a loaf of bread. He knew what John Rosellini's dad did for a living. Booth's dad had been debating politics with Al for several years and Booth eavesdropped from the time he was around 12. "They were polar opposites. Republican vs. Democrat," Booth recalls. "But they liked each other. My dad would say, 'I'm going over to Al's. Do you want to go?' I learned a lot about state government listening to them."

Booth's graudation picture from the Lakeside School yearbook in 1954. *Photo courtesy the Lakeside School.*

Abandoning exaggeration, The Helicopter Story often concludes like this: "At times it would turn into a shouting match between my dad and Al, but that was OK with me. I was learning. This was at a time when the state's mental-health institutions were in disarray, and Rosellini was in the process of bringing them up to standards." Reforming the state's snake-pit mental-health system was a landmark accomplishment for the Democrat from Seattle. Booth's interest in politics, especially social services, grew steadily as he matured, Rosellini recalls.

Inspired by his work with kids in the Central Area, Booth was now even more intrigued by the idea of a career in public service. Rosellini is one of his political heroes. Another is the man who defeated Al in 1964, progressive Republican Dan Evans. Gardner turned out to be a sometimes awkward blend of both. As for helicopters, Booth's chief of staff when he became Pierce County executive in 1981 was Greg Barlow, a former Army Special Forces chopper pilot who had logged a thousand hours of combat, dodging surface-to-air missiles in Vietnam. Booth loved it when Barlow, a National Guard officer, landed a helicopter on the seldom-used pad outside the county offices in Tacoma and sent everyone running to the windows.

Rosellini, his memory still sharp at 99 in 2009, chuckled when asked about The Helicopter Story. He said he'd heard Booth tell it many times.

"It's a true story," he said, "but the fact is we had to kind of push him into running for governor in 1984. He was in Pierce County and kept saying he didn't really know many people outside the county. I knew he'd be a good candidate, so I got two or three people together and set up a luncheon and we talked him into running."

One thing Booth never mentioned when he told The Helicopter Story was his deep-seated real motive for wanting to be governor: For as long as he could remember, Brick had made him feel like a loser. "You're always trouble," he'd hissed when the boy was 4. "I became determined to some-day prove my father wrong," Booth says. Friends say he even daydreamed about becoming president of the United States.

Looking classically preppy in a sweater vest and chinos, Booth belonged to the Oval Club and Sun Dodgers and served as chairman of the Organizations Assembly on the UW campus. He was leafing through *Life*

Frosh Day Queen Jean Forstrom.
1957 Tyee yearbook, pg. 156.

magazine one day when he came upon a photo of a stunning cheerleader from Roosevelt High School in Seattle. He clipped the photo and kept it in a drawer. A year later, there she was again, this time in the *UW Daily* as Frosh Day Queen.

Booth had an office in the HUB, the Husky Union Building. "If you turned right you went into one room, and if you turned left you went into another. I was walking through there one day when I saw her sitting at a desk typing. And I went, 'Oh wow!' You know, love at first sight. I walked right into the door jamb and cut my eyebrow. She had to take me to the nurse. I needed a couple of stitches." Any red-blooded American boy would have done a double take. Jean Forstrom, a freshman from Seattle, was also figuratively a knock-out. A blue-eyed Scandinavian blonde with a Pepsodent smile, she was a future Husky cheerleader and Seafair princess. "He came up with some story about how he needed some extra work done and could I help him with that," Jean recalls with a laugh. "When he puts his mind to it, he can be very charming. You kind of know the story's not true, yet you get sucked in." They started dating, and Jean worked on his winning campaign for first vice president of the student body.

Booth graduated with a B.A. in business in 1958 and attended law school at the UW for a year. He quickly concluded that he wasn't cut out to be a lawyer and went to work for a finance company. Jean, meantime, was still seeing other guys. Booth proposed the day after her 21st birthday, August 13, 1959. "He didn't ask me out on my birthday, so I got another date." That may have made up his mind. "The next morning Booth came over to my house and he had a ring." They were married on July 30, 1960, and moved to Boston. Booth entered Harvard Business School in 1961. Although, Jean's degree was in general business, she landed a job working for the dean of Arts & Sciences at Harvard, McGeorge Bundy, who was tapped for the Kennedy cabinet soon thereafter.

Only a C+ student at the University of Washington because he was spending more time working with kids and being a campus politician than studying, it was a chance encounter that led Booth to Harvard's Business School. "I got a phone call one day from a guy I didn't know very well: 'There's a dean from Harvard coming to campus to meet with some people and our transportation fell through. By any wild chance would you be available to give the dean a ride?' It was snowing hard, but I got out to SeaTac and picked him up. His name was Les Rollins. He's from Massachusetts, so he's used to snow, but he says, 'If this stuff is going to continue for a while I'll get a room at the hotel across the street. We can talk.' " They hit it off immediately. The dean was impressed with the facile young man, unaware that Booth was a member of one of the Northwest's

Booth and Jean as newlyweds. *Gardner family album.*

most prestigious families.

"I came back out the next day to pick him up to take him on his rounds. Les greeted me with 'Why don't you apply to the Business School?' " Booth said his grades weren't good enough. Rollins said, "Well, take the test and we'll talk." He took the test. His math score was impressive, his English score mediocre. The dean told him, "Come back here and take a year of English at Harvard University. We can get you in." It was time well spent, Booth says. "I learned to write. You learn to feel things. I was very good at boxing up things I didn't like. I made mistakes, too—*all the time*. I'd box them up and throw them over my shoulder and forget about them....But if you shut things out you can't write because you don't have any tone or balance."

Norton Clapp, by now president and CEO of the Weyerhaeuser Co., "was as surprised as I was when I got accepted at Harvard," Booth says, smiling at the memory. Clapp's expectation was that Booth would grow into a role in the family business, but a Harvard MBA was a first-rate education with cachet. In his own reserved way, Clapp began telling people his stepson was a bona fide comer. He happily paid the tuition.

Was a Harvard Business School education all that it's cracked up to be? "It was," says Booth, quipping, "but George W. Bush went there, so I don't know—except that he had help getting in." Harvard used the Socratic Method "where you had to be on your toes every day. There were a lot of really bright students there. For the first time in my life I knew that I couldn't get by without studying. I worked harder than I'd ever worked before. Every Friday before we left class they handed us a paper to write—1,500 words due at 6 Saturday night. If you lived off campus you were given until midnight. But if you waited until midnight to turn it in you lost your one night out of the week. So I made it a point to turn it in earlier. I got to know three other Harvard guys who lived in the same apartment complex. We'd get together and talk over our business scenarios, develop themes and make sure we had the facts right. Then you'd write your own paper: What points do you see with the business model? What's wrong with it? How would you change it? Why does this happen after you change it? That kind of critical thinking on real-world business challenges. Harvard was where I really acquired self-discipline. The courses I did well in were finance, not marketing, not production. I learned how to manage money. And to this day I'm better at managing other people's money than my own."

Booth Gardner at Harvard in 1965.
HBS Archives Photograph Collection: Faculty and Staff. Baker Library Historical Collection. Harvard Business School.

When he turned 25 in 1961 he inherited a trust fund most informed sources believe was in the neighborhood of $1.7 million, or approximately $12 million in today's dollars. With advice from the Laird Norton financial wizards, he watched the fund grow handsomely. It included holdings in Weyerhaeuser, Safeco and Puget Sound National Bank, as well as prime real estate. When he was running for governor, his money was in a blind trust that had been established in 1972 when he was a state senator. It was managed by a Seattle investment broker. By the mid-1980s, his fortune was likely at least $38 million, according to a proxy report on his Weyerhaeuser stock. Some said a lot more, although he scoffed at one estimate of $50 million. While he was a skilled executive with a good nose for numbers, Booth was not a shrewd investor like Norton Clapp. He emulated his stepfather's conservatism, however, so his questionable ventures, including partnerships in two soccer teams and a pie company, were never big losers.

"Booth didn't want to be known as a trust baby," says Jim Griffin, his friend since childhood. "After he got his MBA and started working for a clothing firm in Tacoma, he made it clear to me and his other friends that he would live on his salary with no help from his trust income. After he and Jean started having kids, Jean would complain to my wife, Wendy, that Booth wouldn't trade in their VW 'Beetle' for a bigger family car or buy a dryer for their beach cabin. When I talked to Booth about it, he said he couldn't afford either one on his present salary." When she was

First Lady, Jean Gardner told a reporter they bought their first furniture at Goodwill. "He always felt uncomfortable in fancy clothes, fancy cars or whatever," she added. "I really don't know why. Maybe he felt guilty" about inheriting a fortune in the wake of his mother's death.

Brick Gardner always drove Cadillacs, even after he'd stopped selling them. Norton Clapp, who was worth about $450 million when he died in 1995, drove a Buick. It wasn't even the most expensive Buick. That would have been too showy.

Former aides and friends all tell the same stories about Booth never having any pocket money, à la John F. Kennedy, who invariably bummed a buck from aides for a sandwich and a cup of coffee. Rosalie Gittings, Booth's personal assistant, executive secretary and ex-officio mom during most of his years as governor, says, "He never carried any money. He'd say, 'Well, I need 50 bucks.' So I wrote out a check to me and gave it to him to sign. Then I'd dole out the money to him. A woman who had worked for him before said to me, 'He borrows money and never pays you back.' And I thought, 'Well, you dumb-head! What do you put up with that for?' "

Nor was Booth a fancy eater. It was his stepmother, Millie, who broadened his horizons by forcing him to try spaghetti. ("I liked it!") A hamburger and a medium Coke is his idea of a balanced meal. Adele Ferguson, the longtime capitol correspondent for *The Bremerton Sun,* first met him in the 1970s when he was a state senator in a district that included parts of Kitsap County. "He'd invite me out to lunch or dinner and he'd always order a cheeseburger. I figured he must not have any money so I'd order something cheap, too. I said something about it one time to Jack Pyle from *The Tacoma News Tribune.* I said, 'Jesus Christ, this guy never has any money. He always orders the cheapest thing on the menu.' 'Well,' Jack says, 'the thing about Booth is that he's got so much money that he wants to spend yours to make up for it.' The next time I got invited out and from then on I ordered from the *top* of the menu, and I ate *big.* I thought, 'To heck with that. I'm not going to eat any more of these damn cheeseburgers!' "

CHAPTER SIX:

Orphaned

Booth Gardner became a father not long before he lost his own. Doug Gardner was born in Massachusetts in 1962, Gail in 1963 at Lakewood General Hospital. Booth brought his young family back home to Tacoma after receiving his master of business administration degree from Harvard. He took a position as assistant to a division president with Day's Tailored Wear, a long-established clothing manufacturer in Tacoma. Then he spent a year in Southern California with the Bowie Pie Company. Brick Gardner, meanwhile, had sold his two radio stations, completed his master's degree at the University of Hawaii and was teaching at Kalakaua Intermediate School in Honolulu.

"He didn't tell anyone he was going back to school—not me or anyone else," Booth says. He hoped his father was on the wagon and rolling toward stability. One of their conversations gave him pause. Brick said that in grad school he had to cite an example of a behavioral problem and tell how he'd deal with it. "It was the toughest part of the year," Booth recalls him saying. Sometimes he'd just blurt out, "You just shove that kid to the wall, keep him there and don't let him move." Booth says Brick conceded that his son knew "more than his professor about dealing with human beings."

Jean Gardner says she "got along fine" with Brick, "but he had a streak in him that wasn't very nice, and he hurt a lot of people just by words," especially when he was drinking. However, "a lot people really, really liked him. There was just a real close bond with a lot of his cronies from his early Tacoma days. Brick would do anything for them and they would do anything for Brick."

Booth vividly remembers telling his father, "Your drinking is causing problems for not just yourself but for everybody around you. Why don't you quit?" They argued a while. "OK then," Booth offered, "if you can't quit for someone else, quit for me." Brick looked at him intently for what seemed like minutes. "I can't do it for you," he said. "I've got to do it for myself. And I'm going to try again." He did try. Most binges would be followed by a few months of sobriety, "but he always went back to it," Booth says sadly. A former disc jockey at Brick's Honolulu station recalls Brick stopping by with his "snippety" little dog "when the Waikiki bars shut down at 2 a.m."

⌒

Shortly after midnight on Tuesday, January 25, 1966, the doorman at the new 10-story Kahala Hilton Hotel "heard a noise resembling an object falling against the plate glass." He looked around and saw something on the sidewalk near a corner of the building. It was a man, sprawled on his back, showing no signs of life. The doorman asked the hotel operator to call an ambulance and summoned the security guard and hotel manager. When they checked his ID, they recognized him as a recent troublesome visitor. They decided they also needed the police.

Brick Gardner had been at the hotel at 1:15 a.m. the previous Friday. Convincing the night clerk that he was the husband of the woman in Room 917, he obtained a key. About 10 minutes later, the pair came down to the lobby. They talked heatedly for a few minutes before the woman headed for the elevators, remarking to the clerk, "He's a sick man." Gardner started a commotion, then departed in a black Cadillac when a security

Hotel fall kills Kahala man, 60

A school teacher fell to his death today from the ninth floor of the Kahala Hilton Hotel.

Police believe Bryson Ross Gardner, 60, of 4788 Aukai Avenue, Waialae-Kahala, lost his balance and toppled off a beam connecting two balconies while trying to reach an acquaintance's room.

He fell 104 feet and landed on the sidewalk.

He died instantly.

His was the first fatal fall at the hotel.

There were no known witnesses to the 12:18 a.m. fall.

Police believe Gardner was on the ninth floor to visit a friend whose room is on that floor.

Gardner had taught at Kalakaua Intermediate School since 1960.

Gardner formerly owned radio stations here and on the Big Island. His Honolulu station was KHON, now KPOI.

Before he moved to Hawaii in 1954, he owned a chemical firm and automobile dealership in Tacoma, Washington.

Bryson Gardner

The *Honolulu Star-Bulletin* story from January 25, 1966.

guard ordered him off the premises.

The woman told detectives she'd met Gardner some five years earlier on a trip to the islands. They had become "very good friends." After the recent squabble, they'd patched things up, and she visited his home earlier that night. She had made it clear to him, however, that she did not share his "romantic inclinations toward her—that this was goodbye." She was departing for home the next day.

Detectives and the medical examiner took careful measurements. Bryson R. Gardner, 60, had fallen 104 feet to his death from a narrow cement beam while attempting to reach the balcony lanai of Room 917. The crystal on his Omega wristwatch was shattered. The watch had stopped at 12:18. Dust on the ninth-floor beam "had been disturbed." Toxicology tests revealed that Gardner was extremely intoxicated. There was no suicide note. Investigators concluded there had been no foul play. It was the last tragic misadventure of Brick Gardner's checkered life. His alcoholism was compounded by the loss of his wife and daughter and chagrin at having extracted money from Clapp to suffer in some semblance of silence.

"Booth didn't talk a lot about the emotionally charged personal events in his life" when they were kids, Steve Merrill says. When they grew older, however, he confided that he had been haunted by the fear that Brick would kill himself. Merrill says Booth actually took some comfort in the news that Brick's death had been an accident.

The *Honolulu Star-Bulletin* put the story on the front page, together with a photo of Brick, wearing a natty bow tie but looking older than 60. Back home in Tacoma, the *News Tribune* soft-pedaled the story under a one-column headline near the bottom of Page One: **Son of Pioneer Tacoma Family Dies in Honolulu**. The story said nothing about the circumstances of his death other than it occurred "in a Honolulu hospital." Tacoma society was unsurprised but relieved the scandal hadn't happened closer to home. Everyone felt badly for Booth. They were glad he seemed to be going places. For 18 years—until Booth was running for governor—no one in the Northwest media revealed how Brick Gardner had really died.

~~

Shortly after his father's death, Booth was offered the post of assistant to the dean of the Harvard Business School. It was a good time to get away and the job sounded like fun. "I was reviewing applications," he says. "I was the travel squad—flying all over the country for the next year. But I wanted to be governor, and I can't get to be governor from Boston." Jean suggested he fly back home and sniff around for opportunities. The University of Puget Sound in Tacoma needed a new director for its School of Business Administration & Economics, preferably a live-wire young fellow. Booth smiles that "it must have helped" that his stepfather had been a trustee and generous benefactor of UPS since 1933, but his own bona fides were solid: MBA from Harvard; real-world business experience, albeit not a lot; mentor to underprivileged youth; Tacoma native; a winning personality.

Booth and Jean and their two young children moved back to Tacoma in 1967. Booth immersed himself in the job and a host of charitable and social welfare programs, including the Central Area Youth Association, the Central City Learning Center of Tacoma and the Seattle Treatment

Booth meets with a student at the UPS Business School.
Photo courtesy the University of Puget Sound.

Center, a detox program. He built the Seattle Mental Health Institute and helped finance a youth camp on Lopez Island. He was also the adviser to the UPS chapter of Phi Delta Theta and enjoyed joining the students "in Monday night post-chapter meeting fellowship at Pat's Tavern," one of the many places in Tacoma where everybody knew his name. He was at UPS for five years in all, taking a sabbatical in 1969 to head a Seattle School District initiative to develop new programs for schools in the Central Area. Seattle's African American community never forgot him, and the Jaycees named him 1970's "Outstanding Young Man of Washington."

"I enjoyed being at UPS," Booth says, "but I was looking ahead."

CHAPTER SEVEN:

Senator Gardner

Before deciding which office to seek as a stepping stone, Booth realized he needed to pick a party. One thing his father and stepfather actually had in common was that they were both Republicans. Brick Gardner, however, was all fuss and bluster while Norton Clapp was cool and calculating. Clapp gave his time and money generously but strategically, especially in the early 1960s when Washington State sprouted a crop of bright young Republicans. They were led by State Rep. Dan Evans, an engineer from Seattle. Evans was an Eagle Scout who loved to hike and sail. Clapp, by now one of the top Scout leaders in the nation and an enthusiastic boater, liked the cut of his jib. He was also impressed with the rest of Evans' crew, especially the cerebral Slade Gorton, a transplanted New Englander. Clapp was more conservative than they were, but another major Republican donor cut to the chase: "He's a pragmatist, not an ideological warrior."

In "The Last Tycoon," the most insightful profile of Clapp ever written, Nick Gallo of the Seattle *Weekly* summed up Clapp's free-enterprise philosophy: "He lambasted wasteful government, claiming it stifled productivity and creativity. He compared government structure to a 19th-Century stagecoach unprepared to take us into the 21st Century and urged creation of a Metro-like 'megacity' to replace the patchwork of bureaucracies in the Puget Sound area." Clapp was a key contributor as Evans bucked a Democratic tide in 1964 and denied Al Rosellini a third term. The helicopter was now at the disposal of a Republican.

Clapp was in for a shock in 1970. His stepson had decided to become a Democrat, and he hadn't seen it coming. Two years earlier, Booth had publicly identified himself as a Republican in a newspaper ad, joining a list of GOP supporters of the state's formidable senior U.S. Senator, Warren G. "Maggie" Magnuson. "I was a devout Republican by birth, by association," Booth says, "but I was conflicted." He'd been talking politics with Bill Baarsma, a colleague at the University of Puget Sound and a future Tacoma

Norton Clapp by Roger Thias

mayor. Baarsma was an activist Democrat with a strong social conscience. He told Booth that the satisfaction he derived from his work with the kids in the Central Area and Tacoma's Metropolitan Development Council, which administered federal anti-poverty programs, was his heart telling his head which party to join. Jean Gardner suggested Booth talk with the chairmen of both parties "and find out what their philosophies are."

C. Montgomery "Gummie" Johnson, a legendary Republican strategist, "was just 'caveat emptor' all the way," Booth remembers. "His political philosophy was, 'If Jones can't get a job, that's his problem. There are plenty of jobs out there and if he'd keep his act together he'd get a job.' " R.R. "Bob" Greive, the indomitable Democratic majority leader of the State Senate, said, "We're here to help those who can't help themselves. We make mistakes, probably too many. But better to err on the side of serving somebody than not serving them until you're sure where you stand."

Booth went home that night and told Jean they were—*voilà*—newly-minted Democrats. When he broke the news to his stepfather, he says there was surprise tinged with incredulity but no anger. "Norton would have been happier had I been a Republican," Booth allows, smiling at the understatement. When the smoke cleared, Clapp seemed quietly pleased that Booth was exercising independence. The philanthropist in him had always been proud of his stepson's altruism, yet he must have worried whether he was tough enough to make it on his own. Toughness was a trait Clapp admired. Whenever he faced heartache—the loss of his mother, two wives, three sons, a stepdaughter and a brother—Clapp immersed himself in his work and outside activities. Never willing to be lonely, he married four times.

Some say the imposing stepfather and the seemingly mild-mannered stepson had some heated confrontations in the years to come. Booth says they rarely talked politics. What's clear is that even when Clapp's Republican friends were grousing that his stepson was a traitor to his class, he told them to pony up.

After surviving Harvard, Booth had come to "enormously admire"

Clapp's intellect and self-discipline. A few years later, when he temporarily abandoned politics to head the family business, he came to see just how smart his stepfather was. One thing is for certain, Booth says: "He's the reason I was governor. I don't think I could have made it on my own. I just wasn't in the loop. I had done nothing politically."

The first step was a seat in the State Senate.

⤳

Tall and clean-cut, 34-year-old Larry Faulk was a "Dan Evans Republican." He also appeared Kennedyesque. In fact, he'd met JFK in 1960 while a student at Seattle University. Faulk had taken a two-month leave from the Boeing Co. in 1964 to serve as deputy director of the Evans gubernatorial campaign in Pierce County. Two years later, in a flawlessly planned campaign that featured more than a hundred clean-cut doorbellers, Faulk upset two-term Democrat Jack Petrich to become, at 30, the youngest member of the State Senate. The 26th District freshman's accomplishments in the next four years included helping push through legislation to give the state's two-year "junior" colleges autonomy from local school districts. A few minutes before the final vote, a school board chairman in his district called to say he was toast if he voted for it. Faulk was undeterred. He also went nose to nose with a powerful committee chairman from Seattle, Wes Uhlman, to ensure that a division of the new state appellate court would be based in Tacoma.

"Larry was a prodigious worker," Booth says, "and a good guy. Everyone said, 'Run for the House,' but that's a two-year term. I wanted a four-year term. So I took him on. I'm likely a prohibitive loser, but after his victory in 1966 Larry had written a manual on how to get elected at the local level." Booth checked it out from the Tacoma Public Library. Faulk's "master plan" left nothing to chance. It outlined how to stage a coffee klatch, where and when to doorbell and how to get write-ups in all the papers, especially the weeklies, which candidates often overlooked. Emphasizing that "the candidate must be on time," the primer also told how to make a splash at the county convention

Booth on the campaign trail in 1970.
Gardner family album.

to recruit more foot soldiers. "The candidate's band will not be loaned to any other candidate," it said, adding that "girls with chant signs" should be deployed throughout the crowd to build excitement. Bumper strips, lawn signs, car-top signs, even pencils featuring the candidate's name—"the little things"— were also important to the cause. "When I finished reading it," Booth says, "I thought, 'Son of a bitch!' and I said to myself, 'Nobody can do what he did twice.' He'd doorbelled everywhere. He had a good mail campaign. He'd just done everything textbook—and then he wrote the book on it." What happened next is reminiscent of the scene in "Patton" when the inimitable American general fulfills his dream of facing Rommel, the great German field marshal, in an epic tank battle. Patton surveys the battlefield through his field glasses, sees his guys winning and declares, "Rommel, you magnificent bastard, I read your book!"

Money being the ammunition of a campaign, Faulk was also losing that battle. Booth handily won the Democratic primary and never let up. "We doorbelled and turned up everywhere," he says. One day they were campaigning outside Tacoma's Asarco smelter at 6 a.m. as the swing shift was heading home. Faulk was working one side of the street, Booth the other. During a lull, Faulk wandered over.

"Did you read my book?"

"Yes."

"So what did you think?"

"You're losing the election."

"What?"

"Your manual says that if by September 30th you haven't done the following you can't make it up, and you haven't done the following."

Faulk smiled thinly and went back to his side of the street, shaking his head.

"It's a true story," Faulk says, nodding and chuckling 40 years later. Before filing week, "Someone called and told me, 'Booth Gardner's running against you!' And I said, 'Who the hell is he?' It turns out he had unlimited resources and he's a bright guy. Essentially what he did was study my plan and unload on me. Dan (Evans) had convinced us to put an income tax on the ballot and Booth is saying, 'Well folks, Senator Faulk's been down there four years and the budget's gone up 10 percent and he was on Ways & Means and he caused that, and not only that he wants to give you an income tax!' I said, 'Oh my God, I can see it coming now!'

He had automatic typewriters going 24 hours a day; a full-time headquarters; staff people coming out his ears. And here we are. I'm working at Boeing, being a loaned exec to United Way, as well as trying to win this election. I'm being bombarded by everything Booth is sending out in the mail and we can't match it. Oh my God, it was unbelievable!"

Booth was elected to the Washington State Senate with 56 percent of the vote. He and Faulk would meet again on the campaign trail 11 years later. In the meantime, Booth shrewdly also made friends with one of Faulk's campaign workers, Greg Barlow.

26th District Senator Larry Faulk in 1968.
Faulk family album.

Faulk and Barlow had been classmates at Seattle University and were great pals. Both were boxers who'd "just beat the hell" out of their opponents. "Greg was bright and charismatic—a handsome devil," Faulk says. "He was also a Vietnam vet. Booth ran into him during the campaign and was fascinated with him." When he became governor, Booth also hired Faulk's quick-witted wife, Mary, to be an agency head. "Another smart move," Faulk says.

⤳

Senator Gardner's arrival in Olympia in January of 1971 generated a stir in progressive circles. "Booth Gardner, New Bright Light in State Senate; Democratic Stepson of Norton Clapp Sets Tough Goals for Himself," the Seattle *Argus* fawned. "Spending an hour or so with W. Booth Gardner is excellent therapy to help relieve the chronic disillusionment, cynicism and irritating frustration that grip many political observers in Olympia at about this stage of each legislative session," wrote Worth Hedrick, the weekly's Olympia correspondent. "Conversing with the 34-year-old freshman Tacoma Democrat is akin to filling your lungs with fresh air after spending a day in the smoggiest section of an urban area, or comparable time listening to the political wrangling that often pollutes the air of the legislative chambers. Gardner is a supremely confident young man who... also happens to be the stepson of Norton Clapp, chairman of the board of Weyerhaeuser and head of the Seattle Chamber of Commerce—one of the state's foremost Republicans and wealthiest men."

"I have innate confidence in myself—confidence that I can do a good job no matter what I'm asked to do," Booth told the reporter, adding that he had "no axes to grind" and a lot of practical experience in business, education and social services. His basic philosophy was that "before a guy gets into politics he should be well-grounded in community activities. What really counts is getting in and working at the floor-level so you get dirt under your fingernails."

Gardner described himself as an "achievement-oriented individual," but emphasized that he was in "no frantic rush to get things done in the Senate." He didn't plan to "plunge headlong into the legislative treadmill before he learns a great deal more about legislative and political processes." Gardner set three basic goals for his first session: To "understand the structure of state government and inner-relationships"; to learn parliamentary procedure "for that rare instance when you have to be fast on your feet on the floor" and to get involved in "one or two key pieces of legislation." He became chairman of the Manufacturing & Industrial Development Committee,

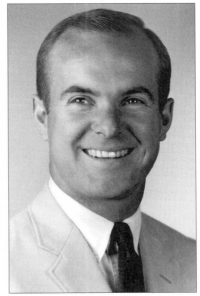

Senator Gardner in 1971.
Gardner family album.

co-sponsoring a bill to diversify the state's industrial base and create more jobs in rural areas. He also backed a bill calling for "tight" seacoast management and, like Dan Evans, championed a state income tax. To the dismay of many, Gardner also promptly signed onto a bill to place the Legislature under the Open Public Meetings Act. Moreover, he refused to sign any bill the first day he saw it, which seasoned Democrats found annoying. "They don't understand what's wrong with me" for not trusting their judgment, he said. "I'm basically nonpolitical. I don't care about politics except as a means of helping me get things done. My only allegiance is to my constituents."

"In the long run," Hedrick surmised, "it may well prove fortunate for the Democratic Party that Booth Gardner believes most Republicans can get along fine without his help."

Maybe not. There were enough curve balls in that welcome-to-Olympia writeup to win a Cy Young Award. As a fledgling legislator, Booth's batting average was way short of the big league he found himself in. Some of the old hands acknowledged he was likable, but also worrisome—a squirrely naïf. Others thought he had real promise. They said he'd come around when he got some real dirt under his fingernails. Fifteen years later, when Booth was governor, House Speaker Joe King, a wily Democrat from Vancouver, said he still didn't get it. Politics, King said, "isn't always pretty, and it isn't always fun. Sometimes you have to hurt people's feelings. Sometimes you have to say no."

Booth was happier when he became chairman of the Senate Education Committee in 1972, but concluded that he was a manager, not a designated hitter. Asked in 2009 to cite his most notable achievement as a state senator, he instantly declared, "None. *Nothing.*" "You're not much of a legislator, are you?" his visitor offered. "I hate legislators!" he blurted out, adding with a chuckle, "Well, I don't really, but I love the administrative aspect of government. I tolerated the legislative aspect of government."

～

Booth was still involved in many community outreach activities, including Northwest Center, a parent-operated organization founded in the 1960s to assist developmentally disabled children and adults. Cecile Lindquist, his UW classmate, headed its board. Katie Dolan, his friend from their Parks Department days, was also in the thick of things, having graduated from outraged mom to sophisticated activist. Katie's repertoire of lobbying tricks included telling fortunes in beer foam, a shtick that won her an appearance on "What's My Line." The Northwest Center's Mother's Guild—dubbed the "mothers in tennis shoes" and "four housewives from Seattle"—began to push the Legislature to approve an "Education for All" act. It stipulated that Washington children with disabilities have a constitutional right to a public school education. After a full court press by Dolan, Lindquist and their equally tenacious pals, Janet Taggart and Evelyn Chapman, House Bill 90 was signed into law with pleasure by Governor Evans in the spring of 1971. "This wasn't an exercise in lobbying or political science," Dolan said. "From our viewpoint it was a matter of life and death."

Education for All was the first law of its kind in the nation. With Gardner's support, Dolan and Taggart, next helped found Troubleshooters, an advocacy agency for families dealing with disabilities. Booth served on their board for several years. Dolan, who died in 2006, "put her whole heart and soul into advocacy for people with disabilities," says Lindquist, who once headed the Washington State Developmental Disabilities Council. "She was extraordinarily creative and driven, which meant she ruffled a lot feathers. But it never bothered Booth. Katie got things done."

A time would come when it did bother Booth.

In the summer of 1971, one of Norton Clapp's board members called Booth to relay an offer he couldn't refuse: President of the Laird Norton Company, with its diverse network of enterprises: Lumber yards and retail building-supply outlets from Alaska to Minnesota; prime real estate in downtown Seattle; shopping centers and industrial parks, plus its major stake in Weyerhaeuser. Booth would also oversee the Medina Foundation and the Laird Norton Family Foundation, two of the Northwest's top philanthropies. Booth's stepbrothers and half-brothers were either temperamentally unsuited, disinclined or not ready to run the family store. Clapp told his stepson he had his full confidence, which sealed the deal. They both understood, however, that Clapp was stepping aside, not going away. That was fine with Booth. "Getting to work for Norton and run a company like that was the opportunity of a lifetime for any manager."

Booth resigned from the State Senate on Dec. 13, 1973, saying the pressure of meeting his business and family responsibilities was too great for him to do justice to the seat. In the wake of redistricting, he no longer lived within the 26th District, so whether he would seek another term had been up in the air in any case. His resignation had been rumored for some time, the *Tacoma News Tribune* noted, adding that "despite rumors he might wish to run for governor or other high office, Gardner denied any such aspiration at this time."

Some speculated he left the Senate because he didn't want to comply with a new financial-disclosure law. But he'd already done a legal end-around, placing his investment portfolio in a blind trust nearly a year earlier after voters approved the law, which had hundreds of public officials in a dither. City council members and citizen-legislators protested that their competitors in the insurance and widget business would crib from their list of customers and "quality people" would be discouraged from entering public service. The asset value reporting categories under the new law were so broad, however, that they offered only vague insight into personal wealth. When he was running for governor 11 years later, Gardner responded to calls to open his blind trust to public inspection. Well, sort of. Citing federal law, the Public Disclosure Commission told Gardner he need only report the assets originally placed in the blind trust. State statutes were also lenient. The value of Gardner's Weyerhaeuser stock in 1972 was listed simply as "more than $25,000." Federal law, however, stipulated that officers and directors of publicly-held corporations had to reveal their stock holdings and transactions. When he succeeded Clapp on the Weyerhaeuser Company Board of Directors on April 15, 1976, Gardner owned 105,240 shares of Weyerhaeuser, worth approximately $4.7 million. He sold 10,000 shares that December at $45 a share. He also became a director of Puget Sound National Bank and stepped up his giving to charities and social betterment programs.

He had work to do at home, too.

CHAPTER EIGHT:

On-the-job training

The executive director of the Medina Foundation, which carefully directed Norton Clapp's philanthropy, was Greg Barlow. Booth recommended him for the job, which ended up boosting his own stock with the boss. A former Boy Scout, Barlow was Clapp's kind of man. He'd been awarded the Silver Star, a Purple Heart and a chest-full of other medals in Vietnam. Combat also italicized his inclination to live like there was no tomorrow. Larry Faulk remembers getting Barlow a job in Olympia when he was in the State Senate. "Greg was staying at our house and he was raising all kinds of hell. He wouldn't make his bed in the morning and he might up and take off with Mary's car." By the time he got to the Medina Foundation, however, Barlow was a detail man, decisive, tough-minded. He got things done. Clapp and Gardner vicariously admired his ballsiness. Barlow also shared the boss's view that charitable money should be invested as wisely as working capital. The Medina Foundation, which has disbursed more than $69 million since it was founded by Clapp in 1947, has concentrated on programs that help the handicapped, feed the poor and educate deserving young people. But if you want a grant, you have to prove you will spend it efficiently. "During the '60s every fool in the world solved

Booth as CEO of the Laird Norton Company and trustee at UPS. *Photo courtesy University of Puget Sound.*

the unemployment problem by setting up his own job development company and applying for a grant," Barlow once observed. "It was silly money." The Medina Foundation, he added, expected "the bleeding hearts" to run an agency that could pass an audit.

Like a tough big brother, Barlow became Booth's fixer. They commiserated when Clapp was underwhelmed by some assignment they'd labored over. One day, Barlow came into Booth's office, shaking his head. "Look at this," he said, forking over a report Clapp had red-penciled like a freshman composition paper. Hardly a sentence Barlow had written had survived intact. "I had to laugh," Booth remembers. "Norton really put you on the spot. You had to be clear. You had to be able to speak concisely and articulate your point, and he didn't like you to try and get away with things. You learned that in a hurry. I saw him once a year for a big meeting to review things. I'd be all prepared, trying to anticipate what he really wanted to know. But he'd always catch you off guard on something. He would sit there and doze off. He was sleeping, but he was still thinking. He never stopped thinking. I had outstanding instincts—way beyond the average person. I was gifted with that, but Norton was brilliant—meticulous and disciplined."

When the Gardner children started elementary school, Jean and her chum, Connie Bacon, bought a gift shop in Tacoma. They were partners for seven years. Bacon, who would become Booth's special assistant for Western Washington when he was governor, described Jean as "kind, generous, caring, bright," with "real depth of character." Several others who knew the couple well during those years said Jean was also "very Scandinavian" and, all things considered, not a good match for such an insecure, ambitious man. Booth was affable on the outside but driven to succeed by those old demons. As he poured himself into the presidency of the Laird Norton Co., overseeing a major expansion of the lumberyards, he was commuting daily from Tacoma to Seattle and struggling to meet his family responsibilities. In particular, he knew he wasn't being a good father—his own being a pluperfect example of how not to do it. Years later, Doug Gardner told a *New York Times* writer, "He provided for us, but he wasn't there for us." Booth admitted, "I wasn't a good father. I didn't give him enough support, so he found it in religion." Like many men of his generation, Booth's priorities were work and success. He even attended seminars where other CEOs and their spouses talked about the pressures. Some of those sessions were like AA meetings, there was so much baggage to be checked.

Jean Gardner spoke candidly to Walter Hatch for his riveting 1987 *Seattle Times* profile of the governor. She said they'd always had a "stormy relationship," even separating for a while in the late 1970s. She resented Booth's bouts of withdrawal, his inability to discuss his feelings. His work and his civic causes seemed to be a higher priority than his family. During those years, he was often absent, she said, and tried to compensate by spoiling their kids, which she especially resented because it meant Mom had to be the bad guy, the one who said no.

⌣

Despite later denials, Booth flirted with the idea of running for governor in 1976, concluding that would be aiming too high too soon, even though it turned out to be a good year for outsiders. For president, a Georgia peanut farmer named Jimmy Carter edged Gerald Ford, who was undone by rampant inflation and his pardon of the disgraced Richard Nixon. Dixy Lee Ray, a former head of the U.S. Atomic Energy Commission, was elected governor, defeating John Spellman, the pipe-smoking moderate Republican who was King County executive. Even members of her own party came to view Ray as a radioactive loose cannon, sort of like Sarah Palin with a Ph.D. and a poodle. From what he read, Booth liked Spellman a lot better than Dixy, but he thought she ran the better campaign. He mused that he could have beaten Spellman too.

The Gardners reconciled and Pierce County voters moved to divorce themselves from a scandal.

⌣

On November 28, 1978, federal agents arrested newly re-elected Sheriff George Janovich in the parking lot of a Tacoma supermarket. In all, 16 members of an alleged extortion ring, "The Enterprise," were handcuffed that day. The other big fish was John J. Carbone. The feds said he was the boss of a Chicago-style gang that extracted protection money from South Tacoma tavern and night club owners and bail bondsmen who offered sex and gambling on the side. The recalcitrant had their places torched, some repeatedly, and a state Liquor Control Board inspector was shot outside his home. When some leading Tacomans had the audacity to suggest the fires were Carbone's handiwork, he had his goons torch his own house while he was on vacation. Not only could he collect the insurance money, he'd look like a victim. Unfortunately, the boys proved to be inept arsonists, Rick Anderson recalled in a *Seattle Weekly* column years later. They had tried to burn down a tavern "by running around at night next to a busy street with flaming brooms, jumping and stretching up to set the roof on fire.... They did get the fire going at the boss's house, all right," but the investigators were no dummies. They looked in the closets and found no remains of clothes or shoes. Walking from room to charred room, they concluded that the good furniture had been removed before the blaze. The net was closed when the sheriff was caught on tape accepting a $1,300 bribe from an undercover federal agent. Janovich, Carbone and five others were convicted on 45 racketeering counts, six other defendants having

The first must be the very best.

TNT 12-16-80

We've made a business decision here in Pierce County. We voted to change our form of local government and to give *one* man, the County Executive we elect, the power and authority to lead the County Council in a total reorganization of every department so that we can have a *united* Pierce County.

It's going to take quite a guy! That's why we're for Booth Gardner.

He is an administrator with extensive management skills. Fifteen years in the top executive positions of government and business, including member of the Board of Directors of Puget Sound National Bank, Weyerhaeuser Company and Council on Foundations, and member of Board of Trustees of Washington Mutual Savings Bank and the University of Puget Sound.

Booth Gardner knows how to make money. As President of the Laird Norton Company and Chairman of the Board of Metropolitan Building Corporation, he has been a businessman *with an obligation to stockholders to operate effectively and efficiently and to make a profit!*

And that's exactly what he has been doing for the past decade. During these very difficult economic times, he has led his companies through inflation and recession with a profit *every* quarter of *every* fiscal year.

Booth is not a figurehead. He is the leader. Handling millions of dollars daily and making the decisions that affect the lives of thousands of people.

Booth's lead-off ad in the race for Pierce County Executive.

pleaded guilty. The disgraced sheriff got 12 years, Carbone twice that, and the county ended up paying the liquor agent and two of the victimized tavern owners a total of $3.7 million for deprivation of their civil rights.

Jolted by the scandal, Pierce County voters in late 1979 elected Larry Faulk and 22 others as "freeholders" to draft a new county charter. They met twice a week for six months, with Faulk as one of the architects of a plan that called for a more businesslike, taxpayer-accountable approach to governance. The voters approved, and elections were set in early 1981 to choose a new seven-member County Council headed by a county executive. The sheriff and other department heads were to become appointed positions.

In December of 1980, Booth's hat was one of the first in the ring for county executive. So was Faulk's.

CHAPTER NINE:

"He's gonna get you next"

As the lone Republican candidate for Pierce County executive in 1981, Larry Faulk had a free ride into the finals on March 10. Booth faced a challenge from Tacoma Mayor Mike Parker in the Feb. 3 primary. At turns flamboyant and abrasive, Parker was a polarizing figure but still considered the frontrunner. "I'm just a runner," he protested. However, when told that Gardner and Faulk thought he was the man to beat, Parker smiled and said, "They must be reading the same polls that I am."

That Gardner was in fact "Booth who?" was confirmed by a poll he commissioned before entering the race. It found that Parker had 96 percent name recognition. Only 40 percent had heard of Booth Gardner. Sixty-five percent held a favorable view of Parker, while Booth's approval rating was 20 percent. It had been 11 years since he had run for elective office in Pierce County. "Nobody knew who I was," he says.

The Gardner campaign launched a $38,000 series of ads that stressed his management moxie and dedication to public service. "The first must be the very best," voters were told in a meet-the-candidate manifesto that took up nearly a whole page. "We've made a business decision here in Pierce County. We voted to change our form of local government and to give

Booth and Larry Faulk at a debate during their 1981 race for Pierce County executive.
© *The News Tribune* (Tacoma, WA) 1981 Reprinted with permission.

one man, the County Executive we elect, the power and authority to lead the County Council in a total reorganization of every department so that we can have a *united* Pierce County. It's going to take quite a guy! That's why we're for Booth Gardner." The next ad asked, "Which man would you hire?" It compared the candidates' qualifications side by side, noting that Booth had an MBA from Harvard vs. Parker's three years of college. Under "Current Responsibilities," it said Booth managed a company with 1,200 employees and an annual budget of $150 million. The mayor's budget was listed as $254,000, with two direct-report employees. The Municipal League rated Booth "outstanding" and Parker "adequate." Parker jabbed that the best outcome for Pierce County would be to elect him and have Booth buy downtown Tacoma.

Booth spent $178,000 in the primary—$139,500 of it his own money. Parker spent just short of $100,000. Booth said he had to spend that much to overcome Parker's name familiarity, the mayor having been in five political campaigns in the space of eight years, including two for the Legislature, one for Congress and one for City Hall. Parker had upped the ante in the beginning, saying he was prepared to spend $200,000 to win. Booth was immediately in, saying he would match that, and everyone knew he could raise the stakes in a heartbeat. "Parker set the rules," he told reporters. "My attitude is that through my efforts I've earned a great deal of money in my lifetime and I can spend it as I choose to spend it." Faulk's scrapbook contains that clipping. He highlighted "my efforts" in red ink and wrote "B.S."

⁓

Parker stumbled badly down the stretch. He hired a right-wing direct-mail fundraiser to send an "Urgentgram" to Democratic voters. Pierce County's 10-member legislative delegation called it "inexcusable" and endorsed Booth. Taking no chances, Gardner bought a half-hour of prime time for $7,000 on the Sunday before the primary to air a "documentary"—an "inside look at Booth Gardner, his family, friends and neighbors."

Booth pulverized Parker on Feb. 3, taking 64 percent of the vote. Standing on a desk at campaign headquarters, balloons bobbing around his head, he surveyed the cheering crowd and declared, "I'm stunned!" He didn't mention that his margin of victory was deceptive. Washington's open primary law allowed Republicans to cross over in droves to support his candidacy. Faulk, who received 8,300 votes to Gardner's 37,500 and Parker's 12,700, was able to conserve his money—although there was precious little of it at the time. He spent less than $5,000 and pronounced it "the best primary election Booth ever bought." Besides the billboards, bus placards, radio commercials, TV spots, yard signs, newspaper ads, two voter surveys, $14,000 worth of postage for multiple mailers and a half-dozen paid campaign staffers, Gardner attributed his win to a "grassroots" effort that featured phone banks and doorbelling. It was Faulk's how-to-win-a-campaign manual on steroids.

The stage was set for a Gardner-Faulk rematch. Booth told reporters

Booth scores a stunning victory in the primary.
© *The News Tribune* (Tacoma, WA) 1981 Reprinted with permission.

he was anything but a shoo-in for the $48,000-a-year job, adding that Faulk was "a very good candidate" and a great campaigner. Philosophically, they differed little. Both characterized themselves as moderates—fiscally conservative businessmen with strong social consciences. They went mano-a-mano 27 times in five weeks on the rubber chicken circuit with Lions and Rotarians from Steilacoom to Puyallup.

Faulk came out swinging, accusing Gardner of a conflict of interest. Before stepping down a year earlier, Booth headed Northwest Building Corp., which had plans to build a shopping center north of Puyallup. He had remained on the company's board until entering the race for county executive. William Clapp, Booth's half-brother, joined the Laird Norton Co. as he was gearing up to re-enter politics and was a corporate officer of Northwest Building Corp. Booth said Faulk was trying to suggest "I'd have trouble saying 'no' to my brother. That would be no problem for me." Gardner's business ties quickly emerged as both an asset and a liability. He was on the boards of the Weyerhaeuser Co., Washington Mutual Savings Bank and Puget Sound National Bank. Faulk said the potential for conflicts of interest was all over the Pierce County map. Booth countered that his connections would allow him to create new jobs and broaden the county's economic base. "I won't have a conflict of interest," he told the press matter-of-factly. "If there is, I'll deal with it when it comes up." He also once again answered Faulk's charge of vote-buying, saying, "If I have the money, don't I have a right to do with it as I wish? I'm not into material things." He was driving a plain-Jane Volkswagen Dasher diesel, and noted that if elected county executive he'd take a huge pay cut.

⌒

"Rich Man, Poor Man," the *Seattle Post-Intelligencer* headlined its election advance. Faulk unleashed a series of crisp, hard-hitting ads that would be effective even today: "THIS COUNTY DOESN'T NEED A BUSINESS EXECUTIVE. WE NEED A LEADER. LARRY FAULK CAN DO BETTER THAN BOOTH." Another asked, "WILL YOU VOTE FOR DAVID OR GOLIATH?" Next came "WHY IS BOOTH GARDNER TRYING TO BUY YOUR VOTE?" Then, down the stretch, with a wicked gut-punch, Faulk reminded voters that Gardner had resigned from the State Senate after less than three years: "THE LAST TIME THE PEOPLE ELECTED BOOTH GARDNER TO OFFICE, HE WALKED OUT ON THEM."

Faulk also ripped Gardner for securing exemptions from state financial disclosure laws. Greg Barlow represented Booth at the state Public Disclosure Commission hearings, asserting that it would cost the businesses in which Gardner was involved considerable time and expense to list all their financial holdings and transactions. The commission accepted the alternative Barlow proposed, allowing Gardner to report his top 10 sources of income from each company and the 10 largest transactions made in Pierce County by each firm over the past years. The commission also granted Gardner's request that the assets of his blind trust not be listed.

With the battle fully joined, Faulk was on the freeway one day when he spotted Barlow tooling toward Tacoma. "I'm driving some old damn beater and he's in his Porsche." They pulled to the side of the road. "What the hell you up to?" said Faulk. Barlow grinned and said, "I'm just bringing down another hundred thousand."

Booth cashed in on his track record of civic activism dating back to his work with the kids in Seattle's Central Area as a college student. He was also the coach of the Cozars, a girls' soccer team that had won the under-19 state championship in 1979. Faulk enjoyed his own solid reputation in the minority community and among advocates for the

Booth consoles a Cozar. *Photo courtesy Dick Baldwin.*

disadvantaged. He was managing a non-profit that hired disabled workers.

The black community in Tacoma summoned Booth to a meeting at the Al Davies Boys Club. They gave him a seat in the middle of the court. The audience was in the bleachers, staring down at the rich white dude. "This is going to be rough house," Booth said to himself. They were making the introductions when all of a sudden "there was just a tremendous ruckus out in the hallway," Booth remembers. "It was three bus loads of black folks from Seattle. They had rented buses and come down because they heard about the meeting and wanted to give me moral support. They said, 'We know we weren't invited but we knew you were meeting with Booth Gardner…and as far as we're concerned this should be a no-brainer for you guys. There's not a person in this state who has cared as much for minority people as he has.' "

⁓

Both candidates brought in their heavy-hitters. U.S. Senator Henry M. "Scoop" Jackson attended two fundraisers for Booth. Newly-inaugurated Governor John Spellman and U.S. Senator Slade Gorton, who had ousted the venerable Senator Magnuson in the Reagan landslide of 1980, campaigned for Faulk. Noting that he usually abstained from involvement in county races, Jackson testified that "Booth represents, decency, honesty, integrity and a decent manager for Pierce County." Likely licking his chops at the thought of Norton Clapp and his friends giving money to a Democrat with cross-over appeal, Scoop declared that Gardner was "manna from heaven." Faulk's campaign got some of that, too. "All the Republican businessmen—the guys who normally would be supporting a Republican in Tacoma and Pierce County—were getting together" at the landmark Johnny's Dock waterfront restaurant to support Booth, Faulk recalls. That "really PO'd" one card-carrying Republican who resented Clapp summoning the faithful to help his stepson. "He told me to go see a guy named Dave Ritter, who owned Fick Foundry. He was a solid Republican. We went to see him and he gave us a check. You never look at the check; you just put in your pocket. I just said, 'Thank you, Dave. We really appreciate it.' When we got outside in the hall, I pulled out the check. Jesus Christ! It's a thousand bucks! Nobody's ever given us a thousand bucks! Dave raised $52,000 for us in 30 days, so we would be able to be competitive."

Faulk laid it on the line when he went to Olympia to ask the governor to campaign for him. "Spellman is sitting there, calmly smoking his pipe and I'm walking around waving my hands because I'm a Slav and I can't talk without my hands, and I said, 'Governor, *we can win this thing*! We need help, and we need it now!' Finally I said, 'Well, governor, let me tell you something: If he gets me he's gonna get you next.' "

⌒

Gardner won the endorsement race. He was anointed by six city council members, 10 legislators, 14 mayors, 15 of the 23 new county charter freeholders, *The Pierce County Herald, The Suburban Times* and *The Tacoma News Tribune*, Pierce County's leading source of news. The *News Tribune's* endorsement editorial said it was "a difficult choice between two good men" but Gardner's "superiority in executive training" tipped the scales. "Gardner's stewardship of a multi-million dollar corporation and his formal education in business administration provide him with impressive credentials," the newspaper said. "It is rare that such a skilled executive would interrupt a successful career in private business to devote full time to local-government service."

On election eve, Gardner and Faulk were at a candidates' forum at a Grange Hall. Booth drew the short straw and had to go first. He had appeared on the same platform with Faulk and the others so many times that his brain was bouncing from the monotony. He started to give his standard stump speech. Then he stopped, smiled mischievously and launched into Faulk's speech. "I had been listening to him for three months solid. I knew his speech by heart," Booth says. Equally bored, Faulk often "kind of dozed off when other people were talking." But as he began to grasp what was happening, Faulk started twitching and fidgeting. "He's kind of a kinetic guy," Booth says, adding that his opponent soon was fully alert and "on the edge of his chair." When Booth concluded, Faulk jumped up, grabbed the microphone and declared, *"He gave my speech!"* Booth took it back and confessed, "He's telling you the truth, folks. I did give his speech. But I've been listening to it for so long I just had to do it. If you want to know what I have to say, he's been with me the same amount of time I've been with him. Let him give my speech." Booth handed the microphone back to Faulk, "but he wouldn't do it, which was a mistake....If he had been on his toes he would have had six minutes to say 'This is too serious a job to be joking around' and things like that."

"It's true," Faulk readily concedes, laughing so hard nearly 30 years later that tears practically come to his eyes. Faulk was usually fast on his feet and outshone Gardner in most of their debates. Booth was faster that night. When he realized what was happening, Faulk says he muttered something unprintable under his breath. You had to hand it to Booth, Faulk says. "He's a nice guy. I couldn't help but like him, and I still do."

Faulk's flummoxed failure to seize that one moment wasn't decisive. On March 10, 1981, Booth survived their rematch by winning 52.8 percent of the vote to become Pierce County's first county executive. Gardner said the conflict-of-interest allegation over the shopping mall probably hurt. For Faulk, more money might have made a difference. Gardner spent some $225,000—including about $150,000 of his own money. It added up to five times what Faulk was able to raise and spend. "The Republican National Committee could have come in with $100,000," Faulk says. "We were closing. Given another week and more money we could have beat him. We had momentum. I could feel it from the streets. But they didn't and he won and, of course, the rest is history."

So is Faulk's warning to Spellman. After his resounding victory in the primary, Booth had told the *News Tribune's* editors he had no plans to run for governor in 1984. He said he'd like to be Pierce County executive for eight years, "then I might go back into private business." But the paper's political writer, Jerry Pugnetti, polled a lot of Democrats who saw the personable 44-year-old as governor sooner rather than later. "If Booth isn't thinking about it, there's a lot of people around here thinking about it for him," one said.

One who thought Booth's road to Olympia was strewn with speed bumps was an old friend, State Sen. Peter von Reichbauer of Vashon Island. A month earlier, von Reichbauer had stunned the Legislature by

defecting to the Republicans out of displeasure with the level of government spending. That gave the R's a 25-24 majority and control of both
houses of the Legislature and the governor's office for the first time in
32 years. Von Reichbauer declared that if Gardner didn't take on Pierce
County's Democratic "machinery" in his first six months of office, "he
will fail." He added that the "narrowness of his victory" over Faulk was
not only surprising, it "will eliminate him as a contender against Gov.
Spellman in 1984."

Spellman, who became King County's first county executive in 1969
by defeating Al Rosellini, congratulated Booth on his victory. Although
he'd backed Faulk, he said he believed Gardner would do well. His advice
was to be assertive. "I suspect that he already knows that. I would just
underline it."

CHAPTER 10:

Earning his "MBWA"

"Being Pierce County Executive was the best job I've ever had," Booth says. Tacoma was his home town, and Pierce County was Washington's second-largest, with a population of 500,000 in 1981. "It was the size where I could get to know everybody I worked for and with." It was there he says that he earned what he called his "MBWA"—the art of Managing by Walking Around.

He took office on May 1, 1981, after eight weeks of 16-hour days. Fueled by fast food and surrounded by mounds of file folders arrayed on the floor in orderly chaos, he literally rolled up his sleeves to immerse himself in the details of county government. He studied the seven union contracts up for renegotiation; took note of the number of middle managers; made flow charts of responsibilities; analyzed who was driving a county car and how many there were; calculated the cost of replacing a stop sign and marveled, "Why does it take *three* workers to do that job?" He discovered that the county's technology was state of the art for the 1950s.

Those who hadn't worked with him before were immediately impressed by his memory—"near-photographic" many said—and ability to focus on the most important details. He'd billed himself as a "decisive administrator

Booth mulls a problem during his term as Pierce County executive. Bruce Kellman
© *The News Tribune* (Tacoma, WA) 1984 Reprinted with permission.

with extensive management and leadership skills," so the pressure was on. Yet he was more energized, more confident and calm than he'd ever been.

For starters, he imposed a three-month hiring freeze because there was, as usual, a curve ball: Not only was the county $4.7 million in debt, America was in its worst recession since the Depression. The Fed's tight money strategy to combat the runaway inflation of the late 1970s had painful unintended consequences. The Northwest was particularly hard hit, with timber and construction hammered. The jobless rate in Pierce County was 9.6 percent. In the next 18 months it would peak at 14.2. Sales tax revenues were down. Cuts in state and federal assistance loomed. Pierce County's new era of "home rule" was impacted by a host of outside forces.

In Olympia, the new governor's task was even more daunting. John Spellman had taken office in January, capping his inaugural address with a chorus of "The Sun'll Come Out Tomorrow," the signature tune from the musical "Annie." Most legislators sang along. They wouldn't have Dixy Lee Ray to kick around any more, but everyone wished there was a Daddy Warbucks. On the campaign trail, Booth had been more cautious about promises than Spellman, who made a "no new taxes" pledge he would bitterly regret. Spellman was also sore vexed by the right-wingers in his own party—"troglodytes" he called them. Booth had a largely collegial new seven-member County Council, but in time he would come to fully sympathize with Spellman's legislative travails. During their terms, many exasperated lawmakers would grouse that both men were wimps. That was untrue and unfair, but they did have a lot in common. Their Irish Catholic great-grandfathers arrived in Seattle in the 1860s. As their counties' first executives under home-rule charters, Spellman and Gardner earned reputations as skillful, honest administrators with the common touch.

⏤〰⏤

Besides "setting a standard for integrity in public service," Gardner's goals included streamlining Pierce County operations, especially the accounting and data processing systems to improve productivity, reduce expenses and provide better customer service. In the world of private enterprise, Booth said he'd never seen the likes of the county's budgeting and auditing functions. They were so complex and confusing, he said, that any two of the three county commissioners in the old government could team up with the county administrator and budget director and rule with an iron fist. In addition to providing checks and balances, a modern budget-information system would let department managers keep close tabs on spending.

The sheriff, no longer an elected official, was now answerable to the county executive. One of Booth's first observations was that he could better deploy his deputies if he had more clerical help and modern record-keeping equipment. That was also calculated to improve morale and professionalism. The younger deputies in particular were anxious to remove the taint of the extortion-ring scandal. Booth's popularity took a hit, however, when he told them they couldn't drive their prowl cars home. (Reflecting on his first year in office, Gardner quipped that in the beginning many deputies waved at him with their whole hand. "Now they use only one finger.") The slackers and malcontents weren't going to like him, Booth predicted, but dedicated, talented employees "would have a chance to shine." One of his first steps was to begin a management-training program for all county supervisors.

~

Three state legislators won seats on the new seven-member County Council, Republican Shirley Winsley and Democrats A.L. "Slim" Rasmussen and Phyllis Erickson. R. "Clint" Richardson, another Democrat, took the fourth new seat. The other three slots were grandfathered to the former county commissioners: Joe Stortini, Jake Bujacich and Joe Vraves. Bujacich and Stortini had opposed the new charter, although Stortini promised to "work 110 percent to see that it works." Taking a cut in pay, as well as a reduction in power, rankled Stortini and Bujacich. "It was a double whammy for them," Winsley says. "All that salary cut did was cause animosity, but it wasn't Booth's fault. The people made that decision when they approved the new home-rule charter."

The council's newcomers, including the often irascible Rasmussen, got along fine. Ironically, it was Rasmussen, an unpredictable fiscal conservative, who pushed the council to hire more staff. "We've got two hands tied behind our back," Slim said, arguing that they needed a budget director

Port official Lew Holcomb talks with Booth and County Council member Joe Stortini.
Russ Carmack © *The News Tribune* (Tacoma, WA) 1984 Reprinted with permission.

and a legal adviser to help interpret the new charter. Stortini jabbed that the new form of government was not supposed to cost more. "Joe would run to the press and say, 'Look what the new council members want to spend money on now,'" Winsley recalls. Outraged at the suggestion he was a spendthrift, Rasmussen would retaliate by reading aloud Stortini's printed comments at the next council meeting in a voice oozing sarcasm.

Vraves, a former mayor of Fife, was affable from the outset and usually voted with the new council majority. "After a while, we all worked together and got along," says Winsley, who headed the new council's Ways & Means Committee. Gardner strived to stay above the fray, praising the council as a diverse "board of directors." He said he appreciated their varied talents. Bujacich, for instance, had "a good grasp" of the budget, he said diplomatically, while Winsley and Rasmussen were also looking out for the county's interests in Olympia. "I love problems," he said, "and I love to solve them."

"Booth did a very good job" of managing a wholesale reorganization of county government, Winsley says. What began as a bumpy courtship evolved into a virtual honeymoon that lasted into fall. Members of a group called Friends of the Charter appeared at a County Council meeting to urge the council not to become too enamored of his charms. The group included several former freeholders as well as members of the Municipal League and the League of Women Voters. "In the case of any love affair there's always a possibility of a certain amount of blindness on the part of both parties," said Dorothy Clark, one of the Friends. She admonished the council to remember that one of its most important roles was to provide "a check and balance" to the executive branch. Erickson, the council's chairwoman, said the council had no substantive complaints about Gardner's decisions, but noted there were times when it felt left out. The biggest dustup found them at odds over whether his top appointments had to be confirmed by the council. Booth said they did not. They said that was the intent of the freeholders but conceded the charter was vague. Erickson noted that Gardner had moved to address their concerns by announcing that "as a courtesy" he would submit two key administrative appointments to the council for confirmation. Erickson had nothing but praise for the cooperation the new form of government had promoted. "It's a love affair, almost, between the council and the county executive."

BBQ Pete's was competing with Frisko Freeze for his mealtime affections. It unveiled the "Booth Gardner Basic Burger"—"a fiscally sound back-to-basics burger with fries."

By November, having solicited more feedback from the council, Gardner had combined key functions of the auditor, assessor-treasurer and purchasing departments into a new Office of Budget & Finance headed by talented young Patrick Kenney, whom they recruited from Michigan. The county payroll had been trimmed by 100, including 75 layoffs and 25 vacancies left unfilled. Through terminations and retirements several $34,000-a-year posts were eliminated and the chain of command was simplified. Some departments owed their existence more to politics than "rational business decisions," Booth said, adding that the old form of government created independent fiefdoms. "Maybe the kings get along, and maybe they don't." Maybe they burn and pillage. "They all loved their perks." As government became more complex and large new suburbs sprang up, Pierce County's problems intensified. It was no longer possible to just throw money at a problem. Labor became more powerful—yet another kingdom. But now the kings were dead, Gardner said, replaced by "real managers." He'd saved some $1.4 million in his first eight months and predicted there would be a budget surplus by 1984. Labor gave him mixed reviews. Rosa Franklin, a leading civil rights activist, praised his efforts to improve opportunities for minorities in county government. "What he has done shows that he wasn't just making words."

A real manager knows how to delegate, and a bouncer always comes in handy. When Booth became county executive he commissioned Greg Barlow as his chief of staff. Barlow had the Medina Foundation "pretty much on auto-pilot" so he had time to do double duty. If Booth had an MBA, Barlow, in the parlance of an old Army first sergeant, had a master's degree in "taking names and kicking ass." Booth said Barlow was "Oliver North with

Lt. Col. Greg Barlow, Booth's chief of staff.
John Cox photo, Washington National Guard.

a conscience." Under pressure, "he's just phenomenal. His metabolism slows down under stress."

Early on, Barlow told Larry Faulk that he encountered a department head who wasn't impressed with either the "Harvard-educated" new county executive or his chief of staff. "Barlow was asking him something and this guy got right up close to him and punched his finger in his chest and said, 'Don't f*** with me, kid.' Well, Greg got a hold of the auditor's office and told them he wanted this guy's office audited, and the report showed bad things." Next, Faulk says, they called the manager into Booth's office. There was not-so-good news and bad news, Barlow said, brandishing two letters. The first was the manager's resignation; the second his dismissal. "If you don't sign the first one, Booth will sign the second." The man gazed at Booth, hoping for a reprieve, saw in his eyes that there was no wiggle room and resigned. Barlow could be "tough as hell on somebody who deserved it," Faulk says, "but on the other hand he can be a very kind, gentle, fun-loving guy." The latter was lost on some Gardner intimates who saw Barlow as Booth's hatchet man. They viewed him as a bad influence.

Barlow believed his mission was to protect Booth from his deep-seated desire to make nice. He liked to be liked so much that he was vulnerable. "Every day someone would ambush Booth on the sidewalk and get him to agree to do something—put a few more dollars in this program or a few more employees in that department," Barlow told *Seattle Times* reporter Walter Hatch in 1987. "I called them 'sidewalk decisions.' My job was to track those people down and ask them exactly what they had asked Booth to do. Once they heard my voice, they usually forgot."

The swagger was unmistakable, Shirley Winsley says, adding that Barlow "always looked like a military guy" even when he wasn't in uniform. "He was always perfectly groomed, like a page out of *Esquire*....He came across as a very smart man, but a lot of us didn't know quite what to make of him. He could have come down to earth a little. That would have helped." She says the image Barlow projected was calculated to annoy the hell out of someone like crusty ol' Slim Rasmussen.

On the other hand, they all liked Booth's legal counsel, Terry Sebring, who was "very competent, congenial and low key," Winsley says. Sebring was able to handle personnel and public works issues without ruffling political egos, she adds, and deserves a lot of the credit for the Gardner administration's successes in modernizing Pierce County government. Booth seconds that motion.

A graduate of the University of Puget Sound Law School's first class,

Sebring had been the chief civil deputy in the County Prosecutor's Office. He was the legal adviser to the three county commissioners before the new charter was approved by the voters. Barlow and Gardner were particularly impressed by the way Sebring handled the new administration's ticklish negotiations with the unions. At Barlow's urging, Gardner tapped him to be personnel director in the fall of 1981. Sebring became Gardner's administrative aide, in essence deputy county executive, in 1982 when Barlow went back to the Medina Foundation and the National Guard. Although Barlow and Sebring were as different as cheese and chalk, Sebring admired him: He was "efficient, organized, very direct and very straightforward. He would tell you where you stood. If you wanted to know, all you had to do was ask." Sebring said Barlow "was probably Booth's closest friend. He'd been with him for a long time...in family circles and business affairs." Sebring adds that characterizing Barlow as "the enforcer" and Booth as too compliant is a misleading simplification. "Neither Barlow nor I ever did anything without Booth's OK. Booth clearly was in charge. We were the functionaries, implementers. I always knew who was in charge—and it wasn't me." And for all the talk about "the man who loves to be loved," Sebring says, "Booth was not one to let faint praise go to his head. He was always very practical. He expected solid staff work...and for you to do your homework, to ask hard questions—due diligence..."

One of the new administration's biggest hurdles from day one was a $200 million sewer project that had been embroiled in litigation for a decade. The project included Lakewood, Winsley's district, and was scheduled to bore under I-5 into Parkland, Clint Richardson's district. "A lot of people had septic tank systems and they also didn't want to see any growth, which of course would come with new sewers," Winsley remembers, while others were simply misinformed. Some of the sewer meetings were like the tumultuous health care reform "tea parties" of 2009, "with people yelling and practically spitting in our faces." Booth was determined to move forward before federal funding lapsed. Wearing a parka and plaid shirt, he usually sat in the audience, listening intently. When his turn came, he was usually able to ease the tension with his calm, folksy manner. Unimpressed was one sewer project foe who paraded outside a meeting with a sign that featured a portrait of a grinning Gardner. "Certain County Officials Must Go!" it declared. "Booth Gardner First." Another carried a "Recall Gardner" placard.

Booth and the new council members emphasized that they welcomed taxpayer feedback. Winsley says she used to get calls saying, "There's this guy wearing a plaid shirt, leaning on a shovel, shooting the breeze with other men, and none of them were working." The plaid-shirt guy was Booth out talking with the sewer-project crew.

Gardner loved to get out of the office, grab a burger and rub elbows with the citizenry and county employees. "I'd go into a supermarket and somebody would wander over and say, 'Hi, Mr. Gardner. I'm on the road crew.' And we'd talk for a bit. They started inviting me over to visit them on the job. Later I saw one of the guys at a movie or something and he said, 'When are you going to go out on the road with us?' I said, 'I'll be out Monday. Get me somebody to ride with.' " Booth tagged along with a worker who was fixing street signs and dutifully lent a hand as they dug holes, poured cement and replaced poles. After a couple of hours, the worker said, "Mr. Gardner, if you don't mind, I think I can do this quicker without your help." Booth took the performance review in stride. The job was not as easy as it looked. He leaned against the truck and they chatted away while the worker got on with it. When he got back to the office, his secretary said she'd fielded a call from an irate taxpayer who insisted on speaking only with the county executive. Booth returned the call. "My mother is elderly," the man told him, "so I picked her up to go grocery shopping and we passed one of your trucks in Lakewood. There was one guy working and the other guy was just standing there." "Was the guy who was just standing there wearing a red flannel shirt?" "Yeah, that's the one. Do you know him?" "*Yes I do,*" Booth said, stifling a chuckle. "I'll talk to him and his boss."

Winsley has heard the story many times but still laughs. "I look at Booth as being the right person at the right time for that new job. He had a positive attitude from the very beginning. I'm not sure anyone else could have accomplished so much in such a short period of time. Instead of coming in with some big agenda, his approach was to take it one step at a time," streamline county operations, get it back in the black and win the confidence of the people who voted for change.

Larry Faulk was also impressed. "I think he did a great job because he brought in a whole new way of thinking," Faulk said in 2009. Although their personalities are dramatically different, both delight in irony and hate political pettiness. When Spellman's nomination of Faulk to the State Pollution Control Hearings Board was bottled up in a legislative committee in 1982, Booth called his friend Ted Bottiger, the Senate majority leader, and got Faulk confirmed. "Classy," says Faulk.

~~~

Adele Ferguson was the first to tell the whole state who Booth was. Her columns were syndicated in dailies and weeklies in every corner of the state. On April 30, 1982, readers from Port Angeles to Pullman read this: "Booth Gardner. Remember the name. He could be your next governor. If a lot of anxious Democrats desperately appraising the quality of the other prospects in the field so far have their way he will be.

"The 45-year-old Tacoma millionaire has been Pierce County executive for only eight months but, facing a $4.6 million county debt when he took office, he has already whittled that down to $3.1 million. He asked county employees to forgo wage increases for a year, and then to accept a 1.1 percent increase. He'd rather keep people working than have to lay off to afford raises ...

"He checked up on the more than 300 vehicles the county owns, other than service trucks, etc., and learned that more than 60 percent of them were being driven home by employees nights and weekends. He put a halt to that, including some usage by deputy sheriffs, who didn't like that one bit. ...

"He made a lot of other changes, some resulting in savings of small amounts of money, 'but you save $15,000 here and $15,000 there and pretty soon you're saving $100,000; he says.

"In short, Booth Gardner, unlike too many other public officials, is an administrator par excellence....Booth Gardner may very well be the rising star of the Democratic Party in this state. Remember the name..."

Adele loved being first on any big story, although on this one she would come to regard herself as a prophet without honor.

In the spring of 1983, with Governor Spellman under attack right and left, Gardner's stated intention of serving eight years as country executive clearly had gone out the window. In politics, "timing is everything," Booth says, and the best strategy is to "get out front early" and discourage would-be rivals. One irony is that when people know you're rich they're less eager to give you money, but he knew Norton Clapp would come through, and he had no reservations about jump-starting the campaign with his own checkbook.

On May 18, Booth's statewide coming-out party continued. The *Seattle Weekly* mulled "The mystery of Booth Gardner: a Democratic dream candidate or a Democratic Spellman?" "He became the Democrats' candidate-apparent last month," Rebecca Boren noted, "when up popped a Booth Gardner committee, complete with a respected treasurer (Seattle businessperson Herb Bridge)...The Gardner campaign is suddenly a palpable force—politicos believe, whatever the scanty evidence, that the almost-candidate is raising money and locking up endorsements. As a result, comments one respected state strategist, 'Democrats look at Booth Gardner and they get an itch. They think, 'My god, he's moderate, he's experienced, he's clean, he—he's rich and he's *ours*!'" But Gardner backer Dan Grimm, the sharp young chairman of the House Ways & Means Committee, noted that what Booth really stood for—besides competence as an administrator—was unclear to most. "Booth in the next few months has to portray his vision of the future. Goals, things he wants to fight for. I don't know what Booth's vision is."

A week later, Booth was addressing the 775-member Seattle Downtown Rotary Club, where the movers and shakers greeted him with the customary shout-out, "Hi, Booth!" Newspaperman John S. Murray, a former Republican state legislator, liked everything he heard. "Booth Gardner," he wrote in the weekly Seattle *Argus*, "is the kind of person we need in the political arena. He is smart and intelligent (they are not the same thing), hard working and incorruptible. The only reason he is in politics is because of the tremendous challenge. There is some talk that Gardner is considering a run for governor. No man in his right mind would want the job at the present time, but if Booth Gardner were to run he could become a Democratic Dan Evans…"

In July of 1983, Peter Callaghan, an exceptional young reporter with the Everett *Herald's* Olympia Bureau, wrote what remains one of the most-quoted Booth Gardner profiles. It was headlined DOES BOOTH GARDNER REALLY WANT TO BE GOVERNOR? Callaghan observed that "for a guy who's getting ready to run for the highest elective office in the state," Gardner seemed remarkably nonchalant, coming across "as someone who won't stay awake at night if he doesn't become the next governor." Some of his supporters worried about whether he wanted the job badly enough. "Booth has to persuade me that he has a fire in his belly," said Grimm. Not to worry, said Gardner. "I come off low-key, but like a duck I try to remain calm on the surface while I'm paddling like mad underneath. But if I decide to do this, I'm going to give it all I've got. I'm a highly competitive person." In the months to come, many would copy Callaghan's observation that Gardner looked "like a cross between Bob Newhart and Tommy Smothers: preppy but likeable." But the lines that drew the most attention were these: "He voluntarily walked into a government best known for its corruption, mismanagement and patronage. In the spring of 1981, Pierce County was $4.7 million in the red. By the end of this year, Gardner expects a surplus of $1 million. …Even his most vocal critics concede he's a master administrator. One of them, Rep. Ruth Fisher, D-Tacoma, suggests that whomever is elected governor should hire Gardner to run the state." Gardner said he considered himself a businessman, not a politician. Of the race for governor, he said, "It's like starting a new business, only I'm the product."

In August, former Seattle mayor Wes Uhlman, who had served with Booth in the state Senate in the early '70s, signed onto his finance committee. He said Gardner would be the strongest candidate the Democrats could field against the vulnerable Spellman. Uhlman urged state Senator Jim McDermott, D-Seattle, who had made two campaigns for governor, to not run again. "Now it is someone else's turn."

In the drizzly days of December, a group of businessmen—most of them well-heeled Republicans—huddled privately with Gardner at the Tacoma Club. They urged him to seek re-election as Pierce County executive, not challenge Spellman. *The Tacoma News Tribune* quickly got wind of it and tracked down some of the participants. Weyerhaeuser executive Edward Soule confirmed that the "basic objective" was to dissuade him from taking on Spellman. "We have high regard for Booth and what he has done for Pierce County," Soule said, adding that they were worried that no qualified candidate would step forward to succeed him if he ran for governor. No more scandals, please. "There wasn't any arm-twisting," said state Rep. Stan Johnson, a Republican from Lakewood. Despite Gardner's success in turning around Pierce County, he said most businessmen were solidly behind Spellman. Booth was non-committal. "Basically, everyone there was a personal friend of mine," he told the paper. And he knew they knew what he knew: He could beat Spellman. His New Year's resolution was that 1984 was going to be his year, although as the date to announce grew near he kept asking himself if he really knew what he was getting into.

"Why do I want to do it?" Booth asked rhetorically during his interview with Callaghan. "I ask myself the same question. I wake up about 4:30 with a knot in my stomach every now and then. The answer is, if people like myself, with capabilities, aren't willing to assume responsibility at some point in their lives, then it's going to be left to those who are less qualified."

CHAPTER 11:

Put on your crash helmets

Booth hired a campaign manager destined to become "one of the most successful political operatives in Washington history." A blend of James Carville and Wyatt Earp, Ron Dotzauer was elected Clark County auditor in 1974, just two years out of college. But by 1983 he was burned out and at loose ends. He'd lost a bid for secretary of state, weighed a run for Congress then won his spurs running Scoop Jackson's 1982 re-election campaign for the U.S. Senate. Jackson's death a year later dazed the state. Dotzauer had grown up in Everett in the shadow of Scoop's home and they had become close. Two very different men from different generations, they were both ambitious Scandinavians who loved politics.

After overseeing the funeral and memorial service, Dotzauer got a call from Sterling Munro, Scoop's former longtime chief of staff who had gone on to head the Bonneville Power Administration. They'd been racquetball pals in Vancouver during Dotzauer's eight years as county auditor. "What are you going to do next?" Munro asked. Dotzauer said he might take a public relations job with a major bank. "Well," said Munro, "Scoop wanted this guy Booth Gardner to be the next governor." What Gardner needed, he said, was someone who knew how to run a campaign. Dotzauer said he'd think it over but doubted he was up for a third state-wide campaign in four years. Another Gardner booster softened him up with a fishing trip to Alaska. Yet another invited him over for a long chat. He ended up having dinner at the Gardners. Jean Gardner

Ron Dotzauer in 2008. *Photo courtesy Strategies 360.*

was "diffident," Dotzauer remembers, "but Booth seemed to be really wanting to do this, and he was Booth's charming self, right?"

Dotzauer moved into the Norton Building in downtown Seattle just before Thanksgiving 1983. Election Day was a year away. "I sat there basically for 30 or 45 days and just said, 'Leave me alone. Let me figure out what we're going to do for the next year.' " The battle plan left nothing to chance—exhaustive opposition research, volunteer coordinators, sharp press people, two pollsters, focused media buys in every region, coupled with "the most massive sign campaign the state had ever seen for a candidate for governor"—27,000 in all, blanketing every legislative district. When Dotzauer decreed it was time to get the sign mill rolling, he arrived at work one day to discover the parking lot now contained 10-foot stacks of lovely Weyerhaeuser plywood. "Holy shit!" he said. "We have enough wood to build half of downtown Seattle."

In the beginning was The Message: "It's the economy *and* efficiency," Dotzauer says. "Booth Gardner's management expertise turned red ink into black. He did it in Pierce County and he can do it for the state. That was our mantra."

Whose idea was "Booth Who?"—the most memorable, and apt, campaign slogan in state history? Dotzauer says it sprang up spontaneously. They were in Spokane during the holidays on one of Booth's first forays into Eastern Washington when someone in a crowd said, *"Who is Booth Gardner?"* Outside of Pierce County, "he had like a 6 or 7 percent name ID," Dotzauer says. Dick Larsen of *The Seattle Times* quipped that at that time Booth "had a name- and face-familiarity that ranged from, approximately, the Steilacoom tideflats to the Poodle Dog (restaurant) at Fife." Dotzauer remembers saying, "Look, why don't we print up some buttons that say 'Booth Who?' Let's just have some fun with this." Booth and Jean Gardner loved the idea. Hispanic groups even produced a "¿Quien es Booth?" button.

Booth had never been around anyone like Dotzauer. He was buoyed by his buckaroo ebullience as the campaign took shape. Dotzauer was there to look him in the eye, straighten his tie and boot him in the butt whenever he needed it. Sometimes tentative, given his natural shyness and insecurity, a good crowd could recharge Booth's batteries. He'd talk about seeing Al Rosellini's helicopter when he was a kid and the importance of public service. "His intuition was amazing," Dotzauer says. "I mean, he just had an instinct for relating to people. His retail politics skill set was as good as they

On the campaign trail in 1984. From left, Ron Dotzauer, Doug Gardner, press aide Tim Zenk, and Booth. *Photo courtesy Ron Dotzauer.*

get. Maybe Scoop's at some levels was better but they both had incredible name recall. And although Booth was a lot more reluctant about campaigning than Scoop, he got good at it. Booth Gardner is an amazingly compassionate guy who just cares for people like nobody I've met. And in terms of the strength of his character, he *really wants people to do well.* He wants to help them get the skills and the opportunities to be successful." Dotzauer says Gardner was reluctant, however, to play up his work with disadvantaged kids. He finally agreed to a TV spot about the Central Area Youth Association but "he really didn't want to talk about it," so they rounded up people he'd worked with and brought them to his house.

"Trying to figure him out was an interesting challenge," Dotzauer says. "There's a whole lot of guilt around Booth, in my opinion." It bothered Gardner that the press kept labeling him the Weyerhaeuser heir who was the stepson of Norton Clapp, as if he'd never done anything on his own. "I think he never really came to terms with all that," Dotzauer says, especially the wealth, "because it happened as a tragedy"—his mother's death.

～

Booth made it official on Feb. 13, 1984, in a series of stops around the state, beginning with breakfast at Fife. "There need be no more speculation and no more headlines asking 'Does Booth Gardner really want to be governor?' " he declared as a standing-room-only crowd of 500 chanted "Booth! Booth! Booth!" In Seattle, he said he would promote "coalition building," emphasizing that labor and industry, loggers and environmentalists, Indians and non-Indians, needed to reason together to solve the state's problems. Governor Spellman did the right thing, he acknowledged, in siding with environmentalists against a Northern Tier pipeline plan and a proposed oil rig assembly plant at Cherry Point near Bellingham. Those were good decisions, he said, but not difficult decisions because "economic growth in this state must come on our terms." In Spokane, the 47-year-old candidate acknowledged he had his work cut out for him to close the name-familiarity gap with Spellman and fellow Democrat Jim

McDermott, a likely contender who had run for governor twice before, including a 1980 loss to Spellman. He planned a $2 million campaign to catch up and pull ahead. Focusing on Spellman, Booth characterized the governor as a weak and indecisive leader who had broken or ignored 58 campaign promises and had "paid little more than lip service to education." Gardner's key promise out of the starting gate was to be "a champion of educational reform," including higher base pay for teachers. While he jabbed Spellman for breaking a promise to not raise taxes, he emphasized that if new taxes were necessary to provide important services "I will be the first to step up and lead that charge."

Based on polling data and his instincts, Dotzauer believed that beating McDermott would be harder than ousting Spellman. The recession had forced the governor to break his no-new-taxes pledge. Although the economy was beginning to rebound, unemployment was still painfully high. "I saw from my research that Spellman's negatives were in the mid-40s, and that's why I knew we could win," Dotzauer says. That poll, plus the aggressive moves to boost Gardner's name recognition and highlight his management skills, was crucial to raising early money, which is like yeast to a campaign. Booth was prepared to jump-start fundraising with $200,000 of his own money but Dotzauer wanted to spend all that and then some on TV spots while McDermott was tied up in the Legislature as chairman of the Senate Ways & Means Committee. "We needed to have an early media buy so I could put Booth in the game. Nobody had ever done that before." Conventional wisdom was that you waited until August, a couple of weeks before the Primary Election, to roll out your TV spots. The Clapp family, with Barlow minding the store, didn't want to write big checks during March. Deep down, Dotzauer says, they didn't think Booth could really win. "I cut a deal with Barlow for the media buy: Whatever I raised he had to match."

Dotzauer stepped on several toes early on. "Running a campaign is not a democracy," he says with a shrug.

The candidate and the campaign manager went to see Pete Taggares. A grade-school dropout with a salty vocabulary and genius for deal-making,

Taggares was the son of a Greek immigrant. He had parlayed a small farm at Othello in Eastern Washington into an agricultural empire. He was worth half a billion bucks—which is a lot of french fries. Everything he owned, including *Spud One*, his corporate jet, was painted white. He liked good horses, tequila with the worm in the bottle and Mariachi bands. He contributed widely to political candidates who struck his fancy. Pete, in short, was Ron Dotzauer's kind of guy. In fact, he had been one of Scoop Jackson's biggest supporters. Dotzauer called him to say there was someone he needed to meet—Washington's next governor. "Who the hell," Taggares said, "is Booth Gardner?"

Pete sent his jet to pick them up for a getting-to-know-you overnighter. He met them at his airstrip in his white Mercedes-Benz, his white poodle beside him. "Jump in," he declared, chewing on an unlit cigar. "Then we went to his *huge* house—a huge house for a huge guy; Pete's 6-4, 300 pounds," Dotzauer says, his voice bubbling with excitement. "I remember all this like it was yesterday. We're in the living room. I'm sitting on a

Bill Wolf, left, a fan, wishes Booth well as he embarks on a seven-city campaign swing in the fall of 1984. Looking on, at center left, is John White, the AP correspondent in Olympia. Over Booth's left shoulder is Press Secretary Jim Kneeland.
Bruce Larson © *The News Tribune* (Tacoma, WA) 1984 Reprinted with permission.

leather couch as long as a wall. Pete is sitting in a big leather chair. Booth is sitting on the hearth in front of the fireplace, and they were having small talk about Weyerhaeuser and business deals. Pete really liked the fact that Booth had a business background and a Harvard MBA." They'd been chatting for about 45 minutes when Taggares' wife, Janet, came around the corner. Pete boomed out, "Ma, I like this guy!" Dotzauer says he barely resisted the temptation to stand up and cheer. "Inside, I'm going YESSSSSS! Booth is just sitting there on the hearth. He didn't say anything." Then Pete slapped his knees, leaned forward and said, "Tell you what I'm going to do: I'm going to make my planes available. I'll help you with money. Anything I can to help. I'm on board a hundred percent. We're going to make this thing happen!" With that, the potato king stood up, said goodnight and went to bed. Booth seemed dazed, finally asking, *"Did he mean that?"* Dotzauer laughed. "Booth, Pete never says anything he doesn't mean. You don't understand yet what this means for us in the campaign. This gives us resources and assets beyond your imagination."

Taggares did everything he said he'd do and more. He told Dotzauer he'd match every dollar the Clapps contributed. "Then money started coming in from all kinds of places I never heard of," Dotzauer cackles mischievously. "It was all legal, but I didn't realize they had so many damn holdings. There was money *all over the place.*" The first round of TV commercials boosted Booth's name familiarity from 7 percent to 30 percent. "We popped 25 points!" Dotzauer remembers, punching the air triumphantly. "It worked."

~⌇~

McDermott, a child psychiatrist from Seattle, was a tough, voluble campaigner who analyzed his opponent as a political dilettante. His strategy was to get in Booth's face and stay there. Their first debate, in late June 1984, was before the Seattle Rotary Club at the Sheraton Hotel. The *Post-Intelligencer's* Neil Modie, an old pro, wrote a lead that was spot on: "It was Booth Gardner's kind of audience but Jim McDermott's kind of show…" Gardner, visibly nervous, failed to counterattack as McDermott flailed him as a double-talker. He claimed to have resuscitated Pierce County without raising taxes, the senator said, but the truth was that the sales tax had been boosted. He claimed to have the common touch, to be a champion of government transparency, yet he had shielded the scope and sources of his wealth in a blind trust.

"As governor, I intend to run this state in the businesslike manner it requires," Booth promised in a voice one wag described as "Elmer Fudd on helium." The Rotarians nodded. McDermott looked right past them and addressed the bank of TV cameras capturing his message for the far larger audience of the 6 o'clock news on all three network affiliates. He said Gardner and Spellman were peas in a pod—former county executives who maintained that "if you've found the right manager, the problems of the state will go away." Landing a withering bipartisan uppercut, McDermott praised former three-term Republican governor Dan Evans. "The last good governor in this state," he said, "was somebody who was experienced in the Legislature and came into the governor's office with no experience in management. He was a man who had learned the process and understood how it worked. Ask your horse. You can lead your horse to water but you can't manage him to drink." Booth smiled thinly. Looking back, he shakes his head at his sorry performance and says he was out of his league. "It was the Yankees in the form of McDermott, and I just got chewed up." Dave Ammons of the AP, who has a knack for being simultaneously honest and empathetic, asked afterward, "You didn't do very well, did you?" "No I didn't," Booth said. "What are you going to do?" "I'm going to take a long walk," the candidate replied, "and I'll be back."

Dotzauer had seen it coming. "Let me tell you why he did horribly," the former campaign manager says, leaning forward. "In late spring, early summer, I said, 'Booth, you have your first debate coming up with McDermott. It's the first time you're going to actually have a side-by-side.

Booth and Jim McDermott during a joint appearance before the State Association of Fire Chiefs. © *The News Tribune* (Tacoma, WA) 1984. Reprinted with permission.

All the rest of the stuff has been posturing. Now, here is a debate training schedule. We're going to carve out X amount of hours each week where we're going to sit down and we're going to do debate prep, including a mock debate.' Well, Booth's way of dealing with things is sometimes to just not show up. So he didn't show up for any of these debate preps. Not a one. He didn't want to deal with it because he hadn't really fully committed to running for governor. I didn't go to the debate because I figured he was going to get his ass handed to him. Jim was smooth, smart and very knowledgeable. He knew the issues and Booth didn't. He was awful. *Awful!* Just horrible. So a couple hours after the debate I'm sitting at the campaign office. Booth walked in, closed the door, sat on the chair in front of my desk and said, 'Ok, I'm ready.' His competitive juices kicked in. 'I don't want that to happen again,' he said, and he apologized to me. He said he had let me down. I could see it in his eyes. Here was this diminutive kind of guy, quiet. Never would you think for a minute that he had this *fiery,* competitive piece to him."

They holed up in a hotel room and did debate prep, complete with podiums. State Rep. Denny Heck, a hard-charging 32-year-old, was McDermott while Dotzauer and the campaign press secretary, the rumpled but wily Jim Kneeland, lobbed tough questions. "In my usual anal fashion, I was prepared beyond belief," Heck recalls. "I had read everything McDermott had written or said about the issues, and of course I knew Jim quite well because we were in the Legislature together. In fact we were at loggerheads a whole lot more than one occasion, even though we were both Democrats." Booth made his opening statement, "then I eviscerated him, making some comments a candidate would never say in public because they are too harsh. But I did them to get to Booth. I was brutal." When Heck finished snarling, Booth stared at him for a second, threw his pen down on the podium, declared "I can't do this anymore" and stomped out of the room. Dotzauer gave chase, bucked him up and brought him back for more. "We kept at it, and from then on," Heck says, Booth was a far better debater, although still inclined to management jargon.

Booth went for a long walk around the perimeter of McChord Air Force Base near his Spanaway area home. When he wanted to give himself a good talking to, he liked to walk, usually on the beach on Vashon Island. The next day, he and McDermott met again before the Metropolitan Democratic Club of Seattle. This time he held his own. His voice was more confident. Looking back, it occurs to Heck, who went on to serve as Gardner's chief of staff, that Booth might have purposely blown the Rotary Club debate to lower expectations, reasoning that "then everything he did after that would be good. I don't think this was true, but I would not put it past him. It could have been something real subconscious. If you're crazy like a fox, your mind is working on a lot of different levels."

⌐

As chairman of the Senate Ways & Means Committee, McDermott had enormous pull with state employee unions. AFSCME, the American Federation of State, County & Municipal Employees, was emerging as a major player in state politics. The Gardner campaign hired a savvy labor guy, Joe Daniels, to help head off an outright endorsement of McDermott. Daniels prepared a three-page backgrounder to prep Gardner for his interview with union leaders, only to have Booth turn in a lackluster performance. Daniels cornered the candidate in the parking lot. "Didn't you read my report?" Booth shrugged, "No, but that's OK. They're going with McDermott anyway." Luckily, key members of the federation doubted

Members of the AFSCME Union rally for Gardner for governor. *Photo courtesy Ron Dotzauer.*

McDermott could beat Spellman. It was the prison guards who turned
the tide. McDermott was a staunch liberal and "they didn't trust him on
the death penalty," Dotzauer says. "We assured them that Booth was OK
with it." Dotzauer, Daniels and his friend Dave Warren, a union business
rep, buttonholed convention delegates all over Ellensburg the night before
the decision. "I think Joe was up in the attic counting votes," Dotzauer
says, remembering Gardner's stunned reaction when he called him from
a phone booth, shouting "We stopped him!" Daniels says AFSCME's dual
endorsement was essential to their second goal—blocking any endorsement
by the Washington State Labor Council that summer. The council opted to
stay neutral for the primary, as did the Washington Education Association.
Booth won the endorsement of the Washington State Patrol troopers, who
were at odds with Spellman and their chief over labor issues. The governor
had vetoed a bill to give them collective-bargaining rights. Dotzauer ordered
a batch of T-shirts that said "No more Hill Street Blues for the WSP."

Still, the campaign was worried about the tenor of the press coverage.
In July, it distributed a three-page letter from Emory Bundy, Booth's college

classmate who had recently stepped down as director of public affairs for King Broadcasting Company. Addressing his "former colleagues of the Fourth Estate," Bundy said he admired a feisty press dedicated to probing conflicts of interest and afflicting the comfortable. "But Booth Gardner has had words and phrases like 'multimillionaire' and 'Weyerhaeuser heir' routinely used as adjectives preceding his name…irrespective of the substance of the story…The effect is obvious. The repetitious, gratuitous use of such words and phrases implies something sinister." Bundy added that it was quite true that Booth Gardner was wealthy, and "the media not only is entitled but is obligated to probe whether he handles his personal affairs in a manner consistent with the responsibilities of public office." However, if it did due diligence, he continued, "I believe you will find a person who has handled his affairs in an exemplary and public-spirited manner…" Bundy noted he himself was wary of Gardner when they served as student body officers at the University of Washington in 1957. Then he discovered that Gardner "was spending countless hours organizing and coaching teams in Seattle's Central Area" in an era when "there was not a department store in the downtown area that would hire a black person as a sales clerk." Realtors and bankers, meantime, systematically segregated neighborhoods, and athletic clubs barred Jews and other ethnic minorities. "So to learn that this young white guy had gone to the ghetto and put together first a team and then entire sports leagues for the kids of the area—and did it in such a quiet way—was a remarkable thing.…So here is a candidate with fine human values, abundantly demonstrated, combined with outstanding administrative skill."

But there's no crying in the big leagues. The media was unchastened. Booth Gardner was rich, and that was his cross to bear.

⌒

Peter Callaghan, who went on to become an influential political columnist for *The Tacoma News Tribune*, was on the campaign trail in 1984 for the Everett *Herald*. "If Booth could make a personal connection with people, he was great," he remembers. "But if it became kind of a wholesale address he was nervous."

McDermott was seldom at a loss for words. Down the stretch to the Primary Election, Callaghan was covering the senator in Eastern Washington. "First of all, he's broke, so it's a very, very low-budget kind of operation. We were told later that Jim really funded the entire flight by collecting money from the newsies. It was the scariest airplane I've ever been on"—a veritable puddle-jumper compared to *Spud One*.

They landed in the Tri-Cities and headed for a Pasco grade school, where McDermott proceeded to offer an interactive civics catechism: "I'm running for governor. Does anybody here know who the governor of the state is right now?"

The kids were shy. Finally a boy in the back raised his hand.

McDermott said, "Yeah, *you,* go ahead. Do you know?"

"Bruce Gardner?" the kid offered.

Close enough for government work. Booth, flush with cash, had blanketed the airwaves. The kid's reply was like a straight pin in a balloon, Callaghan says. "And of course we all look at McDermott. He's got a good sense of humor so he kind of smiles. 'No,' he says. 'It's John Spellman. He's another guy who *wants* to be governor.' " If he didn't know it before, McDermott knew then that he was in trouble. Gardner had a primary election war chest of $1.3 million, including a $500,000 line of credit he extended to his campaign. McDermott had collected only about $360,000. Booth had spent more than that on TV alone.

Steve Excell, Spellman's shrewd campaign manager and former chief of staff, acknowledged that the governor's campaign had spent virtually all of the nearly $900,000 it had collected but flatly denied Spellman's fund-raising was flagging. "We only raise as much money as we need to do the job," he said, adding that they were confidently poised to begin a new push for the Nov. 6 General Election, regardless of the opponent. Excell also emphasized that no one should make much out of what would be a doubtlessly low vote for Spellman in the primary. "There is no question the headlines afterward (will say) there is an overwhelming Democratic

Doug Gardner and his mom applaud after Booth does well in a debate with Spellman.
Jerry Buck © *The News Tribune* (Tacoma, WA) 1984. Reprinted with permission.

vote in this state. But that does not accurately reflect the dynamic of the electorate. Our primary vote…is going to be understated. People tend to vote where the contest is."

Gardner, increasingly confident, given polling data showing him now leading handily, began saying that McDermott and Spellman both represented "old-style politics." Demonstrating he'd learned something about hardball, Booth tagged McDermott as a "two-time loser." McDermott retorted that he alone had a proven track record of leadership in state government—"leadership that money can't buy." In truth, McDermott and Gardner differed little on the substantive issues. Both favored full state funding for basic education, higher salaries for beginning teachers, a better climate for both business and labor and stronger environmental measures. Spellman had his own polls, so he took only fleeting pleasure at the bloodletting. Largely ignored by all sides, including the media, was Democratic dark horse John Jovanovich, a businessman from Burien.

With four days to go, McDermott's hopes took two more blows. Senator Jackson gave a posthumous blessing to Gardner in a letter mailed to Democrats around the state. It was signed by Sterling Munro and two other former Jackson aides who testified that electing Booth governor was one of the senator's "last projects." More surprising was a letter to Gardner from Congressman Mike Lowry, like McDermott a hero to Seattle liberals and heretofore neutral. "I am personally voting for you," Lowry said. Adding that he believed McDermott was also well qualified and party unity was important, he noted that "this is not a public endorsement." Dotzauer, naturally, promptly distributed the letter to the press.

McDermott kept a stiff upper lip. His office door sported a poster of Winston Churchill, complete with a quotation from Britain's darkest hour: "Never give in. Never give in. Never, never, never."

On Sept. 18, 1984, Booth Gardner, buoyed by GOP crossovers, defeated Jim McDermott two-to-one, capturing fully 46 percent of the Primary Election vote. Governor Spellman, virtually unopposed for the GOP nomination, received 26 percent. McDermott was third with 23 percent, a deeply disappointed but gracious loser. He told Booth to not waste much time celebrating. Speaking from experience, he said Spellman was no pipe-puffing milquetoast. He predicted "the most vicious campaign we've seen in this state in a long, long time."

Excell was in the war room, putting the finishing touches on a three-inch briefing book on how to beat Booth, whose lead was as high as 20 points in some polls. For starters, the Spellman campaign handed reporters a fact sheet documenting Gardner's appetite for an income tax, which voters twice rejected in the 1970s. Spellman press aide Paul O'Connor said the governor was coming out "duking," just as he had four years earlier to defeat McDermott. The job this time, he said, was to dispel the notion that Gardner wasn't a tax-and-spend liberal. "There is a presumption that because he's rich, he's a conservative," the pugnacious O'Connor said, adding that Gardner's knowledge of state issues was "candy-coat, shell thin. All he is is a trained dog on the issues." The Gardner campaign dismissed it as more "desperate" duplicity from "the same John Spellman who said 'no new taxes in 1980.' " Gardner spokesman Jim Kneeland warned, "John

Spellman and Paul O'Connor better put on their crash helmets if they're going to try to run on their record."

The gloves were off, battle lines drawn and planes on the tarmac. The finalists both immediately took to the air to barnstorm the state and replenish their coffers.

Their handlers agreed to three televised debates—Oct. 15, 21 and 31—with the governor complaining there ought to be more and not all so late in the game. Spellman said the campaign would be half over before their first face-to-face. The role reversal underscored that the governor was the underdog—and a facile debater. He'd been a national moot court champion at Georgetown Law School. Dotzauer and Kneeland said their guy wasn't chicken; he just had "scheduling conflicts." Then they scheduled one of their own. While Spellman was addressing the Pacific Northwest World Trade Conference in Tacoma on Oct. 1, Booth called a news conference in another room and accused the governor of timing the event to boost his campaign. Gardner said Spellman had failed to do enough to promote international trade and was taking credit for programs developed by the Legislature. Spellman said Gardner's move was "pretty gross." *The Seattle Times* editorialized that it was neither pretty nor gross, just "a meaningless mole hill." Excell called it a hit-and-run strategy destined to fail. A few days later, when Booth said his schedule couldn't accommodate a joint appearance before the Seattle Rotary Club, Spellman said he felt "like a Ghostbuster fighting a phantom." He branded Gardner "a shill for big labor," adding that "inside that Brooks Brothers suit is a carbon copy of Jim McDermott." Outside the hotel a Spellman stalwart wheeled a toy duck symbolizing Booth's no-show.

Weyerhaeuser and Boeing, as well as well-heeled businessmen like M. Lamont Bean, were hedging their bets by making substantial donations to both candidates. Gardner, however, was still some $400,000 ahead with Election Day five weeks out. He was poised to make the campaign another substantial loan and the Clapps were coming through. So were the unions.

The teachers loved it when he said he wanted to be "The Education Governor," and he promised to spend at least one day a month in the public schools.

Next came dueling salvos of press releases, immediately analyzed right and left by the pundits. The Spellman camp said Gardner had made so many "backroom deals" that if he became governor "Washington residents may have to consider using the union label for the state seal." Soon, Booth supporters sported buttons boasting "Hi! I'm a 'Big Labor Boss.'" Gardner called the governor a hypocrite and handed out copies of Spellman's 1980 campaign speech to the State Labor Council convention. It began with an ingratiating salutation to his "Brothers and sisters in the labor movement" and ended with a promise that labor would get its "fair share" of appointments to boards and commissions.

The campaign was growing more nasty by the day and the consensus in the press was that both sides were being alternatively silly and shrill, with Gardner often overreacting and Spellman overreacting to the overreaction, as the Seattle *P-I's* Mike Layton put it. In the *Times*, Dick Larsen wrote: "Good grief! Before our very eyes, The Wimp and The Waffle have turned into The Walloper and The Whipper." Dotzauer wasn't worried. Their tracking polls showed Booth with a 17-point lead. Excell was, but he took hope in the 25 percent undecided and felt strongly that their strategy to puncture Booth's breath-of-fresh-air image was working. The Spellman campaign changed its slogan from "You Can't Beat Spellman!" to "Why Gamble on Gardner?"

A landmark joint appearance occurred in mid-October when the candidates spent an hour answering questions about the environment from the Washington Environmental Political Action Committee. "The environmental movement has come of age as a force in Washington politics," *Seattle Times* reporter Eric Pryne wrote. "Not too many years ago politicians were railing against environmentalists. But you don't hear much, if any, green-baiting this year. And last night a few veteran environmental activists in the crowd of 300 saw the forum as a sign the political establishment finally has bestowed on them and their causes the mark of legitimacy." Spellman noted that in 1981 Booth backed more lenient air-pollution controls on Tacoma's Asarco copper smelter. Gardner said Spellman's zeal for cleaning up Puget Sound was just election-year expediency.

In Tacoma on the 15th, Spellman was crisply forceful in their first debate while Booth surprised most everyone with his poise. Well prepped by his policy adviser, Laird Harris, he accused Spellman of being a "fumbling" governor who had signed more than 80 tax hikes in the space of four years. Spellman countered that Gardner's vaunted management expertise was a sham, charging that he had "ripped off the road fund" to balance the Pierce County budget and "left the county in a shambles." One of the reporters asked Spellman why he broke his 1980 promise not to raise taxes. "No one," he said, "could have expected the worst depression we've had in 50 years"—far worse that the "Boeing Bust" of the 1970s. Spellman could have added that his promise was to raise taxes only as "a last resort," but that might have sounded like equivocating.

Gardner and Spellman chat before their last debate in Spokane on October 31, 1984. *Shawn Jacobsen © The Spokesman-Review (Spokane, WA) 1984. Reprinted with permission.*

The Gardners celebrate victory. *Photo courtesy Dick Baldwin.*

While Booth's TV ads refrained from attacking Spellman, on Oct. 21 in Seattle his team finally got him to come out swinging. Saying he was tired of "catching without a mask," the first words out of his mouth were "John, I think you've run one of the dirtiest campaigns we've seen in Washington in a long time." Spellman shot back nimbly that Gardner was just defensive because "we've scored most of the points." An Elway poll for *The Seattle Times* showed Spellman gaining.

The last debate was Halloween night in Spokane. It produced nothing scary for either side, except that Spellman twice committed the perhaps Freudian slip of referring to Gardner as "Mr. Governor." Spellman said he was proud to stand on his record. He'd made tough decisions to help the state weather the toughest economy in a half century and the recession was almost over. "Philosophically," he said, "I think the State of Washington is on a real high." Gardner said the people knew the real score: "Basically, in the last four years, the governor has done nothing." He headed out for one last lap of the state on *Spud One*. U.S. Senators Dan Evans and Slade Gorton barnstormed with Spellman.

Dotzauer, puffing a cigarette despite a wheezing head cold made worse by the obligatory morning jog with the candidate, was so tired he alternated between caution and confidence. He told one reporter they'd win "by a point or two" and another he figured it would be eight. It turned out to be 6.6. On Nov. 6, 1984, despite another Reagan landslide, Booth Gardner was elected Washington's 19th governor. He captured 53.3 percent of the vote to John Spellman's 46.7. Gardner prevailed in 23 of the state's 39 counties, including every major population center save Spokane, which Spellman carried by just over 2,000 votes. Pierce County gave its native son a 70 percent landslide.

Setting aside the Sturm und Drang, Gardner won because he was a winsome fresh face with an aura of managerial competence. Spellman lost because the brutal recession had forced him to make unpalatable yet fair, even courageous, decisions. He was also hurt by the intransigence of the right wing of his own party. The irony was that Dotzauer could run Gardner like a Spellman, while Excell had to transform his Mr. Nice Guy into the aggressor. "I'm a good manager," the governor had noted on the eve of the election. "I guess maybe I'm not a very good salesman." Spellman conceded gracefully and told reporters he had no regrets about the hardball campaign. It was their only chance. Nor did Excell: "Maybe if we'd had another week or another couple of days…Who knows?"

At Gardner's whooping headquarters, they were touting their man as presidential timber —a "new generation" Democrat who could help his party rebound from Reaganism. Booth was "in touch with a new and emerging wave in American politics," Kneeland told the reporters.

Just as Larry Faulk had warned Spellman that he'd be next if they didn't stop Booth in Tacoma, one of Spellman's post-mortems would prove prophetic for his successor: "In terms of the Legislature, it was a lot worse than I thought it would be."

Dick Larsen, who enjoyed special access to the Gardner campaign and often bit the hand that fed him, just for drill, said the key question for the governor-elect was "Where's the beef?"

CHAPTER 12:

Transitions & Lessons

"Most governors are legislators first, even if being an 'insider' is often an electoral liability," observes former state senator George W. Scott, a legislative historian. Acknowledging that his legislative skills were weak, the governor-elect announced early on that his chief of staff would be Dean Foster, chief clerk of the state House of Representatives for all but two of the previous 12 years. The protégé of a redoubtable former Senate majority leader, R.R. "Bob" Greive, Foster began working for the Legislature as a high school student. "Dean will be my alter ego," Gardner said. "I just think it's going to work beautifully."

Booth's transition team was headed by an efficient trio. The budget-master was Orin Smith, a Harvard MBA with state government experience who was destined to become CEO of Starbucks. Greg Barlow, Booth's aide-de-camp from Pierce County, was the quartermaster, security man and campaign-debt fundraiser. (Booth, tight as a tick, wanted his personal loans repaid.) Laird Harris, a bright young policy wonk, coordinated the issues agenda and oversaw the committees producing detailed workups on every state agency. Harris' role was important and influential, Foster says, because he was so good at it and "Booth wanted to know everything about

Booth takes the oath of office from Chief Justice James Dolliver. Wayne Zimmerman © *The News Tribune* (Tacoma, WA) 1985. Reprinted with permission.

everything." For all the talk about his managing by walking around, Foster says Gardner was a "Harvard-trained business guy who loved to study facts and analyze policy." A diverse array of advisers and talent scouts—many of them unknowns but destined for high-profile jobs in government and business—covered 18 key policy areas. Jim Kneeland handled communications. His aunt, Rosalie Gittings, who had worked for Dean Foster and Supreme Court Justice Hugh Rosellini, emerged as everyone's favorite gal Friday. An old hand in union and party politics, Gittings would become Booth's personal assistant. Mary Faulk, a versatile hospital administrator who was married to Booth's old Pierce County rival, crunched numbers for the team as a loaned executive from Tacoma's Consolidated Hospitals. Indispensable was former state senator A.N. "Bud" Shinpoch, a hard-nosed old liberal who had been chairman of the Ways & Means committees in both chambers and "knew the budget backward and forward." Gardner spent countless hours on cabinet selections.

A pre-inaugural poll by *The Seattle Times* found that 71 percent of the respondents expected Gardner to be either excellent or good at managing state government. Sixty-one percent also gave his leadership qualities high marks. Women tended to rate him higher than men.

～

On January 16, 1985, William Booth Gardner became the governor of a state that was slowly emerging from a crippling recession, with unemployment lingering at nearly 9 percent. The forest products industry was hemorrhaging jobs. Slade Gorton and Dan Evans, who had succeeded Washington's gold dust twins, Jackson and Magnuson, in the U.S. Senate, were warning that the Office of Management & Budget's plans to boost the Bonneville Power Administration's interest payments and accelerate its debt repayment could shutter aluminum mills and other heavy users of industrial power and usher in a regional depression. The state and the cities ringing Puget Sound were facing a costly federal mandate to reduce sewage contamination. One bright spot was Boeing, which expected to hire 3,000 more workers in the next 12 months.

Booth labored over his inaugural address, doing most of his writing and editing in a small room off the library in the Temple of Justice. He was making changes right up to the moment it had to go to the state printer.

"Nearly 200,000 of our citizens who want work cannot find it," the governor told a joint session of the Legislature. "Much of our abundant agricultural harvest has no market....Overfishing and poor management have vastly depleted our salmon resources ...Pollution threatens our shellfish harvests. Roads, bridges and public buildings are in critical need of repair at a time when our revenue base simply will not permit us to address all our needs. And many people have lost confidence in the ability of our public schools and institutions of higher learning to provide quality education....I want to achieve excellence at all levels and in every classroom of our K12 and higher education systems. ...The challenges we face are difficult, but difficulty is an excuse that history never accepts. And we do have the chance—a golden opportunity—to make history …. History lies in transforming Washington into the Gateway of the Future."

He set four priorities. The first was to develop a diversified, cutting-edge economy that would make it possible to achieve a host of other goals. In the meantime, services necessary to help the needy had to be sustained and "the practice of pushing our problems into the future and onto the shoulders of our children" must end, "whether the subject is pensions or repairs to our infrastructure." Rainy days were inevitable, he said, emphasizing that the state needed a budget reserve large enough to "absorb unanticipated drops in revenue without having to resort to session after session and service cut after service cut to balance the budget."

Gardner next took a moment "to talk directly to my fellow state employees. In the weeks since the election, I've spent a good deal of time observing your work first hand. In agency after agency, I've seen the hard work and dedication to the common good that I expected. I want you to know that I have faith and confidence in you. Our challenge, working together, is to make the people of this state *proud* of their government." Echoing Dan Evans' often-recounted declaration in his own 1965 inaugural address that he'd "rather cross the aisle than cross the people," Gardner said he couldn't solve the state's myriad problems without the help and support of the Legislature. "In each house there is an aisle which separates the two political parties. Between the two houses there is a corridor which separates them. One floor in this building separates the executive from the legislative branch of government. …Never has it been more essential for state government to be united."

Noting that the state's centennial was just four years away, Booth said "the Age of the Pacific" was already here, with the world's focus turning toward the nations and states of the Pacific Rim. "In a spirit of rediscovery, rededication and renewal," he said, "we should spend the next four years actively preparing for our second century."

Fans hailed it as an uplifting "breath of fresh air." Critics said it was

The governor gives the First Lady a twirl at the Inaugural Ball. Jerry Buck
© *The News Tribune* (Tacoma, WA) 1985. Reprinted with permission.

long on vision and short on specifics. One observed that it sounded a lot like John Spellman.

That night, the Triscuits and salami ran short as 4,000 cheering revelers crowded under the Capitol dome. They prodded the tuxedoed governor into taking a few dance steps with the First Lady, who was stunning in a sequined pink and rose sheath as he twirled her. The toast featured California champagne because the Inaugural Committee couldn't find any in-state bubbly within its budget. Tomorrow, the governor said, barely audible in the din bouncing off all that towering marble, it would be time to get to work.

~

Beginning on a bipartisan note that drew praise from political friends and foes, Gardner decided to retain Karen Rahm as secretary of the labyrinthian Department of Social & Health Services and Amos Reed, a 69-year-old veteran of prison management in several states, as secretary of the Department of Corrections. Eight other less influential Spellman appointees were also reappointed. The back story was that Booth wanted everyone vetted so carefully that he ran out of time on some appointments and resolved to go with the flow for a while to see who was and wasn't up to snuff; if holdovers generated some political capital at the outset, so much the better. "Nobody is permanent," Orin Smith emphasized. Rahm didn't last long and Reed was gone by the next summer.

Smith was named to head the Office of Financial Management, while Shinpoch was turned loose on the Department of Revenue. Richard A. Davis, a highly regarded executive with Pacific Northwest Bell, was commissioned to unravel the rat's nest of problems at Labor & Industries. Its convoluted, money-losing worker's compensation program was derided by both business and labor and targeted by Gardner during the campaign. Davis quickly named Joe Dear, the 33-year-old chief lobbyist for the State Labor Council, to serve as temporary assistant director. Dear's job was to transform Vocational Rehabilitation from chaos to a reasonable facsimile of efficiency. He became a star.

Joining Dean Foster as key internal staffers were Harris as policy adviser, Kneeland as press secretary and Terry Sebring, Gardner's trusted legal adviser from Pierce County, as the governor's attorney.

The appointment of Bellevue City Manager Andrea Beatty to head the

Booth meets with members of his staff. Standing from left, the governor, press secretary Jim Kneeland, press aide Jim Richards and policy adviser Laird Harris; sitting, chief of staff Dean Foster. Wayne Zimmerman © *The News Tribune* (Tacoma, WA) 1985. Reprinted with permission.

Department of Ecology proved controversial. The 39-year-old was a total unknown to the environmental community, which had done a lot of soul-searching before deciding to back Booth over McDermott. Her defenders praised her as "a fast study" and a skilled manager. Smith acknowledged that her lack of environmental chops represented a risk, but he said the governor wasn't interested in conventional wisdom. (Beatty, later Andrea Riniker, came to be known as "The Velvet Hammer" as Ecology came down hard on heavy industry, including Weyerhaeuser. Beatty's successor in 1988 was an intensely bright deputy attorney general, Christine Gregoire.)

Agricultural interests were surprised and disappointed when Gardner bounced Spellman appointee Keith Ellis from the Department of Agriculture. Alan Pettibone, acting dean of the College Of Agriculture at Washington State University, got the job. Richard Thompson, Puyallup's city manager, who had worked closely with Gardner in Pierce County, was named director of the Community Development Agency. Dick Virant, a former commander of McChord Air Force Base, was picked to head General Services. Isiah Turner, 39, an African American, was elevated from assistant commissioner in the Department of Employment Security to agency chief.

Disgruntled State Patrol Troopers were rewarded with an affable new chief, George Tellevik, who had risen through the ranks to major. That he wasn't on the troopers' short list underscored Gardner's independence. In Tellevik, the governor saw a leader with street smarts. He turned out to be one of the administration's best choices. After a couple of clashes with union leaders, Tellevik won over the troopers, who realized he was a solid manager and "just an all-around decent, nice person." Tellevik was with the administration for its entire eight years. He nearly doubled the number of troopers on the road, emphasizing not just enforcement but assistance to motorists with disabled vehicles. He dramatically improved the Patrol's facilities, updated its fleet of cruisers and persuaded the Legislature to fund a computerized statewide fingerprint network. On his watch, Washington highways became some of the nation's safest.

Booth's intuition was first-rate, Foster says. But by no means infallible.

Turner was destined to make an embarrassing exit from Employment Security, which stung twice as much because he had been an innovative manager and the point man for Gardner's commitment to diversity. Theresa Aragon, 41, director of human services for Seattle, was tapped to head the Department of Licensing. A Chicano studies activist, she was also a former university professor. Her talents turned out to be better suited to academics, although supporters said the governor and legislators never gave her a fair chance to correct management deficiencies in the agency. Gardner strived to promote minorities and women, with mixed success. The Latino community was angry over Aragon's departure from the cabinet in 1988.

A great pick was Mary Faulk, whose appointment to head the State Lottery riled some Democrats accustomed to patronage. In the throes of the heavily-caffeinated transition, Faulk had impressed Smith as a versatile manager with strong people skills. Mary remembers him saying, "Why don't you give me your resume?" Laughing her infectious laugh, she scoffed, "Are you kidding? The governor wouldn't offer me a job." A couple of days later as she and Larry were finishing a late dinner, the phone rang. It was Booth. "How'd you like to be the director of Lottery?" Surprised, flattered and excited at the challenge, she declared, "That sounds wonderful." (When the word came down that Smith and Gardner wanted her at the Lottery, Barlow told Larry Faulk that someone in the back of the room quipped, "How many doorbells did she ring?" "Zip," Barlow shot back, "but she's good!" And she was. In the years to come, Booth would plug her in wherever he needed a steady hand—next at General Administration, then to Licensing to succeed Aragon. The Faulks divorced, amicably, in 1990 and the following year Mary married Gardner's second prisons chief, Chase Riveland. In 1993, Governor Mike Lowry named her to succeed Chris Gregoire at Ecology. Mary Faulk Riveland was Ms. Fixit, and the Rivelands were one of the state's power couples.)

With economic development as a cornerstone of his administration, Gardner's prize catch was John Anderson, whom he wooed back from Oregon to lead his "Team Washington." Before moving to Oregon in 1982,

Booth with some of the outstanding women he appointed. Chris Gregoire is seated, third from left. Next to her, fourth from left, is Mary Faulk. *Photo courtesy Mary Faulk Riveland.*

Anderson had been acting economic development director, then deputy director. Earlier he had headed the Puget Sound Economic Development Council. In Oregon, Anderson stressed statewide economic-development teamwork and brought thousands of high-tech jobs to the state. Oregon's Republican governor, Vic Atiyeh, was loath to lose him. Gardner persuaded the state salary commission to boost the pay for the post from $55,700 a year to $71,000, some $18,000 more than Anderson was getting in Oregon. The governor also won more money for the budget director and ecology chief, asserting the state needed to be able to recruit top-flight managers.

～

Booth was optimistic about the legislative session, with Foster as chief of staff, Democratic majorities in both chambers and three members of the "Pierce County Mafia" in leadership positions: Wayne Ehlers as speaker of the House, Ted Bottiger as Senate majority leader and young Dan Grimm of Puyallup as head of Ways & Means in the House. The wild card was Jim McDermott, who lost the election but was still in the cat-bird seat as chairman of Ways & Means in the Senate, where the budget would originate.

With revenues projected to perk up, teachers, troopers and other public employees were clamoring for salary increases; environmentalists, educational reformers and mental-health advocates were demanding ac-

Booth with a House page in 1986.
Gardner family album.

tion. Colleges needed new buildings; bridges, dams and sewage treatment plants were in disrepair—$2 billion worth of public works projects alone. Moreover, the state's pension funds, a huge piece of unfinished business, had to be shored up. Reaganomics had caused the federal deficit to soar and the states saw their "revenue-sharing" reduced to a trickle. Washington's tax system, heavily dependent on consumer spending, was revealed as more problematic than ever. Dan Evans, whom Gardner regarded as the exemplar of gubernatorial excellence, had tilted twice at the income tax windmill. Yet Booth believed that if he could "restore trust in government" tax reform was "doable." He was about to get a crash course in the perils of governance. But he was off and running, literally, at least three times a week, prompting honks, waves and double-takes as he jogged the three-mile Capitol Lake loop. When, as promised, he took time out for his first field trip to a school he was totally in his element. The kids at Northwood Junior High in suburban Spokane gave him rock star treatment, screaming for an autograph, handshake or hug. "He's so cool," one ninth-grader said, admitting that she didn't know anything about him except that "he's the governor." Gardner said that any time he heard people complain about what a cushy job it was to be a teacher, he'd say, "I've got a deal for you: You work from now until Christmas as a teacher, and I'll cover your job for you. At the end, you tell me if you don't need two weeks off at Christmas."

In Olympia, the honeymoon was over even before the ides of March, when Booth warned that salary increases for public employees, teachers and college faculty were unlikely in 1985. The reserves for the current biennium were practically gone, he said, and the state could face a deficit in the next two years "unless we begin to pull back" on spending. Then came the news that revenue collections were down $25 million. "We're in trouble," said Grimm. Gardner responded with a cautious $9.3 billion budget that gave top priority to economic development and the cleanup of Puget Sound. He earmarked nearly $299 million for contingencies and included $40.6 million, pending a hoped-for negotiated settlement, to begin phasing in "comparable worth" pay hikes to some 15,000 mostly female state workers who'd prevailed in a landmark sex-discrimination case. State

Booth meets the press. David Ammons of the AP is seated at his immediate left, with Bob Partlow of Gannett standing behind him with a clipboard. Seated, second from left, Dale Folkerts of the Everett Herald. Next is Peter Callaghan of the Tacoma News Tribune. Dean J. Koepfler © *The News Tribune* (Tacoma, WA) 1992. Reprinted with permission.

Patrol troopers, who'd gone nearly two years without a raise, got a 4 percent boost in his budget. Gardner also recommended raises of 4.6 to 8 percent for faculty at the state's two major universities to help them compete with other four-year research schools. However, "The Education Governor" was proposing a $4.2 billion budget for the public schools, $117 million less than Spellman had suggested. That was also nearly $600 million below what the state school superintendent, Frank "Buster" Brouillet, said it would take just to maintain the status quo, which was rapidly losing its status. Booth's budget made "any talk of education excellence a cruel joke," said John Cahill, communications director for the state's largest teachers' union, the Washington Education Association. Its outgoing president was Booth's Phi Delta Theta UW fraternity brother, Reese Lindquist, who had prodded the union to back him for governor. "I'm very disappointed," Lindquist said. "We're extremely disappointed." It was the beginning of a topsy-turvy, eight-year love-hate relationship between the governor and the WEA. Gardner vowed that salaries would be his No. 1 priority in 1986.

Also bitterly disappointed were the other state employee unions, whose lobbyists crowded into the news conference where the governor unveiled his budget. "The way you set priorities in state government," said Mark Brown of the Federation of State Employees, "is you put your money where your mouth is." Senator McDermott, however, pronounced Gardner's budget "very prudent," and some Republicans were also impressed with his fiscal restraint. Then more bad news: The Forecasting Council said state revenues would be $154 million less than predicted in December, the fourth decline in 12 months. Gardner ordered an immediate freeze on hiring, purchasing and travel. When he learned that the commission planning the state's 100th anniversary in 1989 was proposing a $152 million birthday party he was "stunned and astonished," saying, "The state doesn't have that kind of money." He said it had to be a "grassroots" celebration involving school children and tapping the creativity of every community in the state. He named First Lady Jean Gardner and Secretary of State Ralph Munro to head the centennial celebration.

On March 28, Gardner cut short a trip to Eastern Washington and in a move he would later describe as one of the worst mistakes of his first year, amped up the crisis atmosphere. Striving to demonstrate forcefulness, he went on statewide television to warn that painful budget cuts and possible tax hikes would be necessary in the wake of a new report showing the revenue shortfall for the biennium ending June 30 could be as much as $60 million. With the sales and business and occupation taxes highly sensitive to economic downturns, state government was balancing its budget on a two-legged stool. Editorialists said the crisis was a golden opportunity to push for an income tax, given Gardner's connections to the business community and astounding popularity with the proletariat.

Wherever he went that winter, people kept shouting, "Hey, Booth. You're doing a great job!" Habitually gruff Shelby Scates of the *Seattle Post-Intelligencer* declared, "We've got a phenom in the statehouse."

In the parlance of the newsroom, Gardner was "good copy"—a story-making machine. Whole forests fell to feed the presses and ink arrived by the tanker truck as a diverse cast of gifted writers chronicled the adventures of Booth and his retinue. Besides Scates, the *P-I's* coverage featured Mike Layton, Neil Modie, Laura Parker and Joel Connelly. *The Times* fielded Larsen, Lyle Burt, Doug Underwood, Don Duncan and Walter Hatch. *The Tacoma News Tribune's* team included Callaghan and Rick Seifert. Ammons at the AP and Gordon Schultz at United Press International were two of the best wire-service reporters the state had ever seen, while Bob Partlow covered the Capitol for Gannett News Service. Adele Ferguson's columns appeared in dailies and weeklies all over the state. Henry Gay, the Menckenesque sage of Shelton, was a big-league writer in a small town. David Brewster's Seattle *Weekly*, which made its mark covering Dixy Lee Ray's meltdown, featured the witheringly witty Rebecca Boren. One day, she stood watch in Gardner's outer office as "a ghastly procession of state budget experts" trooped out of "Macbooth's" inner sanctum. "First came State Revenue director Bud Shinpoch, his expression frozen, looking neither to the right nor to the left. He was followed by Senate Ways & Means chair Jim McDermott, his face as gray as his charcoal suit… Out, out brief candle. March 28 turned out to be the day the 1985 legislative session died. While Governor Gardner was out doing his prairie-dog routine—popping up in Sunnyside schools—his money mavens were being whacked by the week's bad news. …The governor's panicky response drew pans from political pros across the spectrum."

⌣

Everyone took a two-day pass in the middle of the battle of the budget to note Greg Barlow's promotion to brigadier general to oversee Washington's Army National Guard. It was the No. 2 post in a Military Department headed by Spellman appointee George Coates. Clearly the model of a modern major general, Coates made the appointment with the blessings of his new commander-in-chief. He praised the former Green Beret chopper pilot as "a super soldier." Barlow's promotions had come so fast that Congress hadn't had time to approve them. He'd been a lieutenant colonel just eight months earlier. Many members of the Guard had backed Gardner for governor because he promised to shake up the Military Department. Now a number of officers groused about political patronage—on condition of anonymity, of course. Barlow had been 31st on the seniority roster. If they hadn't seen him coming, that spoke volumes about their political combat readiness. They conceded he was a true "blood-and-guts warrior." What they didn't realize was that he was also a crack military administrator. Unfazed by it all, Barlow said Booth had actually offered him the No. 1 job in January. "I could have been an immediate two-star general," he told reporters, "but I didn't want the troops to think it was a political thing."

Some members of the Gardner team were relieved to see Barlow back in uniform, but he never lost Booth's ear. He got his second star and was named adjutant general by Gardner in 1989. One of the craftiest operatives the capital has ever seen, Barlow was paid $85,000 a year to head the state's National Guard and $85,000 a year as executive director of the Medina

To Our Commander in Chief: Thanks for your total support! Greg
Annual Training 1987

Booth and Barlow on maneuvers in 1987. *Gardner family album.*

Foundation. He also collected as much as $20,000 more for weekend drills with the Guard. Norton Clapp said Barlow was so good at his job that neither he nor the foundation's board were the least bit worried about his telecommuting. No other state agency director held a second full-time job. By all accounts, however, the general was a dazzling juggler. Adele maintains that one of Gardner's biggest mistakes as governor was not naming Barlow his chief of staff. "Greg ran Pierce County for Booth and Booth got all the credit," she says, adding that she wishes she had known that when she was touting Gardner in her column and doubtless helped get him elected. "I wrote one time that Booth had a guy working on his campaign who was blowing his money. ...I was walking through the Legislative Building one day when here comes this really handsome silver-haired guy in uniform. It's Greg Barlow. He said, 'You're Adele Ferguson?' I said, 'Yeah.' And he said, 'I just want to thank you for the column you wrote....I went down yesterday and picked up his checkbook!' Barlow didn't mess around. Booth should have taken Barlow to Olympia with him." Dean Foster says that would have been a bad idea. "Barlow intimidated me," the former chief of staff says. "He intimidated most everybody, and he had a negative view of government that in my mind would have hurt Booth very rapidly. He did make decisions and he did chop off heads. They're a little more used to that kind of stuff in Pierce County. Down here we play a little softer." Ron Dotzauer, not known for playing softer, admired Barlow's toughness and loyalty to Booth, but he believes "it would have been a disaster—an unmitigated disaster" to have Barlow as chief of staff. "We all worried about that."

⌐

To the Republicans' delight, the majority Democrats "degenerated into an inter-house, inter-generational, self-destructive feud" over relatively minor spending differences. On April 28, after 105 days, the lawmakers went home without passing a budget for the 1985-87 biennium. Grimm and McDermott and their Ways & Means staffs exchanged unpleasantries. "…[T]hey just piss at each other," the governor said, revealing his frustration. Hoping a cooling-off period would break the logjam and that the next revenue report would be rosier, Gardner decided to postpone a special session until June. He admitted wearily that he'd been idealistically naïve to "really believe" that the executive branch and the Legislature could set aside distrust and egos and just "work closely together and build a consensus—do what's right." His favorite song had been the hit inspired by the schmaltzy jingle for his beverage of choice, Coca-Cola, "I'd Like to Teach the World to Sing in Perfect Harmony." Reaching for something stronger, he said he was a fast learner and observed that "a lot of what Dan Evans accomplished was in his second term."

In the meantime, there was progress on several fronts. Gardner signed an ambitious $552 million construction budget that would finance new buildings and remodeling projects at schools, colleges, prisons, parks and hatcheries. He also signed several environmental bills, including measures to expedite a comprehensive plan to clean up Puget Sound and give workers information about hazardous materials. Other bills authorized home schooling and returned state civil service to a seniority-based system. With mixed emotions he signed a dozen "educational excellence" bills, well aware that the budget crisis could leave many of them unfunded. Notably, the push for standards-based education, a hallmark of his eight years as governor, began with House Bill 141, which required achievement tests for all high school sophomores, and Senate Bill 4140, which boosted high school graduation requirements. Another bill he signed into law that day, May 20, 1985, launched a program of free preschool for underprivileged children.

After some horse-trading by Gardner before the gavels dropped, the special session lasted only two days. The lawmakers approved his request for a sales tax deferral to help lure new industry and authorized bonds for new schools and other state construction projects but failed to approve a plan to clean up Puget Sound and killed a House-passed plan to raise $56.5 million by hiking cigarette taxes. Teachers and other state employees, including the troopers, got no raises. Only $173 million was left in reserves. Flanked by Speaker Ehlers and Senate Majority Leader Bottiger, the governor gave the special session an "A." Skeptical reporters noted that the water quality legislation, one of his top priorities, had gone down the drain. "OK," he said, "an A-minus —I'm an easy grader." Reminded that he had asked for a rainy-day reserve of $200 million to $300 million, the grade deflation continued. "I guess I'll give them a B," he said with a shrug. *The Tacoma News Tribune* gave them an A for speed and C for performance. *The Seattle Times* gave both the governor and the legislators an F, saying their failure to finance a Puget Sound cleanup program was "inexcusable." Senate Republicans took their lumps for rejecting a compromise effort to launch some sort of cleanup program.

One of the highlights of the administration's first year came that summer when the state landed a $200 million semiconductor plant for Clark County. RCA-Sharp, a U.S.-Japanese joint venture, planned an initial hire of 600 workers. The average salary, Gardner and Anderson told a packed press conference in Vancouver, would be $40,000 per year. One legislative staff report had estimated that the sales tax deferral would cost the treasury a lot more than Gardner claimed as businesses that were planning to move to Washington anyway took advantage of the new loophole. But Team Washington was off to an impressive start. Booth noted it had been one year to the day since McDermott humiliated him in their Seattle Rotary Club debate. After plunging to 41 percent in May, his approval ratings bounced back to 57 in June. "He comes across as being sincere," a 35-year-old woman from Port Angeles told pollsters. Dan Grimm, who had wondered out loud if Booth had what it took to be governor, said, "The heart is there, and I had questioned that. Now it's not 'does he want to be a good governor and do things?' It's now a question of what he wants to do."

He wanted an income tax. "I'll vote for it," the governor told the CityClub of Seattle that summer, recalling that the issue was last placed on the ballot in 1973. "I'm a business person, and I would rather be taxed on profits than on my gross." Booth emphasized that the only way to sell the voters on the plan was to make it a flat tax tied into a package with the sales tax and the business-and-occupation tax. As one went up, the others would have to be reduced. The voters' chief fear, he said, was that adding an income tax to make the state's tax base "less regressive and more equitable" was just another song and dance to make their pocketbooks lighter and government fatter.

He also wanted a lot more of those family-wage jobs and barnstormed Japan for two weeks to promote Washington as a great place to do business—"The Gateway to the Pacific" and the front door to American consumers.

When he returned, he made his first cabinet change, replacing Karen Rahm at the Department of Social & Health Services with Shinpoch, aka "Bud the Knife." Having cut two layers of management at the Department of Revenue in the space of seven months, Shinpoch would immediately become acting director at DSHS. Gardner said Rahm wanted to go back to Bellevue, but "were she willing to stay, I'd be very happy to have her." Shinpoch, who could detect BS at 100 paces, told reporters, "Some of the constituent groups are very well organized. They went around her back to the governor, and then when it came time to make a decision, he didn't back her up." Dean Foster says that was classic Shinpoch. "Bud was a great numbers guy, but his skills in communication would not have made him eligible to be a high-level diplomat at the U.N." George Scott, a Republican, recalls admiringly that during a legislative hearing Shinpoch once dressed down a bureaucrat by thundering, "I don't want to hear any more goddamn lies. I want to know what you're doing with the money!" Shinpoch's mission, which he chose to accept with relish, was to "de-layer" the 14,000-employee, $3.5-billion-a-biennium agency. Grimm cheered him on, saying, "There's something wrong when a chairman of Ways & Means who has been serving four years says that DSHS baffles him."

The governor was feeling run down and underwent a series of medical tests. A rarity in that he was addicted to junk food *and* exercise, he was diagnosed with hypoglycemia—low blood sugar. He routinely started work at 6 a.m., finishing up 14 to 16 hours later. He knew every burger joint from Aberdeen to Pullman. What the doctor ordered was more relaxation and fewer Cokes and burgers. The cook at the Governor's Mansion was told to serve less red meat, more fruit, whole grain bread and juices. After several weeks, the first lady said he'd had a new burst of energy, but she found a Frisko Freeze bag in his car. Frisko Freeze was trying to get with the program, even at the risk of offending one of its best customers. One day while the State Patrol was driving him through Tacoma, he used the mobile phone to call in an order for a double cheeseburger and a chocolate shake. The counter clerk asked for a name. "Gardner," he said. The clerk paused for second, then asked, "You're not supposed to be doing this, are you?"

When Seattle's 3,700 teachers went on strike for 19 days that September,

Gardner received high marks for helping to mediate a settlement. He "more or less banged heads together and kept people up around the clock until an agreement was reached."

That fall, Doug Gardner, Booth and Jean's son, departed for Africa to be a relief worker. A tennis ace at Pacific Lutheran University, he earned a degree in business administration and became a born-again Christian. Describing himself as "a babe in Christ," the 23-year-old said, "I have confidence in the Lord and he has confidence in me that I can do this." The Gardners' daughter, Gail, was majoring in economics at Dartmouth.

As the 1986 legislative session drew closer, the governor began lobbying for more operational control over the state's 400 boards, councils and commissions, most notably the Game Department, the Transportation Commission, the Parks & Recreation Commission, the Community College Board, the Liquor Control Board and the Gambling Commission. "I run an organization that was designed to fail," he said.

While the reviews were mixed on his transition from candidate to governor, Booth, his staff and his cabinet were invigorated. Things didn't exactly "work beautifully," as he had predicted at the beginning, but they were happy to have survived the first year with no scar tissue. The Gardner Administration was a never-ending field day for the reporters and political junkies. But the gushing and gnashing in the press and the posturing by the players amounted to Polaroid snapshots. They rarely captured the big picture. Basically—to use Booth's favorite word—1985 was a learning year. In many ways, however, it was also a microcosm of the next seven.

CHAPTER 13:

"Where are we going?"

Thanks to Jim Kneeland's genius at staging photo-ops, Booth was a familiar face on the nightly news and front pages—standing in a boat on the polluted Duwamish River, surveying the site of a new electronics plant in Clark County, helping pick up litter near Ocean Shores. (Rest assured that Kneeland made sure there actually was litter.) *The Wall Street Journal* and *Business Week* hailed "a bright new face in American politics." Gardner artfully used the news media to boost his popularity. One day he handed out bumper strips that said "Support the 1st Amendment—KISS A REPORTER." The AP's David Ammons observed that "before he was elected, he was an uptight, scared little guy. …He's just blossomed, both as a governor and in his relationship with the press." The GOP leader in the House, Sim Wilson, said it was all smoke and mirrors. "Who the heck is the governor," Wilson scoffed, "Jim Kneeland or Booth Gardner? I'd give him an A for PR and a C-minus for substance."

After Dixy Lee Ray, who was in a perpetual snit and named the pigs on her Fox Island farm after her least favorite reporters, and their bouts with Spellman's testy press secretary, the reporters enjoyed their ready access to Gardner. Joshing punctuated many of his press conferences. They kidded

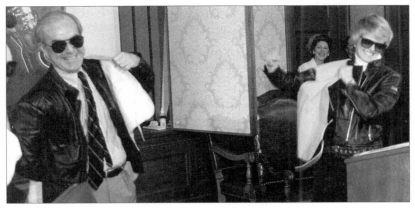

To promote "Motorcycle Awareness Week," Booth and Mary Faulk, then director of licensing, donned Harley Davidson leather jackets. *Photo courtesy Mary Faulk Riveland.*

him about his jargon, goading him to drop a quarter in a jar every time he lapsed into MBA-speak. He knew them all by their first names and asked about their spouses and children. He disarmed everyone with his repertoire of sure-fire stories, many of them self-deprecating, such as the time he jogged home from the Olympia YMCA after a vigorous workout with barbells. "The blood was pumping and the adrenalin flowing and I was really feeling full of myself," he says. "Then I hopped into the shower, which was even more invigorating. As I exited the shower, Jean walks in and I gave her one of these," he says, flexing his biceps like Charles Atlas. "I said, 'What do you think the people of the state would say if they could see me now?' And she said, 'I think the people would say that I must have married you for your money.' "

"Everybody is used as a prop by him. He could make a living as a stand-up comedian," Bob Partlow of *The Olympian* said early in 1986. "It's hard not to be charmed by the guy."

Critics said the press was overly smitten with the governor. A backlash was predictable. It's the natural order of things. No self-respecting reporter wants to be seen as a lapdog rather than a watchdog. When the new wore off and Gardner stumbled, the media let him have it. Gardner was actually less thin skinned that most imagined, but when Dick Larsen dubbed him "Prince Faintheart" it pinched a sciatic nerve. "It was devastating to Booth," Dean Foster says. "Booth thought that he and Dick were friends… and friends don't do that to friends." *The Seattle Times* writer had been granted exclusive access to some of Gardner's most important strategy sessions, a move that backfired when he showed the colors by biting the hand that fed him. Dick Milne, Kneeland's successor, remembers arriving for a Saturday morning meeting on tax reform "and Dick Larsen is sitting there. I was the press secretary and I wasn't even told. I pulled someone aside and said, 'This is not good—not only because of what he's going to do with that potential ammunition that nobody else has, but what am I going to tell Walter Hatch and all those other people?' I was dead. The rest of the press corps was in my face."

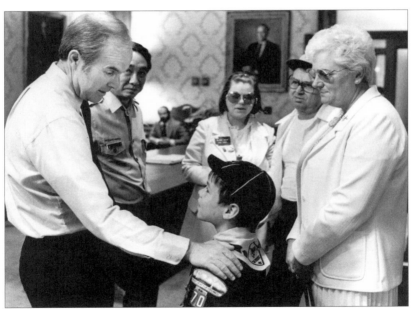

Booth greets Cub Scout Billy Joe Thomas and his parents. Wayne Zimmerman
© *The News Tribune* (Tacoma, WA) 1985. Reprinted with permission.

Still, Booth was so likable that state Sen. Barney Goltz of Bellingham christened him "The Cabbage Patch Governor," the cuddly cloth dolls being the toy sensation of the season. Representative Grimm, pointing to the governor's rapport with children, said he was more like Mr. Rogers. Ken Nuckolls, a veteran political operative said, "He's a nice guy, but nice guys finish last. I'm not sure he can get mean." Sam Hunt, chairman of the Thurston County Democrats, said, "I think the biggest question people have is 'Where are we going?' There are all these issues out there. What is going to happen? What does he want to happen?"

When it comes to being governor, "style is probably at least equal to substance," said Mark Brown, the lobbyist for the Washington Federation of State Employees. "He has a winning style. He has an air of confidence, but not arrogance. It's not a question of getting along. Booth Gardner genuinely cares about people. When he says 'I'm only as good as my fellow state employees,' he means it."

He also meant it when he said he would promote diversity. On Christmas Eve 1985 Gardner issued an executive order banning discrimination against gays and lesbians in state employment. Gay rights activists called it a courageous step forward for the State of Washington. Opponents, many of them evangelical Christians, flooded his office with letters of outrage and declared it would cost him "any prospects of re-election in 1988." Gardner's order also encouraged state agencies to hire people with limited English language skills. "My administration will not tolerate discrimination," he said. "We only intend to discriminate against one group: those who are not competent to do the job. If a worker can do the job in a professional manner, then state government has no right to intrude in his or her private life."

In 1990, a cross-burning outside the Whidbey Island home of a mixed-race couple and several gay-bashing incidents prompted an outraged Gardner to propose some of the most aggressive malicious harassment legislation in the nation. He was thwarted repeatedly by conservative senators who asserted that extending protection to gays amounted to an endorsement of their "lifestyle." The Persian Gulf War in 1991, though brief, sparked an outbreak of threats against Jewish and Muslim Americans. The governor said the best way to honor the diverse group of men and women in the armed forces would be "to ensure their civil rights and freedom are protected here at home." Gardner was able to establish a statewide program to monitor hate crimes and secure funds to train law enforcement on ways to combat racist groups like the Aryan Nations and skinheads.

Gardner said his first six months were exhausting. "I just couldn't catch my stride. ...You've got to go through your first legislative session, and that isn't fun." As it was in the beginning, it would be at the end nearly eight years later: When the lawmakers left town, he was liberated. Looking back, he says he was never comfortable with the rough and tumble of legislative politics. "I hated it."

Rosalie Gittings, his personal assistant, recalls his mood swings, especially in the afternoon when his attention deficit was at its worst. She believes his eating habits were a big part of the problem. She scolded him whenever she found a cache of Coke in the office refrigerator. Even more disconcerting was his habit of disappearing. "All of a sudden, he would decide to run out of the office and I would catch him on the stairway. He would want to avoid going someplace to make a speech or having to meet with someone. I just told him, 'Booth, you can't do

Booth meets with Rosalie Gittings, his trusted personal assistant. Wayne Zimmerman © *The News Tribune* (Tacoma, WA) 1985. Reprinted with permission.

that. It throws everybody in a turmoil." We had several little sessions out in the stairwell." Gittings says many don't grasp the fact that Gardner is fundamentally shy. "He feels most comfortable around kids. It's not just some act."

If anyone knew the real Booth Gardner, it was Gittings, according to many former staff members. "Rose Gittings is the most intuitive person I have ever known," says Mari Clack, a University of Washington classmate who became Booth's Eastern Washington representative. "She was the mom," Gardner says with affection.

The Seattle Times conducted a poll to give Gardner a first-year report card. It found that 63 percent rated him good to excellent at managing state government, but only 45 percent rated him effective at initiating new programs. Jim McDermott disagreed. He said Booth had been "the most effective first-year governor I have ever worked with."

"I don't think you can do this job in just one four-year term," Booth said as 1986 approached. "I fully intend to go for two terms." When he was feeling upbeat, he told himself he wanted at least three consecutive terms, to match Dan Evans.

~

Pete von Reichbauer, Booth's old friend (he had been an usher at the legislator's wedding) was one of the most vocal of the Republicans asserting that Gardner's request for the power to hire and fire the directors of the Game, Transportation and Parks departments and appoint the members of the state Board of Education was an effort to "turn the clock back to the era of pork barrel politics." The state senator warned that "the people who decide which lakes and streams are stocked with fish, or where the next state highway is located will be beholden to the political powers in Olympia." The proposal also riled many members of the state's passionate contingent of fishermen and hunters. The Game Department had been created by initiative in 1932 when steelheaders carried the day in a battle with commercial fishermen and packers. In 1945, Governor Mon Wallgren persuaded the Legislature to give him the power to appoint the game director.

The Sportsmen's Council promptly filed a referendum, and Wallgren's plan was soundly defeated by the voters. "Two years later, we beat Wallgren," one veteran angler recalled. "It will happen to this guy (Gardner) too." At a House committee hearing on the governor's plan, anglers demonstrated that they belonged to no organized party. Jerry Pavletich, a leading member of Trout Unlimited, a steelheader group, backed Booth, saying, "The buck should stop with the chief executive of the state. The bottom line is the present system does not work." Next up was Dean Fellows of the Federation of Fly Fishermen, who said Booth's proposal would give governors a license to "sell the appointment to the highest bidder."

"Whenever we've tried to abolish or merge or change any state agency, by God you'd think the world was coming to an end," said Rep. Max Vekich, a Democrat from Grays Harbor who strongly supported the reorganization plan. Booth did have the support of anglers, tribal leaders and fisheries professionals as he steamrollered opponents to the reappointment of a sharp young lawyer, Bill Wilkerson, as state fisheries director. One of John Spellman's best choices, Wilkerson was an apostle of Gardner's policy of peaceful negotiation to manage salmon runs.

⌒

Boosting the state's cigarette tax by eight cents to a national high 31 cents was the linchpin of Booth's plan to finance half a billion dollars worth of water-quality projects over the next decade. The tobacco lobby and smokers yowled, but the Lung Association and Cancer Society were jubilant. Jeannette Hayner, the Republican leader in the Senate, was in favor of good education and opposed to lung cancer but she likened the tax hike proposal to "burning books to heat the school." She predicted revenues would decline if the cost of smokes became prohibitive, a classic Catch 22.

The governor asked for a 3 percent raise for teachers and other state employees. That and acquiring more power over an un-elected bureaucracy and the water quality program were his highest priorities for the 60-day 1986 legislative session, sure to be fraught with partisanship. All 98 seats in the House and 24 of the 49 seats in the Senate would be up for election that fall.

In his first State of the State address Booth emphasized that he couldn't make government more efficient with one hand tied behind his back. Commissions and boards had become the fourth branch of government, making "major decisions about the life of our citizens, yet you never have the opportunity to vote for them or probably even know who they are." He predicted that opponents would "talk about politics creeping into government. My response to that is: Do we really need to protect government from the people?" The governor said he was already looking ahead, doing his homework, to ensure that 1987 would be the year when they focused on education. That likely would require an income tax, he added, because there was no way to improve the schools without additional resources. "I recognize that I'm battling the odds," he said, "but education, both K-12 and higher education, has more responsibility for the future well-being of our people and communities than any other part of state government."

Al Rosellini and Dixy Lee Ray supported Booth's government reorganization plan but Dixy scoffed at the need to spend hundreds of millions on water quality programs. Most of Puget Sound was "a very healthy body of water," the marine biologist told the Tacoma Rotary Club, and in any case "far cleaner" than when she was a child. "Puget Sound, if left alone, will flush itself," Dixy declared. "If you start disturbing the bottom, all you do is mix it up and spread the pollution around a wider area. ...The main thing is to stop pouring things into it."

In January of 1986, Amos Reed, with the governor at his side, announced he was retiring at the age of 70 after five years as head of Corrections. In the three years before Reed took control of what he described as a "filthy jungle," there had been 15 murders in the state's prisons and several riots. On his watch, there were only two homicides and no major disturbances. "His countless hours of selfless devotion have led to a very highly disciplined and safe prison system," the governor told reporters.

After several minutes of sayonara pleasantries, it was time for Q&A. Adele Ferguson cut to the chase: "Didja get canned, Amos?" Reed bristled. "It's time for me to retire and I've retired," he said. "It's just that simple. ...My relationship with Booth Gardner has been excellent to outstanding. He's my friend, he's my employer... I'm still young and vigorous and could whip most of the men in this room!" Did he regret the million-dollar cost overrun for the new prison at Clallam Bay on the Olympic Peninsula? "I left a will leaving that to you to enjoy; to have and to hold, as the saying goes." Any advice for his successor, who would be the subject of a nationwide search? "I wish my successor every good thing that can possibly come. If I shook hands with him right now, I'd say, 'Start counting the days because your days are numbered.'" Legislative relations were not Reed's strong suit. He chafed at being portrayed as a lock-'em-up-and-throw-away-the-key administrator. That wasn't a fair appraisal, but the governor and other progressives wanted more emphasis on programs to fight drug and alcohol abuse, boost job skills and create a safe and effective work-release system. McDermott said Reed had outlived

Booth addresses striking woodworkers, who marched to Olympia to protest wage and benefit cuts proposed by the Weyerhaeuser Co. in July of 1986. Jeff Larsen © *The News Tribune* (Tacoma, WA) 1986. Reprinted with permission.

his usefulness and Sen. Mike Kreidler, a Democrat from Olympia, asked, "How much can we afford to spend on prisons at the expense of education, social services and cleaning up the environment?"

Reed's successor was 43-year-old Chase Riveland, the director of Colorado's Department of Corrections and regarded as a rising star nationally. "He's part of the new wave of bright young corrections officials," said Barry Krisberg, president of the National Council on Crime and Delinquency. Riveland was a backer of lower-cost alternatives to incarceration for non-violent criminals. Most inmates were going to be released some day, he emphasized, so rehabilitation and job skills were the keys to reducing recidivism. Simultaneously progressive and tough-minded, Riveland proved to be an excellent fit. He was asked to stay on by Gardner's successor, Mike Lowry, and headed Corrections for more than 11 years.

⌒

Dan Grimm, a budgetary whiz, was the administration's point man in the House to keep the $482 million Comparable Worth settlement rolling. The landmark plan to create pay equity in state government was ratified by the Legislature on January 31, 1986. After decades of gender discrimination by the state, nearly 35,000 mostly female workers would receive substantial raises. Rep. Bob Williams, a feisty Republican from Longview, said the plan was "fatally flawed" and sure to lead to a tax increase or reduced services. Poppycock, said Grimm. "Once we shear away all the rhetoric, the only real vote is your commitment to comparable worth." The Puyallup legislator said the governor and his staff had driven "a pretty hard bargain" and not backed down. U.S. District Judge Jack Tanner signed off on the compromise, calling it "a miracle."

Christine Gregoire, then a senior assistant attorney general newly arrived from Spokane, supervised the attorney general's comparable worth team. "That's how I met Booth," the state's 22nd governor recalls. "We worked hard, unbelievably hard, and he would come in and see us."

Booth frequently gave his State Patrol Executive Protection Unit fits by disappearing. Gregoire was caught up in one of his nocturnal escapades. "Way, way late one night," Booth waltzed into the conference room and motioned to her. "We're going to go out, but don't tell anybody," he whispered. "So we sneak out the back way, get in a state car and drive downtown. The speed limit is 25 and we're going 40." I go, 'Booth, when is the last time you drove a car?' And he goes, 'It's been a long time. Isn't this fun?' We get a Coke and a hamburger and we're coming up the private back stairs. At the top are two State Patrol EPU officers, arms folded. I said, 'Uh-oh.' And he said, 'I'll handle this.' So he walks right up, goes 'Excuse me' and walks right through them. I think, 'OK, I'll say the same thing.' I go, 'Excuse me' and they don't budge. They start lecturing me. Booth is right behind them going 'Neener-neener-neener.' Then he walks away." The troopers proceed to chew her out royally. "It's shame on *me!*" Gregoire remembers, shaking her head and laughing. "One, there's his diet; two, he needs protection; three, 'Why did you let him drive the car?' And I'm saying, 'This is the governor of the State of Washington…What was I supposed to do?' "

⌒

Booth was definitely feeling frisky. When his water-quality legislation was bogged down, he called the two Democrats who were blocking it and persuaded them to change their votes. "It's too soon to say that he's turned from a caterpillar to a butterfly," Grimm said, "but he is showing signs of metamorphosis.…He's sounding like a governor to me."

The Washington Education Association demanded a 5 percent raise and threatened to call a strike. Whatever will be will be, said Booth; the state couldn't afford 5 percent. His stand was buttressed in late February when Chang Mook Sohn, the director of the state's Economic & Revenue Forecasting Council, warned that the state could face financial problems by the summer of 1987.

In the closing hours of a hectic session, a coalition of Republicans, conservative Democrats and worried bureaucrats scuttled Gardner's government reorganization plan, 25-23. "We'll be back," Booth vowed, savoring his victories. He'd won a sales tax deferral to woo new industry, secured a package of bills to revamp industrial insurance laws, prevailed on comparable worth, secured raises averaging 3 percent for teachers, college faculty, troopers and other state employees and, best of all, won approval of the cigarette tax hike to fund his Puget Sound cleanup plan.

At 59 days, it was the first time in 60 years that the Legislature had been able to adjourn early. The *Post-Intelligencer* said the governor had become "a force to be reckoned with." "He has the ability to twist your arm without it hurting" said Rep. Pete Kremen, a Democrat from Bellingham.

For good measure, the legislators gave themselves, the governor and other statewide elected officials, who hadn't had a pay increase in six years, hefty raises. Booth would see his pay jump from $63,000 to $74,900 on Jan. 1, 1987, then to $86,800 a year later.

The governor signed the cigarette tax hike during a gala ceremony in the Capitol rotunda. A year earlier he had quashed a huge bond issue to celebrate the state's centennial in 1989, calling instead for a water cleanup program to create "a lasting legacy." Jean Gardner and Ralph Munro, co-chairmen of the celebration, unveiled the centennial logo. The first lady tried to sell the governor a $2 centennial lapel pin. His pockets were empty, as usual, so she bought it for him.

To the surprise of all and the chagrin of fellow Democrats, trial lawyers and labor, he also signed a sweeping tort reform bill that placed a cap on pain-and-suffering awards. It limited the liability of "deep pocket" defendants and shortened the statute of limitations for filing malpractice lawsuits. Proponents had predicted at least a partial veto. Calling it the toughest decision he'd faced as governor, Booth weighed his decision for three weeks before concluding the bill was a reasonable compromise. He had misgivings about many of its provisions, but realized the bill was too complex to tinker with via veto. "I really think the tort system has gone too far," he said. "Let's do this and see if it works." He warned the insurance industry to keep its end of the bargain and lower rates. Otherwise, "I think you will see insurance reform with a vengeance in the Legislature" in coming years.

In the summer of 1986, Booth announced that the state would file suit to try and remove Hanford from the running as a site for a national nuclear waste repository. He called a one-day special session of the Legislature, which voted resoundingly to place a waste dump referendum on the Nov. 4 ballot, although some Republicans said it was just a plot to goose up the Democratic turnout.

Bud Shinpoch stepped down as acting secretary of the Department of Social & Health Services that June after 11 eventful months. Booth patted him on the back but his praise was unmistakably tepid. He called the changes "just meat and potatoes." Shinpoch begged to differ, saying, "It's the most massive reorganization I've ever been involved in, and I was involved in a lot of them in my 25 years at Boeing." The former state senator said he had eliminated 1,300 forms and 70 manuals at DSHS and diverted nearly $13 million from management to delivery of services. He said the new administrative structure would allow his successor to manage an agency that many maintained was unmanageable.

Shinpoch fans, and there were many, asserted that Gardner got cold feet when special interest groups began to bleat. Shinpoch had made the unions mad as hell, Dean Foster recalls. They counter-attacked on multiple fronts, including the "Depth Charge News," a parody of Shinpoch's monthly "Depth Study News" bulletins. Sen. Kreidler and Rep. Jennifer Belcher said Shinpoch was too bull-headed. "I'm not sure they had a game plan other than to go over there and shake it up," Belcher said, adding that Shinpoch created paranoia and refused to accept advice from bureaucrats who'd long been in the trenches. "He'd make a great military-type commander," said Kreidler. "But when you're talking about a large agency like DSHS and you try to do it in lockstep, you're sure to end up with anarchy."

Shinpoch's successor was Jule Sugarman, the award-winning founding father of the national Head Start program. His impressive resume also included key administrative posts with Atlanta, New York City and the Carter

Administration. Sugarman was an innovative social activist but the DSHS job was a career-breaker, fraught with rising welfare caseloads and the fallout from an epidemic of drug use and child abuse. Caseworkers routinely faced life-or-death decisions. Sugarman's managerial and political skills were immediately found wanting. Republicans managed to pigeon-hole his confirmation and he served in a tumultuous limbo. After he fired the director of the agency's mental health division, Lyle Quasim, one of the state's highest ranking black officials, he was taking flak from all sides. His performance became a major issue in Booth's campaign for re-election. Sugarman resigned in late 1988, 31 months after he arrived with fanfare and two weeks after the governor proposed breaking up DSHS into separate human and health services departments. The governor named Dick Thompson, most lately his director of governmental operations, to succeed Sugarman. Managing DSHS clearly was a daunting task. (Quasim, who charged that he was fired for refusing to lie to the Legislature, sued for defamation and was awarded $240,000. He got his whack at running DSHS in the 1990s, first under Governor Mike Lowry, then Gary Locke, and lasted longer than most.)

Gardner told reporters that at least for the near future he had rejected the possibility of a state income tax to fund improvements to K-12 and higher education. "An income tax would require bipartisan support, which does not exist today," he said in a speech to the Seattle CityClub, promising to work "in good faith" with both parties and all of the other interest groups to achieve consensus on a tax reform plan. Until then, the 1987 Legislature would need to enact some combination of higher taxes because "the centerpiece of all economic development efforts is education. Education is, and has always been, an investment in the future of this nation and our state," he said. "It has a crucial role in helping us meet emerging competition" from around the world "by producing highly skilled workers—people who are able to think critically...people who can generate the best technology available." Unfortunately, he added, "there's a certain group of people who

have refused to sit down and have a reasonable discussion on tax policy."
Indignant was Rep. Williams, who'd become the top Republican on the
Ways & Means Committee. He said he'd politely asked for an audience
to discuss tax—and spending—reform, only to be told the governor was
booked solid for the next two months. "Bob Williams would be able to
fill two hours of the governor's time twice a day every day if he let him,"
Kneeland said. The press corps nodded knowingly. The former federal auditor could talk your leg off. That he had a formidable head for numbers no
one could deny, but his high-pitched voice and tendency to drone negated
the appeal of his boyish earnestness. Someone dubbed him a "gadfly" and it
stuck. Williams was a favorite of the "moral conservatives" being mobilized
by TV evangelist Pat Robertson for his 1988 presidential bid. There was
something ironically delicious about a Weyerhaeuser accountant leading
the loyal opposition to Booth Gardner.

Kneeland, who had been with Gardner since the 1984 campaign, left
in August to join Ron Dotzauer in his public relations firm, Northwest
Strategies, with the promise of more money and fewer hours. Keeping
pace with the governor was a daunting proposition, even for a 33-year-old,
Kneeland admitted. It was exciting but "almost always like a controlled riot
situation." Dick Milne, Kneeland's deputy, got the job.

Other significant comings and goings found Dick Virant moving from
General Administration to the state Tax Appeals Board, and Mary Faulk
leaving the Lottery—where she'd overseen an impressive turnaround—to
head General Administration. Gardner said Virant "asked for reassign-
ment." A month earlier a state audit report blamed GA and the Department
of Corrections for nearly $6 million in cost over-runs in the construction
of the new state prison at Clallam Bay. Gardner's style was to push you
out with one hand and pat you on the back with the other. The media and
his foes saw it as a sign of weakness. For better or worse, it was his nature.

What no one could deny was that his managers were transforming Labor
& Industries. The governor called a news conference to announce that for the
second year in a row there would be no workers' compensation rate increase.

Dick Davis and Joe Dear were rapidly erasing the $225 million deficit the administration faced when it took office. The savings were achieved through better claims management, strong anti-fraud efforts and legislation removing the requirement that all injured workers receive vocational rehabilitation. The Association of Washington Business was very pleased.

An energized Gardner hit the campaign trail in the fall of 1986, hoping to preserve Democratic majorities in both houses of the Legislature. The candidates were eager to tap into his charisma. Former Seattle congressman Brock Adams drafted him as his honorary campaign chairman in his bid to unseat U.S. Senator Slade Gorton. Surveying a new poll, Shelby Scates marveled that Gardner was nearly as popular as Scoop Jackson. His numbers were "far above anything ever registered by Dan Evans, a political scientist's selection as one of the 10 great governors of the 20th Century." Gardner's sobering challenge, the *Post-Intelligencer* pundit added, was the mounting evidence that the state was sliding downhill economically. Personal incomes were dropping steadily behind the national average and prospects for job

Booth kibitzes with Thriftway checker Joe Short, right, as he campaigns in Gig Harbor in 1986 for Democratic legislative candidate Ron Meyers, center. Bruce Larson © *The News Tribune* (Tacoma, WA) 1986. Reprinted with permission.

development were anemic. Exhibit A was the Clark County computer chip plant. It fizzled like a damp sparkler on the Fourth of July a year after the hoopla when RCA and its Japanese partner, Sharp, called the whole thing off. "This isn't going to set us back a lick," Gardner boasted.

Prodded by Dean Foster, his chief of staff, Booth stumped 40 legislative districts and headlined 26 fundraisers. He even made a foray into Oregon to campaign for the Democratic candidate for governor, Neil Goldschmidt. Booth reveled in his popularity, hugging pretty girls and making senior citizens giggle. He won cheers by urging a college band to play "Louie Louie." Dotzauer quipped that "babies are born with higher negatives than he's got."

The battle to maintain control of the State Senate in 1987-88 was trench warfare. "If we don't win this one, we're incompetent," Dan McDonald, the Republican floor leader, said before the election. McDonald was chagrinned and livid when the Democrats eked out a 25-24 majority. With Gardner's help, Rick Bender scored a come-from-behind victory to keep his seat in the pivotal 44th District in northern King County and southern Snohomish County. "He really took the gloves off," McDonald said, charging that Gardner had besmirched the integrity of Bender's challenger, Jeanine Long, who had vacated her seat in the House to run for the Senate. "He certainly demonstrated that it's 'no more Mr. Nice Guy,' " McDonald said. Larsen devoted his *Seattle Times* column to a post-mortem of the bitter contest, observing that to Republicans Gardner had now become "a grinning, vacuous handshaker who was willing to involve the state's highest office in some slightly deceitful political tactics and who, as a result, now carries some indelible mud on his immaculate image."

The Republicans had also lost several seats in the state House and, worst of all, the U.S. Senate race. Gardner and Adams barnstormed the state on election eve. Gorton was also hurt way more than helped by a campaign stop in Spokane by President Reagan, who made a weak statement about the state's concerns over the prospect of Hanford becoming America's nuclear waste dump. While Gardner gained some IOUs in both Washingtons, things were too close for comfort in the State Senate, where blue dog Democrats, notably Brad Owen of Shelton and Slim Rasmussen, resisted the leash. "It's a 'Slim' majority," quipped Karen Marchioro, leader of the State Democratic Party. Booth would need Republican help to achieve anything big in 1987 and 1988 when he'd be up for re-election.

The governor moved Bill Wilkerson from the Department of Fisheries to the Department of Revenue because he needed a talented salesman to help him raise taxes to improve public schools and universities. Appointed fisheries director by Governor Spellman in 1983, the 40-year-old lawyer helped negotiate a new U.S.-Canada fishing treaty. He waded into even more troubled waters to try and resolve the tricky resource management disputes between the tribes and non-Indian commercial fishermen through negotiation rather than litigation. Joseph Blum, the deputy regional director of the U.S. Fish & Wildlife Service in Portland, succeeded Wilkerson at fisheries.

～

Booth's sweeping $520 million education-reform package for the 1987-89 biennium was unveiled just before Thanksgiving. Washington's kindergarten through third-grade classrooms were among the most crowded in the nation, Booth said, emphasizing that the early grades were crucial to learning basic skills, forming good study habits and developing character. He said the state needed to spend $67 million to hire 900 new teachers and also proposed extending the teachers' work year by five days to give them more time to prepare lesson plans and strategize with their colleagues. That move was estimated at $82 million. Some $14 million was proposed for teachers' "in-service" continuing education, while about $6 million should be earmarked for drop-out and drug and alcohol-abuse prevention programs, the governor said. Higher education, meantime, needed an infusion of $190 million, with most of that earmarked for sorely needed faculty raises of up to 20 percent. The 43,000-member Washington Education Association heard a lot to like. It was wary, however, of merit pay in disguise and "unalterably opposed" to Booth's plan to establish a statewide salary schedule. WEA President Terry Bergeson said a uniform pay scale

Booth works the phones late at night in preparation for the opening of the Legislature.
Bruce Larson © *The News Tribune* (Tacoma, WA) 1987. Reprinted with permission.

would make it more difficult for urban districts to compete for quality teachers. Also criticized as expensive and impractical was Gardner's proposal to scrap undergraduate degrees and require every teacher to have a master's. Gardner countered that the result would be better trained and better paid teachers. The governor maintained that the WEA opposed the plan because it tied the infusion of money to higher standards and more days of professional development.

In a speech to nearly a thousand school board members and administrators meeting in Seattle, Booth warned that infighting among education's stakeholders could doom his push to thrust Washington State into the forefront of educational reform. "The entire education community needs to be united," the governor emphasized, asking every district to field a team of 25 to help lobby legislators.

The speech stands as his oratorical landmark. It summarized everything Booth Gardner passionately believes about education's power to transform lives—all the lessons he'd learned in the Central Area and at Harvard rolled into one. His agenda dovetailed with the findings of the Carnegie Commission on Higher Education, which emphasized the need for innovation and excellence. Intervening early on in the lives of children, particularly those at risk, yields incalculable dividends, the governor told the educators. Prenatal care and programs to inculcate parenting skills and improve nutrition are all part of the equation. So too programs to assist special-needs children and their families. "Everyone matters," Booth said, noting that it cost the state $25,000 to $30,000 a year for every individual who fell through the cracks and ended up on welfare, in a rehab program, in jail or prison. He said his program could save the state millions of dollars and untold grief. "You can pay me now," he said, "or you can pay me later—and later is going to cost a whole lot more." Booth ended with an appeal to their business sense and their hearts. "Education is like no other box on the budget scorecard. If it's neglected, society will pay for it over and over again."

Laird Harris, Gardner's policy adviser, recalls intense "skull sessions" in the basement of the mansion in the summer and fall of 1986. Experts from around the country came to share their ideas, and Booth consulted with his many friends who were teachers and school administrators, notably Bill Gerberding, president of the University of Washington. "Some people underrated Booth because he was sort of folksy," Gerberding says, "but he had a lot of self-confidence. He was very bright and also well connected in many ways—business, politics, higher ed. He knew a lot of heavy hitters. He wanted ideas."

Before the year was out, Booth announced that he would seek a second term, putting to rest speculation that he might be a candidate for the U.S. Senate should Evans decide to not seek re-election. In a statement that revealed a major truth about his own abilities and the nature of the U.S. Senate, Gardner told reporters, "I think there is a major difference between an administrative and legislative personality. You don't have to go much farther than Dan Evans to see that....He's said to me on several occasions that it's a lot more fun being governor."

Being governor was not going to be much fun in 1987.

CHAPTER 14:

Taxing times

"The future of the state is a lot more important than who is governor," Booth said on the eve of the 1987 legislative session. If pushing higher taxes to achieve educational reform cost him re-election, so be it. "I can live with that. There is life after politics." It wasn't just rhetoric, his former aides emphasize. "Creating the nation's best schools" was his highest priority.

With charts, handouts and a platoon of aides, Booth outlined his plan to simultaneously cut some taxes and raise others to make up the difference and still leave $510 million for better schools and universities in the 1987-89 biennium. He wanted to reduce the sales tax, trim the business-and-occupation tax, provide tax breaks to small businesses and make other adjustments that would cost the state a total of $717 million. Concurrently, he had a plan to generate $1.2 billion. Extending the 6 percent sales tax to "professional services"—doctors, dentists, accountants and lawyers— would bring in $948 million. Extending it to "consumer services"—barbers, beauty parlors, health spas, cable TV and other entertainment—would bring in another $113 million. He'd raise an additional $70 million by taxing the fees charged by financial institutions (with an exemption for residential mortgages), and $17 million more by boldly going where no one who

Booth takes stock of his administration's accomplishments following adjournment
of the 1986 legislative session. Flanking the governor are House Speaker Wayne Ehlers,
left, and Senate Majority Leader Ted Bottiger. Jerry Buck © *The News Tribune*
(Tacoma, WA) 1986. Reprinted with permission.

solicited the support of those who buy ink by the barrel had ever dared to
tread—a tax on newspaper sales and advertising.

The governor pointed out that the cities and counties stood to gain
some $272 million by charging their own local sales taxes on services. All
this would be a tough sell, he acknowledged—impossible, in fact, without
bipartisan support. Republicans pronounced the plan dead on arrival. "We'd
like him to spend at least half the time he's spent on increasing revenue on
reforming spending," said Bob Williams. A new poll revealed that education
was far and away the top issue for registered voters, but 61 percent disap-
proved of the governor's plan to extend the sales tax to services.

School was still out on his plan to give teachers and other state employees 3 percent raises in September of the next two years. Booth said his
budget accomplished that without hiking taxes. He also called for welfare

reform—"workfare"—and endorsed McDermott's plan to provide basic health care coverage for the uninsured.

The lawmakers were facing the first session in six years where slashing would not be the order of the hour. Although the economy was improving, estimates indicated there wouldn't be enough revenue to accomplish what Gardner wanted to do in both K-12 and higher education. The question became not whether taxes would be needed but what kind and how much. His staff presented several piecemeal options. He chose the most ambitious and controversial route for two reasons: He did not want to give up on the most costly part of his plan—boosting the caliber of teaching—and the change in tax structure was a step toward full-scale reform.

Booth urged the legislators to not "spend 105 days making excuses" why they couldn't halt the state's "slide toward mediocrity." The Republicans were stoic, the Democrats curiously subdued and the teachers loaded for bear. Not once was the governor's 1987 State of the State message interrupted by applause. "Even the anecdotes were the same," someone yawned. Looking back, Gardner says one of his biggest frustrations was "this politics of perception and posturing."

~~~

Booth told reporters he planned to call up General Barlow to help make the case for tax reform. "Everywhere I go I talk about education, but there's a quid pro quo there," the governor said. "The public has to decide if they want to make the investment, but at the same time we have to show we can run our business as effectively as possible." He admitted that he didn't bring Barlow on board when he first took office because "the staff still has a certain apprehension about Greg—which isn't all bad." Nor all wrong, says Dean Foster. "We made it pretty clear to Booth that we didn't want Barlow to have an office in the Capitol. I knew he would wreak havoc, so they found one for him down at GA (General Administration) and his role was ill-defined. He was an exceptional guy with an unbelievable amount of energy, and he ran right over the top to do things for Norton and Booth," the governor's former chief of staff says. That style was not calculated, however, to win friends for the governor and influence legislators.

During Booth's eight years in Olympia, business interests always worried that those damn tax-and-spend liberals had the upper hand in the governor's office, Foster adds, so he believes it's possible that Barlow was dispatched by Clapp to make sure Booth wouldn't give away the farm. Adele Ferguson said that was precisely the case. "Well, here comes Rambo," she wrote. "But it may be too late." Foster says he never saw the direct influence of Norton Clapp on the governor, "but I knew it was there." Booth says his stepfather's friends gave him more free advice than Clapp, although Norton did "suggest" it might be a good idea to call up Barlow. "I just thanked him" for the advice, but "I didn't feel I needed it." In other words, did he humor Clapp by bringing back Barlow for a while? "Yeah," Gardner nods with a conspiratorial smile.

Other critics took note of the tension in the inner circle and stoked the coals. They said it seemed as if Orin Smith, the budget chief, had more influence on the governor than Foster or Harris. Becky Bogard, the governor's legislative liaison, was said to be a weak link. Foster was respected on both sides of the aisle. Why not move him into that job? And why did such a hot-shot manager need 17 more staff members than Spellman?

Minority Republicans pointed to a better-than-expected revenue forecast and said they could fund many educational improvements without new taxes. They were licking their chops at the prospect of hitting the campaign trail in 1988 with a no-new-taxes budget. Lawyers, CPA's and hair dressers were certainly impressed. In the Senate the GOP found allies in three defecting Democrats and created an impasse that forced Gardner to call a special session. When the smoke cleared, they had dramatically diluted his public school education-reform plan. What he got was considerably better than nothing, although the teachers' union gave it a "D" and sent him to the corner. The package featured approximately $141 million

Booth meets with representatives of the Washington Education Association.
Leon Horne, left, of Tacoma, played a key role in the WEA. *Gardner family album.*

for new programs and enhancements, notably $28 million to modestly decrease class sizes in K through three; $24 million for teacher raises (a minimum of 2.1 percent); $6 million for early childhood education; $5.5 million for dropout prevention and $50 million in block grants to school districts. There was also seed money for "Schools for the 21st Century," Gardner's pilot program to allow 21 schools the freedom to experiment with innovation.

The Washington Education Association asserted that "The Education Governor" had been exposed as a wimp. It decried the "paltry" raises and Booth's failure to produce more new teachers and a higher beginning salary. Harris says the teachers' frustration blinded them to a major truth: Booth Gardner was not their enemy. Dan Grimm, the House Ways & Means chairman, who won many new admirers during the session with a maturing blend of idealism and pragmatism, said the WEA's intransigence undermined the governor's attempts to form a pro-education coalition. Grimm called the WEA the most ineffective lobby in Olympia. The teachers would not be moved, asking, "Would you compromise on your children's future?"

Harris says the Gardner team underestimated the fact that they were in a two-front war and was caught off guard by a change in the weather. "Booth knew his teacher-education reforms would not be popular with the WEA," the former policy adviser recalls, "but he believed they would come around because of the higher salaries that would follow. He knew that education was at the top of the business community's policy priorities, but we did not accurately gauge its opposition to tax increases to pay the bill. If he had known about the improved revenue forecast, he might have reduced the tax package but I doubt that he would have abandoned it. Although the session was regarded by many as a failure for Booth, I think a fair retrospective shows that his initiatives were ahead of their times. He was trying to reform K-12 years before 'No Child Left Behind.' His 'Schools for the 21st Century' would be recognized by the first President Bush and now Obama as laying the groundwork for public charter schools."

Higher Education had a far happier outing. To stay competitive in the global economy, Washington simply had to have world-class universities, Gardner said. On this the governor and Senate Republicans in the catbird seat could agree. The Legislature allocated $155 million more in the 1987-89 biennium, with raises of 6 to 8.5 percent for faculty, including community college instructors, the stepchildren of higher ed. UW President Gerberding and the governor had emphasized the dangers of a brain drain.

Booth with UW President William Gerberding, right, and Seattle bank executive John Mangels. *Gardner family album.*

With salaries lagging far below peer institutions, the university's ability to recruit and retain world-class academic talent was compromised. Gardner wanted the Legislature to close 80 percent of the salary gap. He got it to 72 percent for both his alma mater and Washington State University, a major victory in such a contentious year.

~⁓

Gardner's sweeping government reorganizational plan, packaged as a constitutional amendment, died in the House. But there was a consolation prize. The Legislature funded the cash-strapped Game Department from the state's General Fund for the first time in its 55-year history—renaming it the Wildlife Department. The revenue from hunting and fishing licenses was falling far short and layoffs had loomed. Sen. Brad Owen, who sided with the Republicans on the budget, was Gardner's guardian angel on this one. The maverick Democrat from Shelton pushed through the legislation, and Booth won the right to appoint the department's director. Opponents in the sporting community vowed to file a referendum but couldn't muster enough signatures to place the issue on the ballot.

Also on the upside, the "Family Independence Program," the governor's visionary plan to reduce the welfare rolls through a combination of job training and education, was approved in a slightly less ambitious form. It presaged the landmark Clinton-era welfare reforms.

With strong support from House Speaker Joe King, Jim McDermott's dream of establishing a state-subsidized basic health insurance program for the working poor finally came true in the form of a $19 million pilot project for 30,000 workers. It was the first program of its kind in the nation. McDermott and Gardner predicted that one of America's biggest crises in the years to come would be a relentlessly increasing number of citizens who couldn't afford health insurance. "If I were to pick the moment in my political career that I enjoyed the most, it'd be about two seconds ago," the senator from Seattle said as Gardner handed him the pen he used to sign the bill.

Booth was energized, as usual, by his popularity and confident of re-election, despite his appetite for an income tax that the electorate repeatedly balked at swallowing. He and Wilkerson said it could take two years, maybe four, to sell the skeptical public. Tax reform was "*the* issue of the late '80s," the governor said. Wilkerson noted that "70 percent of the people we've surveyed think we need change. But 70 percent also think change will make things worse."

In Olympia, skepticism was epidemic. Booth was panned as indecisive. June brought personnel changes, the sort of mid-course corrections governors invariably make to deal with burnout, infighting and their own errors of judgment. Saying "this isn't a career, it's an experience," Orin Smith departed for the far greener pastures of private industry, not to mention fewer 16-hour days and less aggravation. Booth hated to see him go. Adele flat out wrote that the budget chief had threatened to quit if Barlow was going to be sniffing around his yard, which prompted Booth to call off his pit bull. She also wrote that Barlow had hurt himself with Norton Clapp by talking too freely about Booth's widely perceived gumption deficit. Smith says there's "no question" that he and Barlow had their differences, which was inevitable "because there were no shades of gray with Greg." However, he says he made no such threat. It was just time for him to move on after years of public service. Smith said Booth's inability to push his tax reform program through the Legislature was a setback, but he pointed to the governor's accomplishments in welfare reform, higher ed financing and K-12. "Nothing in the Ray or Spellman administrations compares to the agenda Booth put before the Legislature," Smith said. "I don't think, in the last 12 years, a governor has so dominated the agenda of the Legislature."

Smith was succeeded by Dick Davis, who had shaped up Labor & Industries. Joe Dear, only 36 but a deft manager, moved up to head L&I. Dick Thompson left the Department of Community Development to move into the inner circle. His title was "governmental operations director." Becky Bogard resigned, a victim, some said, of male chauvinism in the Senate. Dean Foster's talents were redirected toward "external operations," namely legislative affairs, where he had a world of experience and good will to spare. Laird Harris left for the private sector and wasn't replaced. Peter Callaghan's take was that "the brilliant policy guys like Laird" were out and those with more political chops were in. Foster says Booth was narrowing his focus to try to achieve more.

On July 26, 1987, *The Seattle Times'* Sunday magazine featured one of the most compelling biographical profiles the state has ever seen. It was headlined "The Governor Who Loves to be Loved." Surrounded by children who had arrived to watch him sign a proclamation saluting Young Entrepreneurs, Booth beamed from the cover. Inside, tranquility was in short supply. *Times* reporter Walter Hatch contrasted the governor who could use "his cheery charm and mild manner to entertain a group of Pleasant Valley school kids" with the one who "with a ghostly white face" left a late-night meeting with impatient legislative leaders looking "exhausted, battered, even defeated."

Skillfully avoiding sensationalism, the profile nevertheless laid it all out—his parents' messy divorce; his "squirming under the thumb of an alcoholic father"; the plane crash that claimed his mother and sister; his fateful meeting with Norton Clapp; the Central Area Youth Association; Harvard; Brick's fatal fall; his first forays into politics. Hatch interviewed Aunt Lou, Booth's childhood friends, even his junior high school band teacher, as well as Barlow and the First Lady. Jean Gardner was remarkably unguarded about her husband's quirks. The governor was candid, too, saying he had compartmentalized the pain from his childhood. "I built a ceiling on top and a floor below to protect myself from expectations and disappointments. I shielded myself."

The piece was the talk of the town.

A quickie special session in August to deal with a U.S. Supreme Court decision impacting the business-and-occupation tax was marked by bipartisan cooperation. Gardner won high marks for greasing the skids. Foster's new role was already paying dividends. The session also produced a law to help Boeing and other business mainstays resist hostile corporate takeovers, as well as progress on funding toxic-waste site cleanup. In October, the governor called another special session—1987's third—to resolve the "Superfund" hazardous waste dispute between environmentalists and industry and fully fund the 2.1 percent pay raise the teachers had been promised. Some called it the "session-of-the-month club." Gardner was

Booth and Revenue Director Bill Wilkerson take their tax reform show on the road. Peter Haley © *The News Tribune* (Tacoma, WA) 1989. Reprinted with permission.

criticized by a number of Democrats, including Rep. Jolene Unsoeld, open government's tireless champion, and Sen. Phil Talmadge, a future Supreme Court justice. They charged that the governor had subverted the initiative process and improperly appointed a task force of legislators to draft a bill behind closed doors. However, many Olympia insiders and the press said he was finally exercising "true leadership."

In the spring of 1987, King County Prosecutor Norm Maleng, a gentle-manly Republican in the Dan Evans mold, began testing the waters for a race against Gardner. Party Chairwoman Jennifer Dunn was enthusiastic. Pointing to his tough-on-crime record and strong social conscience, she called him the "credible" candidate the party had been hoping for. Fall produced a surprise wild card: Bobby Williams was running, too. Most observers rated the lawmaker from Longview a long shot against Maleng, a popular politician from the state's biggest county.

Gardner and Wilkerson took their tax reform dog-and-pony show on the road almost every week all winter. Without tax reform, "you're dreaming, absolutely dreaming" to think that the business-and-occupation taxes won't keep soaring, the revenue director warned the Association of Washington Business. To lunch-bucket groups, they declared that the state's tax system was patently unfair. With more than half of its revenue generated by the second-highest sales tax in the nation, Washington put the greatest burden on those least able to pay. Booth said a bipartisan consensus on tax reform was crucial and emphasized he wasn't wedded to an income tax. "My goal is to create a better business climate." He said he hoped to submit a plan to the Legislature in 1989, then to the voters to cap the state's centennial year. However, if the Republicans made it a partisan issue, the governor said he just wouldn't go there, and the cause might be set back decades. Maleng and Williams said that was classic Booth Gardner—vague details and veiled threats. "I think it's time he comes up with a specific proposal and take it to the people and become a leader," Maleng said. Gardner was cornered by reporters a few weeks later and admitted that his personal preference was an income tax. "See," said his rivals.

Gardner appointed a 16-member Committee on Washington's Financial Future to develop a "revenue neutral" tax reform plan—one mean feat—for the 1989 legislative session. Wilkerson and Dick Davis, the director of Financial Management, were named co-chairmen. The panel included the mayors of Seattle and Spokane, the superintendent of public instruction, representatives of business and labor, tax attorneys and accountants. Senate

Republicans would have no part of it.

Pollsters hired by both parties sampled the electorate at year's end and reached the same conclusion: Voters hated the idea of an income tax but loved their governor. The GOP poll actually rated him higher than the one commissioned by the Democrats—65 percent favorable vs. 61 percent. Republicans spun the two-to-one opposition to an income tax to assert that Gardner was in "a weaker position for re-election than expected." A *Seattle Times* poll revealed the magnitude of their challenge. Gardner's positives were at 76 percent, Maleng's at 21 and Williams' at 7. Fifty-seven percent of the respondents had never heard of Maleng and 81 percent had no idea who Williams was.

Responding to widespread speculation, Booth denied any interest in the U.S. Senate seat being vacated by Dan Evans or the vice presidency. "I am committed to this job for eight years," he said, "but after that, who knows?"

Skimpy revenues in a supplemental budget year made Gardner look like Scrooge. Agency requests outstripped available funds by nearly 14-to-1. He ordered a one percent across-the-board spending cut to boost the budget surplus to a still-worrisome $600,000 and head off election-year attempts by the Republicans to portray him and his fellow Democrats as profligate. For the 60-day 1988 session, the GOP had an outright 25-24 majority in the Senate. They'd won a hotly-contested special election to fill a vacancy in the Vancouver area by fielding an attractive new conservative, Linda Smith. With 25 of the Senate's 49 seats up for election that fall, including 14 held by Republicans, the GOP would be on offense and defense simultaneously. The Democrats were hoping their popular governor had coattails. Gardner would face a Republican majority in the Senate for the remainder of his tenure as governor.

In an introspective interview with *The Olympian* as the 1988 session got under way, the governor acknowledged that Olympia insiders saw him as a weak, inconsistent leader. "It's the way I come off," he said with a shrug.

"...Talk to my kids. They would probably give you the same review... I'm one to listen to the other side of an issue. I'm one to change my opinion at times. I don't like to jam things at people." The comment about his kids was yet another glimpse into Booth's complicated psyche. When the kids were growing up, Jean was the enforcer because Dad was so often gone and, in any case, hated to say no.

Goaded by Adele Ferguson, the press analyzed transcripts of his recent press conferences and concluded that he had been remarkably noncommittal on any issue more controversial than his soccer team. "I don't know yet" and "I'm waiting for others to decide" were two of his stock answers. Booth says he was more gun-shy than indecisive. His staff had pointed out that familiarity can breed contempt.

As expected, the 1988 Legislature also punted. Beyond a progressive decision to raise the level of compensation for injured workers, its achievements amounted to $100 million for construction projects and a bill authorizing a bailout of the Trade & Convention Center in Seattle. Even with a two-day a special session, they couldn't agree on how much to raise the state's $2.30-an-hour minimum wage. Although both parties agreed it was embarrassingly low, a compromise degenerated into finger pointing. The governor was disgusted and the feeling was mutual.

~⁓~

After adjournment, they were off and running. One of the first polls found Gardner with 57.5 percent and his rivals registering barely a blip. Many were surprised to see Williams leading Maleng, with a whopping 3.8 percent to his 3. The undecideds were at 35 percent. Both Republicans were hoping they would be buoyed by opposition to an income tax.

Maleng had been elected King County prosecutor three times, the last two without opposition. Raised on a dairy farm, his undergraduate degree was in economics. His track record was impeccable—compassion for victims, no quarter for rapists and killers. With a warm voice that radiated integrity and well-tailored suits, he was the governor you'd get if you called

Central Casting. Maleng said the voters had a clear choice: "Vote for just a nice guy, or a nice guy who can get the job done."

A slight, bespectacled figure who often wore a rumpled raincoat, Williams made Gardner look positively macho in comparison. Some of the reporters called him "Gomer." He was so persistent that many considered him a pain in the neck. But to conservatives, particularly evangelical Christians, Bobby Williams had a head-full-of-numbers charisma all his own. He'd been a legislator for a decade. Adele asserted that few understood the budget better. He was a happy little warrior—and a crafty one, too, busy building a grassroots base. Williams' theme was this: Booth Gardner was a well-intentioned man who wanted things to be good and hoped for the best. "But that is not the mark of a good leader. That's the mark of a good cheerleader."

Gardner retrieved his tux from the cleaners. An elegant $1,000-a-couple bash in the Grand Ballroom of Seattle's Westin Hotel raised $700,000 for his re-election campaign. "One item that definitely was not on the menu was campaign finance reform," Gannett's Bob Partlow observed acerbically. A few blocks away, he noted, "the poor, homeless, hungry, handicapped and dispossessed were supping on scraps and trying to survive another cold, wet winter night on Seattle's streets." It reminded him of nothing quite so much as the opening scene in *Doctor Zhivago* where the revolting peasants were mowed down outside the czar's palace, where chandeliers twinkled and caviar was consumed by the gallon.

As the campaign got going, the governor made a decision that threatened his standing with the environmental community and had his staff in a dither. On a hunch, he named Chris Gregoire to head the Department of Ecology when Andrea Beatty Riniker departed to manage the Aviation Department for the Port of Seattle. Outside the Attorney General's Office, Gregoire, 41, was a virtual unknown. "She has said she's not an environmentalist; even Ronald Reagan said he was an environmentalist," said an incredulous David Ortman, the Northwest representative of Friends of the Earth. "She also said she's not a manager. Well, what does that leave? What's this person doing in the Department of Ecology?"

Booth said she was going there to unravel a thicket of litigation and replace bureaucratic nincompoopery with common sense. "When Chris was working on the Comparable Worth case, she really impressed me with her ability to analyze issues," Gardner says. A national search for a new director at Ecology produced "some attractive candidates. But one night I thought to myself, 'I think Chris can do the job. I'm going to appoint her.' " The next morning, when he revealed his decision to his staff, "all hell broke loose—I mean there was pandemonium. Everybody said, 'No, you can't do that. She has no profile. People in state government don't know who she is.' "

Gardner would not be dissuaded. Gregoire was stunned, almost reduced to stammering: "Gosh, Booth, you know, I'm flattered but I'm a senior assistant attorney general. I'm a lawyer and that job just doesn't make sense to me. Why would you want me to do that?"

"Because they've got nothing but lawsuits. We're not making any progress."

"Well, I can help you from over here at the AG's office. I don't have a big track record as the world's greatest environmentalist."

"So, are you telling me 'no'?"

"Well, let me think about it.'"

Gregoire called back the next day to turn it down, saying, "Booth, I am so flattered. Maybe someday. I'll help you over here. But I can't be the director.' "

A week later he called back and invited her to a clandestine lunch at the Governor's Mansion. "He's a very persuasive guy," says Gregoire, shaking her head at the memory of the day in 1988 when her life began to accelerate beyond her wildest imagination. She went on to win bipartisan praise for the job she did at Ecology, then became attorney general and, in 2004, the state's second female governor.

"Many people say that if I hadn't spotted her she wouldn't have been governor. I have good instincts for good people," Booth says with pride.

"In the years since he called me that day (in 1988), some of the best advice he's given me is to 'go by your gut,' " Gregoire says. "That time, he went by his gut, when too often he did not. He tells me he can't recall an occasion where he went with his gut and failed. He wished he'd done it more."

⁓

Because Booth had such a huge lead, a ton of money and public affection that Dick Larsen described as ranking "somewhere between Donald Duck and fresh-baked bread," the media redoubled its efforts to hold his feet to the fire. He supplied the kindling. There was a guffaw fest when the campaign made the patently preposterous boast that Gardner's first-term achievements were in the same league with Governor Mike Dukakis' celebrated "Massachusetts Miracle." The governor grew cranky and his one-liners fell flat. In Spokane, KHQ-TV reporter Hugh Imhof asked the governor about his flip-flop on a budget item boosting a controversial technology center in the city. Playing to a crowd of supporters, Gardner said, "I think you've got your descriptive nouns all backwards. And that's why you're a reporter and I'm governor." That did it. Next, in a speech in Vancouver, B.C., he made an arrogant wisecrack about the caliber of higher education in British Columbia vs. Washington state: "you can take a UBC diploma, frame it and stick it in your windshield and we'd let you stay in handicapped parking."

"He thought that was funny," marvels Pete Callaghan, who wrote a column about the governor's attitude problem. Booth seemed bored and cynical, the Tacoma reporter said, and he deserved to get smacked around. It was "quit acting like you're giving everybody the service of your time."

May of 1988 was a month Gardner wishes he couldn't remember. Was he really temperamentally cut out to be governor? "There've been periods when I've questioned that myself," he admitted.

⁓

Mike Murphy, a lanky Grays Harbor County commissioner, was one of the earliest members of Booth's kitchen cabinet. Murphy had a boyish smile, the common touch and political smarts learned at the knee of his father, C. "Tab" Murphy, one of the most popular politicians in the history of the Harbor area. Mike had been state president of the Jaycees, a congressional aide and a leader in the Washington Association of Counties. He was a consensus-builder, respected by businessmen and environmentalists, Indians and sportsmen. He'd fished the fabled Humptulips River, hunted from Matlock to Montana and hiked the Olympics.

Having won the right to appoint the director of the new Wildlife Department, Gardner urged Murphy to apply for the job. Murphy's emotions were deeply mixed. "It's the one job in the world I'd have done for free," he says. Still, he felt duty bound to suggest that the appointment might prompt accusations of cronyism that could wound Gardner's bid for re-election. Booth called back a few days later and said not to worry—he'd be perfect for the job. Murphy quickly amassed endorsement letters from sportsmen's groups, legislators, tribal leaders and influential businessmen.

After a nationwide search by a well-known headhunter, Ted Ford Webb, the field was narrowed to Murphy, Curt Smitch, a Gardner staffer who handled natural resource issues, and two game directors from other states. Next came a series of interviews with a selection committee that included Dick Thompson, Mary Faulk, Dick Davis and Webb.

"Are you going to be home Saturday morning?" Booth called his friend to ask. "Sure," said Murphy, who could tell by the governor's tone "that he wasn't driving to Elma to tell me I was going to be appointed."

Booth drove through the Black Hills by himself, got lost and found a sheriff's deputy to give him directions to Murphy's place. They sat down in the living room. "He told me he was giving the job to Smitch. He said he was sorry he'd put me through all that. I appreciated that he came to tell me in person, but that didn't make me any less disappointed."

Despite a dozen years as a county commissioner overseeing a $45 million budget and hundreds of employees, the panel told Gardner that Murphy didn't have enough management experience. "The governor spends $30,000 on a headhunter in a nationwide search and then settles for a guy across the hall," said one of Murphy's legion of disgusted supporters.

A few weeks later, the governor was the keynoter when the county officials had their annual convention in Vancouver. He never mentioned Murphy by name but they all knew who he was talking about when he confessed, "I embarrassed a good friend of mine and yours. We all have our character flaws and one of mine is a tendency to kick my friends... while I'm trying to win over my enemies."

Murphy went on to lose narrowly in a bid to become state lands commissioner and was appointed by Gardner to the Liquor Control Board. Smitch angered non-Indian sportsmen by signing off on an agreement that opened state land to tribal hunters and allowed the tribes to set their own seasons and bag limits. "Curt is a good guy," says Murphy, "but he didn't know the issues and the players like I did."

⌣⌐

Katie Dolan also encountered "the tendency." She was the remarkable mom who came to the playfield with her autistic son when Booth was a university student. Dolan helped found a group called Troubleshooters in 1972 and became its executive director. Troubleshooters won a federal grant and became the nation's first developmental disabilities advocacy agency with government standing. Booth served on its board for several years. He and Dolan were dismayed when, just as he was poised to run for governor, the progress they'd made bogged down in internecine squabbling. In an extraordinary 594-page oral history conducted in 1988-1990, Dolan talked about the dangers of the "unbridled vengeance" that grips many parents and advocates for children with developmental disabilities. "I've always thought of the narcissism that we have as being a survival mechanism to try to make some sense out of the world," she said, adding that parents of children with developmental disabilities keep asking themselves "Why me? How could a loving God allow this to happen to me and my child?" Paranoia, single-mindedness and martyr complexes can take hold, Dolan said. It's all part of the brain struggling to deal with all that pain. "...I can remember feeling that none of these families were ever going to be satisfied until the special-ed director and therapist and teachers and principals were all nude hanging by their thumbs in the center courtyard of town with signs around their (necks) saying, 'The parents were right (and) we were wrong.' "

When Dolan found herself embroiled in a special-needs advocates' turf war, she appealed to Governor Spellman. He was not just sympathetic, he was appalled. Dolan soon realized, however, that governors come and go; bureaucrats run the show. She was drowning in alphabet soup. The Client Assistance Program (CAP) of the Department of Vocational Rehabilitation (DVR) thwarted her. DSHS was a maze. She was outnumbered and outmaneuvered. Service providers characterized her as a strident radical, which she readily acknowledged was often absolutely true. Dolan was first and foremost a passionate defender of the civil rights of the disabled. Then in the nick of time, the former chairman of the Troubleshooters board—her friend Booth—became governor. "He was charming and educated at Harvard and a divine person and he always loved us."

Two whirlwinds collided when Dolan ran afoul of a lobbyist for the Advocates for the Mentally Ill. "I just want you to know," the woman said, "that I'm going to fight you every step of the way." Dolan protested that there was "plenty of money and plenty of room for everybody," but the battle lines were drawn. Dolan's adversary was also close to Booth, who tried to stay neutral, insisting that both groups prepare grant proposals. Then he started getting complaints about The Troubleshooters in general and Katie in particular. In 1986, she was told the governor had concluded she probably had to go, that "it's gone too far." Dolan said Booth told a mutual friend, "Don't worry about Katie, she'll take care of herself."

Dolan stayed overnight in Olympia and went to see the governor at 6 a.m. to plead her case. "Help me," she said. "He more or less gave us a feeling like it was going to be fine and he'd take care of it." She asked him to appoint someone he trusted "as kind of a monitor on the whole system."

He sent Barlow, whom Dolan regarded as a "wonderful man" who had lent the Medina Foundation's support to the Troubleshooters. But Barlow "saw a board that was out of hand, a staff that was out of hand and, after all, I was the executive director and I think he knew that if I couldn't handle that then I shouldn't be there." On Nov. 17, 1986, she got the word unceremoniously that she was on suspension for two months and not allowed in the office. By February, it was all over—a case study of how the road to bureaucratic hell is paved with good intentions. Katie's story also illustrates how much fun it isn't to be governor, or at least Booth Gardner caught in the crossfire.

Dolan felt betrayed and "tormented." It was former State Senator Mike McManus who "literally saved my life and helped me redirect my energies," she said. "I had called him because he's a very close personal friend of the governor's. He explained to me a little bit about the governor—that he really cannot resist a lot of forces like that and often lets his friends down mainly because they're his friends. He might go for a stranger easily, but his own friends he thinks of them as being either maybe stronger, not really needing (his) help or that it would be wrong of him in some way to go out and help his friend. His friend is supposed to make it on his own... The governor has said he has a little problem with that kind of thing."

They created a Katie Dolan Advocacy Award. In 1988, Booth presented it to Katie Dolan.

~~~

Booth made history and won widespread praise in the summer of 1988 when he named Charles Z. Smith to the Washington Supreme Court. The court's first ethnic minority, Smith was born in the segregated South in 1927, the son of a Cuban auto mechanic and a cook whose grandparents were slaves. With his brilliant mind, winning smile and impeccable manners, Smith had been breaking color barriers in the state's legal profession for 35 years. Impressed by his work as a young deputy prosecutor, Attorney General Robert F. Kennedy plucked Smith from King County in 1961 to head the team of Justice Department lawyers that successfully prosecuted Teamsters President

Justice Charles Z. Smith, the first ethnic minority on the Washington Supreme Court. *Photo courtesy Josef Scaylea.*

Jimmy Hoffa for corruption. In 1965, Smith became Seattle's first African American municipal court judge. Governor Evans named him to the King County Superior Court bench a year later. Smith had been a professor and dean at the UW Law School and a lieutenant colonel in the Marine Corps. He was also one of the nation's leading Baptist laymen.

Carl Maxey, a pugnacious, charismatic civil rights leader from Spokane, was also advertised as being among the finalists for the Supreme Court seat. Retiring Justice William Goodloe did Maxey no favors by injudiciously suggesting him as his successor—a breach of decorum that also offended the State Constitution. However, Goodloe's curious behavior had no influence on the governor's decision. Although Maxey's widow believes the governor was "scared to death of him," Booth says that's not so. He says he respected Maxey but wanted a conciliator, and Smith stood for civility as much as civil rights. The governor believed Smith had "the potential to bring a new level of balance and direction" to a court that regularly produced 5-4 decisions on its toughest cases.

The behind-the-scenes story, Smith says, is that the job was his for the asking. He says he was invited to meet with the governor, who cut to the chase. The conversation went like this:

"I understand that if I offer you an appointment to the Supreme Court you would turn it down."

"Why don't you make me an offer?"

"OK, I'm offering it to you."

"Fine, I'll take it."

Smith says the governor's press people asked him if he would object to keeping his appointment on the QT for few weeks while they floated the notion that Maxey and others were still under consideration. No problem, the judge said, smiling at the penchant for "playing games."

When confronted with what he considered racism, the normally mild mannered Smith demonstrated he was no shrinking violet. In 1990, he told a Tacoma City Club forum on race relations in Washington State that "Even though I am at the top of the judicial system, there are still people... who believe they can call me 'nigger' and get away with it." Smith said "a cabal" of his colleagues conducted a "reign of terror" between 1990 and 1993 in an attempt to make him so angry that he would resign. The incident revolved around the firing of one of Justice Smith's law clerks over sexual harassment allegations.

Former chief justice Gerry Alexander, who served on the high court with Smith for eight years, believes picking Smith was one of Gardner's best decisions as governor. "Charlie Smith was probably the perfect guy to break the color barrier," says Alexander. "He's a remarkable man."

Terry Sebring, Gardner's legal counsel until Booth appointed him to the Pierce County Superior Court bench in 1990, says the governor carefully weighed his judicial appointments. Marsha Pechman, Robert Lasnik and Ricardo Martinez, who became federal judges, were first appointed to the Superior Court bench by Gardner, as was future Supreme Court Justice Bobbe Bridge. William Downing, a former prosecutor whom Gardner named to the King County Superior Court bench in 1989, emerged as one of the state's most thoughtful and civic-minded judges.

⁓

With a free ride into the General Election in November, Booth had a fundraising field day, collecting $1.1 million, compared to $260,000 for Maleng and $174,000 for Williams. And while his Republican challengers concentrated on winning the primary, he was being gubernatorial, buoyed by an economy that owed much of its rebound to a high-flying Boeing.

Smokers fumed but the reviews were mostly positive when Booth banned smoking in any state office or vehicle over which he had executive control, effective January 1, 1989. He also raised once again the issue that would be one of the hallmarks of his years as governor: standards-based education. To counter the disturbing dropout rate in urban school districts, he proposed a plan to require grade-school students to demonstrate minimum levels of competence in reading, writing and math before moving on to junior high. A program of tests, tutoring and re-tests should be implemented to help children develop "these crucial basic skills and a sense of success rather than a sense of failure" that leads to dropping out, the governor said. Exemptions would be made for students with learning disabilities. Gardner said he was more interested in holding educators responsible for student achievement than holding back kids with litmus tests.

On Sept. 20, Williams' enthusiastic network of 14,000 "family values" volunteers out-hustled Maleng's mainstream Republicans. Williams took 20 percent of the primary vote. Maleng, who many believe would have been a great governor, won only 15 percent. Williams' ebullience in victory was overshadowed by the stunning vote of confidence for Booth Gardner, who captured 57.6 percent. In the previous 40 years, the best any incumbent governor had done in a primary election was Dan Evans' 43.4 percent in 1968. "This will be fun," said Gardner, immediately rejecting Williams' call for five debates. Two would be plenty, he said, adding that he expected Williams to be more of an irritant than a threat: "He'll be like a mosquito in a closed room." But Williams warned that he could "sting like a bee." He went on to stage several debates with a cardboard cutout labeled "Booth Gardner." The real thing, he said, was a bleeding heart, tax-and-spend liberal who coddles criminals.

Dixy Lee Ray visited the Tri-Cities to stump for Williams. Displaying her usual political acumen, she said Gardner better watch out—Williams was closing the gap. Polls projecting Gardner a landslide winner were suspect, the former governor said, because pollsters can easily slant results "by the way they put the questions."

When Williams finally got Gardner on the same platform, he was so frustrated that he came out swinging wildly. Gardner dismissed the attacks with an analogy that wasn't altogether flattering. He said Williams was "like a flea boring in on a sleeping dog." (With mosquitoes, bees and fleas, the campaign could have used some metaphorical insecticide.) Williams, in any case, was never able to get an inch of traction. He was crushed like an ant. Gardner won a second term with 62.2 percent of the vote.

Al Rosellini congratulates Booth on his re-election. Jim Davidson photo, *Gardner family album*

CHAPTER 15:

Tough choices

On January 11, 1989, Booth delivered his second inaugural address, "The Centennial Challenge." It was capitalism with a conscience. "We stand on the threshold of a new century of statehood," he said, and "we have the opportunity to do something extraordinary." The choices were clear: "Either we respond to international competition or we doom ourselves and our children to a dramatic slide to second-rate status in the world." Microsoft was demonstrating that "the computer has become the pencil of the 21st Century—the basic tool that must be mastered by all who expect a good job. ...How we respond to that competition is perhaps the greatest challenge this state, and this country, has ever faced." For the first time since the dawn of the Industrial Revolution, Gardner said, "a good business climate is also a good living climate....The things we have always wanted for people in our society are now the very things business needs from the workforce." So in addition to the moral commitment to create a fair and just society, "we now have an economic imperative to help our people become well-educated, productive citizens."

He spoke with unusual passion. "I implore you to understand it is not just some abstract 'they' I am speaking of. It's our children—yours and

Denny Heck, Booth's second-term chief of staff, and Ecology Director
Chris Gregoire visit Booth at the mansion. *Photo courtesy Denny Heck.*

mine—who are not being educated for the 21st century....And it will be our
children who will be the first generation in America's 200-year history that
will not achieve, much less exceed, our standard of living if we aren't willing
to commit to a public agenda of excellence for the common good."

A huge stumbling block to business investment was the state's tax structure. Basically unchanged since the Depression, it was "unbalanced and
unfair," the governor said. "To the members of the Legislature, I say this:
Now is the time to hear the people's voice on tax reform. Do not stonewall
it. Let the people decide."

Loggers and other blue-collar workers seeing their jobs chopped by
environmental restrictions and new technology must be retrained, the governor said. Further, "the health of our citizens, particularly our children,
is an issue that goes right to the heart of our quality of life." He called for
the creation of a new Department of Health. Crucially, the governor said,
"we must start thinking of ourselves as world citizens, competing inter-
nationally, with the best years of our lives ahead of us....The future is not
predetermined. It will become what we make it."

Gardner decided he again needed a chief of staff to help him hunker down for an ambitious second term. Dick Davis came over from the Office of Financial Management, and was succeeded by his No. 2, the capable Len McComb. Denny Heck, a former legislative leader, became deputy chief of staff and the governor's top legislative strategist. At mid-year, Davis, who was 53, returned to the private sector, having paid his public-service dues. Heck became Booth's right-hand man for the rest of his tenure as governor. A political prodigy, Heck was elected to the House at 23. He served five terms, rising to majority leader before resigning in 1984 to succeed Dean Foster as chief clerk. He lost to Judith Billings in a photo-finish race for superintendent of public instruction in 1988. Heck was intense, self-disciplined, confident, confrontational, fast on his feet and extremely bright. Over the next three years, he says he learned to be "more mellow." Foster, a friend and admirer, chuckles at that: "Put it this way: There were times when Denny was less intense."

Determined to advance his legislative agenda, Booth sent Heck and Foster into combat. Foster carried a first-aid kit and Heck a club. "It was my role to bust knuckles," Heck says. "I was the enforcer." By April, resistant Republicans and even some Democrats were sporting buttons that said "Blame Governor Heck." Looking back, he says it all began at the Inaugural Ball that January. "I was walking around in my tuxedo kind of full of excitement that I was joining the Gardner Administration. I was talking with a lobbyist, who made what I thought was a highly offensive joke ridiculing Governor Gardner as being a non-factor legislatively. And I said, '*We're* going to change that.' " It came across as hubris. Mark Twain once observed that "we" should be reserved for kings and people with tape worms.

"I think that's the start of Denny's mellowing," says Peter Callaghan. "Suddenly he fully realizes he is not just speaking for Denny. It really upset him when the 'Blame Governor Heck' buttons came out. He doesn't want to be the focus of attention, for obvious reasons: It gets you in trouble with the boss, who doesn't want some employee of his getting attention and making it look like he's the power behind the throne."

Booth, who has a wry sense of humor, thought the buttons were funny, but Heck was embarrassed—and the wiser for it.

No one in the administration was amused by the "Booth Buster" buttons that angry teachers, state employees and other union members wore when they descended on the Capitol in March, demanding bigger raises from a projected $400 million revenue windfall. The buttons depicted Gardner as a smug cheapskate with a "3%" pin on his lapel.

Gardner's executive request package was pushing a hundred bills when Heck came on board. "That's not the way this can work," he insisted. "The governor has to be for three or four big things. Our priorities have to be clear." Heck was determined to reassert Booth forcefully into the legislative process. The Cabbage Patch Governor became The Terminator. Booth shot down nearly 18 percent of the bills that arrived on his desk in 1989, using his veto a record 83 times. Overall, he vetoed 14 percent of the bills sent to him, more than Dan Evans in his three terms. Gardner was also more forceful with the veto pen than Dixy Lee Ray, John Spellman and his successor, Mike Lowry.

Weary after nearly five months of tax reform horse-trading and peeved at Gardner's new cheekiness, the 1989 Legislature overrode his veto of a bill creating a new crime, residential burglary. The lawmakers wanted to emphasize the threat to human life created by a home invasion. The House vote was 97-0; the Senate 46-1. Booth said he supported the idea, but vetoed the bill on the grounds that the longer prison sentences prescribed in the legislation would strain the budget. Dan Evans promptly sent him a letter

Booth listens intently during a visit to Pacific County in 1989.
Kathy Quigg © The Daily World, Aberdeen.

that Booth had framed. Today it hangs prominently on a wall in his office. "You're not a governor," Evans said, "until you have been overridden."

Gardner, Heck and Foster had decided to pave the way to an income tax with a plan that boosted the gas tax and reduced the sales and business-and-occupation taxes. In "Sine Die," a fascinating guidebook to the Washington legislative process, Edward D. Seeberger offers the anatomy of the dustup that ensued: "The Senate took politically tough votes to pass one gas tax increase at seven cents and another at five cents. Gardner let it be known he would veto both efforts without overall tax reform, so much-relieved House Democrats let the proposals die. To make up for their earlier tax increase votes, senators passed a transportation budget with no gas tax increase at all and the House concurred." The first special session ended on that note. Although he still lacked a deal, the governor called a second special session. Two days of arm-twisting made the lawmakers even crankier. Gardner said he would accept a four-cent increase, "but by then few legislators cared. ... Leaders made it known they were prepared to vote to override six more Gardner vetoes if he called another special session."

"Booth Gardner is the antithesis of a politician," House Speaker Joe

King told a reporter. "The process is still difficult for him. I continue to think that's why the public likes him so well. He seems like the opposite of a politician—and he is." On this King and Jeannette Hayner, the GOP majority leader in the Senate, could agree. She admired Gardner's popularity with the voters, "but that doesn't translate into legislative skill. If it did, my gosh, he'd be able to do anything."

"They tried to change Booth Gardner's image," said Vito Chiechi, the political strategist for the House Republicans. "In doing so, they went too far." Maybe, says Heck, "but he had to be a player." Vito got fired the next year. Denny got a raise.

An income tax was, is and may always be the toughest sell in Washington politics. Foster recalls seeing a letter Gardner wrote to Norton Clapp defending his plan. "It said, 'You've always taught me to look at the facts. And here's how I see the facts involving our budget situation, how we raise money and why the income tax is more equitable.' I never saw the answer."

The Gardner legislative team—Heck, Foster and Wilkerson—regrouped. Over the next three years they pushed hard for the lawmakers to send a tax reform plan to the voters. "Try as we might, we just weren't able to get anything passed," Foster says. Dan Evans and Gardner commiserated on that one, too. Campaigning outside the Weyerhaeuser pulp mill at Cosmopolis in 1973, Evans offered his hand to a night shift worker heading home. "My wife always votes for you," the guy said, "but I just want you to know that I'm not voting for any f***ing income tax!" Seventy-seven percent of the voters agreed with him that year.

Some important victories in the first year of Booth's second term were overshadowed by the noisy debate over tax reform. Gardner and Gregoire, who quickly proved to be an aggressive and effective manager at Ecology, goaded the feds into ruling out Hanford as a repository for the nation's

Booth receives the blessing of former U.S. Senator Warren G. "Maggie" Magnuson in 1989. *Gardner family album.*

high-level nuclear waste. They also won a "Tri-Party" agreement with the federal Environmental Protection Agency and the U.S. Department of Energy that the nuclear waste at Hanford, dating back to the atomic bomb project in World War II, would be systematically cleaned up over the next 30 years. Old waste tanks were perilously close to the Columbia River aquifer. The governor also banned any further shipments to Hanford of low-level radioactive wastes from other states. That decision was largely upheld by the U.S. Supreme Court in 1992. Booth had done some hard bargaining with 10 other states to ensure his stance wouldn't be undermined. The Legislature also backed his plan to retain and broaden the reach of the Puget Sound Water Quality Authority and approved creation of a Department of Health.

Booth said it was only fitting to celebrate the state's centennial by reaching out to the ancestors of the original Washingtonians. He signed an accord with the tribes, pledging the state to a more formal collaborative relationship to solve natural resources issues without litigation. The latter-day treaty was the first of its kind in the U.S., and it made a significant difference. In 1992, Indian leaders from around the state presented Gardner a ceremonial cedar mask and a poem honoring him as a great leader "for

Indians and non-Indians alike." Billy Frank, the chairman of the Northwest Indian Fisheries Commission, said the new spirit of cooperation had improved natural resource management as well as economic and social relations. Joe DeLaCruz of the Quinaults, chairman of the World Council of Indigenous Peoples, said the agreement became an international model. "Booth had been warned that he risked his political future if he didn't 'stand up to the Indians,'" Laird Harris recalls. "He was unfazed," following through on overtures to the tribes by Spellman and Wilkerson.

The centennial turned out to be a moveable feast and a coming-out party for the first lady. When Booth first took office, Jean Gardner, despite her winning smile, was shy inside. She wasn't comfortable being such a public person—constantly on display. Being first lady is hard work, as Nancy Evans, Mary Lowry and Mona Locke will attest. Teaming Jean with Ralph Munro, who exuded zest and could transform a Genealogical Society bake sale in Enumclaw into the event of the year, was a marriage made in heaven. If the Gardners had gotten along that well, life at the mansion would have been bliss. They christened the tall ship *Lady Washington*, inspected children's murals, saluted writers and artists, dedicated trails. "She was

Ralph Munro and Jean Gardner kick off Washington's Centennial Celebration in 1989. *Photo courtesy Louie Balukoff.*

phenomenal," says Munro. "During one of our first planning meetings, she looked nervous. I looked down at her lap and her hands were shaking. Without saying anything, I reached down and took her hand. We bonded. Public speaking didn't come easy to Jean, but she got to be very good at it, and people loved her. We still get letters from people saying they have just completed their centennial projects they started in 1989."

Jean notes that some people will tell you that the only thing worse than having to give a speech is dying. "I was in that category. I would throw up beforehand and say weird things." It started with Booth's first campaigns, she says, "and it took a long time for me to get over that phobia of public speaking. You're trying to sound intelligent and know what you're talking about—trying to get people enthused. ...But it was so much fun working with Ralph on the Centennial. And by the time I was president of the Seattle Symphony Board (in 1993) I could stand up and talk to anybody about anything."

⌇

Just as timber towns were slowly rebounding from the painful recession of the early 1980s the U.S. Forest Service proposed to drastically reduce the harvest on the Olympic Peninsula to protect the Northern Spotted Owl, soon to be declared a threatened species. Environmentalists said it was the proverbial canary in the coal mine for an entire old-growth ecosystem.

January 19, 1989, was the day the world turned upside down for Monte Dahlstrom and Tom Mayr, a pair of second-generation Grays Harbor loggers, and thousands of others whose livelihoods were rooted in the woods. Mill owners assembled at the Quinault Ranger Station, expecting the Forest Service to announce that 90 million board feet of timber would be available. They could live with that. Jaws dropped when they were told that the new guidelines for protecting owl habitat would reduce the cut to 42 million board feet. Rex Holloway, a Forest Service manager, warned that it could be 20 million board feet in the years to come. "This will be economic devastation for Grays Harbor," said Dahlstrom. "It will

Booth with Werner Mayr, a pioneer Grays Harbor logger, during the height of the
Spotted Owl controversy. *Kathy Quigg © The Daily World, Aberdeen.*

be a different place to live." It was no exaggeration.

Booth had been a strong supporter of the landmark Timber, Fish &
Wildlife Agreement of 1987. "TFW" was a consensus-building approach to
maximizing timber harvests while minimizing environmental impacts—all
the while striving to resolve conflicts through negotiation rather than litigation. Now he created a Timber Team to coordinate assistance programs,
including wide-ranging efforts to help communities diversify their economies and retrain workers. He also lobbied the Forest Service for more liberal
harvest levels. Rich Nafziger, one of Gardner's most versatile staffers, headed
the team, coordinating outreach by state agencies and helping lobby the
Legislature for assistance. The plight of timber communities resonated with
Gardner. He was determined to help and saddened by the despair he saw
during his frequent visits to Aberdeen and Hoquiam, Longview, Kelso and
Port Angeles. He also held meetings in Raymond, Forks and Morton, even

smaller towns where timber was all there was. This time, Gardner found many allies in the Legislature, which provided funds for worker retraining and economic development, including money for new infrastructure. In 1991, the lawmakers extended unemployment benefits and offered assistance with rent and mortgage payments. Still, there were "too many food banks and not enough family-wage jobs," the governor said, shaking his head during a visit with his friend Jim Coates. The former Weyerhaeuser millwright headed a food distribution network in Hoquiam that was struggling to meet demand. "I'm fed up with the feds," Booth told a community awards banquet in Aberdeen, adding that Oregon Governor Barbara Roberts was equally exasperated with the Bush Administration. "They express their concern over endangered birds by turning themselves into ostriches," the governor said. "They should give us back control of our timberlands and let us manage them under a regional authority." Fundamentally a free trader, Booth reversed course as the timber supply situation grew more dire and called for limitations on log exports, even though it would cost the state upwards of $60 million a year in lost revenue.

In his farewell State of the State Address in 1993, Gardner said he felt compelled to share an epiphany from his last visit to Grays Harbor. "There are plenty of trees left in those forests," he said, "but no longer many jobs. Supply, demand and environmental issues have conspired against Hoquiam. I've been there many times, most recently this past fall, just after a permanent mill closure put another 600 people out of work."

He told of speaking at a high school assembly. "When I looked out at those young women and men, just embarked on adulthood, full of hope for their future but perplexed and scared by what was happening to their parents, I was moved. I told them that nothing is permanent—not even the town where they had been born, or the woods and the mills that gave it life. I told them that while their parents and grandparents had lived good and productive lives in Hoquiam, that same life might not be available to all of them. I advised them to look ahead and not cling to the past. I urged them to continue their education and to look, perhaps, beyond

Hoquiam, beyond the mills they could see and the trees that surrounded them toward the more prosperous economies on I-5. I thought it was a pretty good speech," Booth told the legislators. "It was honest and it made sense. It had hope. It was doable. Apparently it was heard because at least one student went home and told her parents. At the community forum that evening, one of the parents asked me to share what I had told the students. When I was finished, a man rose from the crowd. You could see 25 years of working in the woods on his face and hands—25 years that had ended a month before with a pink slip. He said, 'Governor, what you say is all right for my kids, but what about me? I'm 45. I have a wife and four children. My mother is sick. Do you really think I can start over again?' I didn't have much of an answer.

"Since that evening, I have thought about that man a lot. And I have thought a lot about what I could say to you that would be useful—useful to the many new legislators who are here today, useful to the veterans who've been here for years and risen to positions of leadership—and useful to the

Booth talks with Hoquiam High School students in 1992. Many of their parents were impacted by the logging restrictions. *Kathy Quigg © The Daily World, Aberdeen.*

people of this state. …Here's what I've seen from this perspective: First and most importantly, I've seen that everybody matters. That man in Hoquiam matters. His children matter. His sick mother matters.…There are no 'little people'—only little minds that fail to grasp the basic truth of our common humanity and our common future."

Booth usually gave few instructions to his last speechwriter, a gifted wordsmith named Jill Severn. "But for that portion of his farewell address he made me sit down and listen carefully to the story about the lesson he learned from his visit to Hoquiam," she remembers vividly. "He told me, 'I want you to write it *exactly* like that'—talking to the kids, then the dad asking him if he really thought he could start over. It was something he felt deeply. We'd often have fabulous conversations about all these great state-of-the-world ideas. He was always interested in new ideas. I would bring him articles, then he'd wander in and we'd just talk about anything and everything. That was what was so magical about working for Booth." He could turn a good phrase, too, Severn says. "Governors are the expansion joint," he told her one day when they were discussing the politics of balancing a budget. "The feds are pushing down, and the people are pushing up."

⁓

Booth's sixth year as governor, 1990, began with the good news that revenues likely would be $600 million higher than expected. That meant the "short" 60-day session—ostensibly a non-budget event—would be a fiscal free-for-all. About half the seats in the Senate and all 98 in the House would be on the ballot that fall. Tired of "getting peanuts instead of apples," teachers demanded a 10 percent raise. Gardner, backed by budget writers for both parties, said that wasn't "doable this year." Welfare caseloads were rising, school enrollment was up and the prison population was higher than expected in the wake of tough-on-crime legislation. In short, the bow wave from earlier approved expenditures was already too big, the governor said. He was worried, too, about the outlook for the 1991-93 budget and advocated socking away $233 million of the projected surplus.

Booth earmarked $70 million for school construction and some $50 million for other programs to improve education, including smaller classes in the first three grades. He also championed a plan that made many educators nervous—open enrollment. However, "Learning by Choice" won the Legislature's approval. It was hailed by parents, who gained the right to send their children to any school where there was room. President George H.W. Bush borrowed several ideas from Gardner's Schools for the 21st Century program to launch "American 2000," his own campaign for innovative education. Year-round schools, team teaching and grouping students by ability rather than age were among the innovations explored by Washington state educators. "Good ideas are at work out there in the state of Washington," Bush told reporters after a White House meeting with Gardner, Lt. Gov. Joel Pritchard and some Washington educators.

Welfare programs that focused on the needs of children received another $70 million in the governor's proposed supplemental budget. He was also reprising his gas tax plan, advocating a 5-cent hike over the next three years

Northwest region members of the Washington Education Association rally in Everett on February 13, 1990. *WEA photo.*

to raise $1 billion by 1995 for the state's neglected highways and bridges.

The Northwest Region of the Washington Education Association announced a one-day strike—an "Awareness Day"—on Feb. 13, 1990, to protest
the failure of the governor and lawmakers to meet their demands for "a real
raise" and smaller classes. The other regions and local district WEA affiliates
agreed to mobilize on the same day, some by refusing to report for work,
others by leaving early or staging after-school rallies. In all, 25,000 teachers
around the state participated, including 7,000 who assembled at Everett's
Memorial Stadium on a picture-postcard winter day: Sparkling sunshine
and a light blanket of snow. Three-thousand Seattle teachers marched down
Fifth Avenue. Still others picketed outside ferry terminals with signs that
said, "Pay the toll, Booth." That summer, in a development that seemed
heaven sent, the Education Commission of the States held its annual convention in Seattle, with Gardner presiding as both host and chairman. On
opening day, WEA President Carla Nuxoll and her vice president, C.T.
Purdom, led a noisy procession of 6,000 teachers brandishing banners and
balloons. "No more hot air!" they chanted at the top of their lungs.

⁓

Gardner's $72 million package to crack down on predatory sex offend-
ers would be the slam dunk of the 1990 legislative session and one of
his finest hours as governor. His actions demonstrated the empathy that
reverberated from his fractured childhood, his outrage at senseless crime
and his common sense.

On the evening of May 20, 1989, 7-year-old Ryan Hade asked his mom
if he could go for a bike ride in their South Tacoma neighborhood. She told
him to be back before dark. Ryan's sad fate was to encounter a profoundly
deranged man. With a doughnut as bait, Earl Shriner lured Ryan into the
woods, raped him, strangled him with wire, cut off his penis and left him
for dead, naked and caked in blood and mud. Shriner, who was 40, had
an appalling track record of violence and perversion. At 16, he killed a
schoolmate. Too young to be charged with homicide under then-prevailing

state laws, he was first committed to a school for juvenile delinquents, then to a mental hospital. Diagnosed as slightly retarded, he fell through the cracks of a system that found it difficult to differentiate between the mentally ill, the developmentally disabled and criminals with frontal lobes fried by drugs and alcohol—a cautionary tale in and of itself. The ensuing years found Shriner in and out of jail for assault, kidnapping and animal mutilation. The case provoked outrage statewide. Talk-radio went ballistic and Gardner was hit by an avalanche of demands for a special session of the Legislature. "Many of our political leaders are counting on your anger to blow over," one critic told a rally at Cheney Stadium in Tacoma. Others wanted to summarily castrate every pervert in sight.

The governor said he was sickened by the crime, but an emotional response was no rational way to write new laws and reform a complex system. He appointed Norm Maleng, his former rival, to head a 24-person task force. It included representatives of the criminal justice system, mental health professionals, defense attorneys, victims and their relatives, notably Helen Harlow, Ryan Hade's mother, and Ida Ballasiotes, whose daughter was raped and murdered in 1988 by a fugitive from a work-release center. Maleng was an inspired choice for chairman. Booth respected his ability as a prosecutor and knew he had the perfect personality to ensure the process wouldn't be tainted by the emotionalism of the moment. His appointment also gave the task force a bipartisan cachet.

The only truly controversial issue was whether an involuntary commitment law was constitutional. Under the legislation presented by the task force, with Gardner's strong endorsement, violent sexual deviants still deemed a high risk to reoffend after completing their prison sentences would be confined in a "Special Commitment Center" for as long as it took to ensure public safety—maybe forever. Washington was the first state in the nation to enact such a law. The plan called for expanded treatment programs, especially those designed to rehabilitate young offenders. It also provided more assistance for victims. The Community Protection Act of 1990 was enacted by the Legislature and survived Federal Court scrutiny several times in the years to come.

Earl Shriner was sentenced to 131 years in prison. Ryan Hade's story has nothing approximating a happy ending. He underwent reconstructive surgery and saw counselors for years. He sometimes became angry or physically ill around the anniversary of the attack. As he grew older, however, he gained confidence. He went to technical school and learned the upholstery trade. He loved snowboarding and skydiving. In 2005, he bought himself a brand new motorcycle—bright yellow—only to be killed in a collision with a pickup truck a few days later. That's when the public finally learned his name. The former "little Tacoma boy" was 23.

The "Tennis Shoe Brigade" Harlow and Ballasiotes helped organize played an important role in building support for tougher sex offender laws. The Legislature also authorized law enforcement to notify the public when sex offenders are released from prison or move from place to place.

As freeways became rush-hour nightmares and farmland sprouted subdivisions and strip malls, land-use planning in Washington evolved from a hodge-podge of municipal zoning regulations to efforts at comprehensive planning. King County, where the voters had a front row seat for what happens when you pave paradise and put up a parking lot, led the way. The Evans Administration was in the vanguard, producing the State Environmental Policy Act and the Shoreline Management Act.

Although environmentalists said it was a watchdog with a muzzle and Booth had his own misgivings, the Growth Management Act stitched together by the 1990 Legislature was a landmark. Speaker King and Rep. Maria Cantwell, two agile and ambitious politicians, were key players. King hoped to become governor, while Cantwell was aiming for Congress.

Gardner appointed a Growth Strategies Commission in 1989 after a bill backed by the speaker died in the Senate. However, its report wouldn't be ready until after the 1990 session. Believing the momentum was still there, King deputized Cantwell to coordinate the work of six committees—each headed by a female legislator—drafting a revised bill. It was one of the most complex undertakings in modern legislative history.

When the Senate's amendments to make the act less aggressive proved unacceptable to the House, Gardner called a special session. A conference committee finally produced a compromise that won bipartisan approval on the last day, April 1, 1990. Gardner fully supported the key requirement that the state's 15 fastest-growing counties adopt comprehensive growth-management regulations. Using his veto to remove several sections he viewed as problematic, the governor signed the act into law, and asked his commission to fine-tune revisions. Its recommendations, notably the creation of three regional boards of appeal, were enacted in 1991 after some hard bargaining. The governor also won the power to withhold tax revenues from cities or counties that failed to comply with rulings. In 1992, his last session as governor, Gardner and his allies turned back efforts to weaken the act.

The 1990 Legislature approved Gardner's Learning by Choice plan. In addition to open enrollment, it features Running Start, which has become one of the most popular and effective "advanced placement" programs in

Booth flexes his muscles for Arnold Schwarzenegger during the actor-bodybuilder's visit to the UW campus in 1990. Schwarzenegger was in town for the opening of the Goodwill Games. *Davis Freeman, UW Columns Magazine.*

the nation. Running Start allows exceptional high school juniors and se-
niors to attend community colleges full- or part-time for free. Since its inception, thousands of Washington students have graduated simultaneously
from high school and community college and gone on to earn bachelor's
degrees at substantially less expense.

~~~

Isiah Turner's largely successful tenure as commissioner of the
Department of Employment Security came to an unhappy, headline-mak-
ing end in October of 1990. Turner resigned after a state audit authenti-
cated a *Seattle Times* investigation that revealed he had misused at least
$14,000 of state money for travel and telephone expenses. The taxpayers
had paid for hundreds of nights in upscale hotels not far from his home
and office and scores of personal calls. An auditor called it the worst case
of expense-account abuse in recent state history.

Turner, who was paid $79,000 a year, was the only African American
in Gardner's cabinet and an important liaison to the black community.
"Saddened and heartsick" at his ouster, members of the minority community and other supporters pointed to his achievements. Turner had created
the most diverse workforce in state government and streamlined delivery of
services. Noting that Turner had apologized and made restitution, many saw
an undercurrent of racism in his ouster. Several suggested that a white person with a similar track record would have been reprimanded and retained.
When Gardner named Vernon Stoner, the state's first African American city
manager, to succeed Turner it took the edge off the furor. *The Times* took
more heat than the governor, but the scandal wouldn't go away. It got worse
when Ernie La Palm, Turner's well respected deputy, was dismissed at year's
end. La Palm, 56, said he was sacked because they believed he squealed
on his boss. (Eric Nalder, the *Times* reporter whose stories brought down
Turner, said La Palm was not his source.) The Gardner Administration flatly
denied that was why La Palm was let go. Rather, "considering the revelations
and problems in the department," they felt it was important for Stoner to

appoint his own management team and make "a clean slate." La Palm shot back: "That they are now saying there are all these problems in the department is an interesting observation in light of how Gardner pronounced Isiah Turner the greatest commissioner in the history of the agency."

The governor attended farewell events honoring Turner, including a reception that drew a crowd of 400 to Seattle's Mount Zion Baptist Church. "This state has lost the best employment-security director it has ever had," Booth said. Dick Larsen scathingly hailed it as a singular duplicitous moment in "Chapter III of the Adventures of Prince Faintheart."

Also embarrassing was a projected $18 million cost overrun and conflict-of-interest allegations in connection with ACES, a welfare system computer project at the Department of Social & Health Services. Its $20 million predecessor, COSMOS, was scrapped in 1989 when caseworkers demonstrated they could compute welfare eligibility by hand about twice as fast. COSMOS began in the Spellman era, but the twin snafus dogged the Gardner Administration for the rest of its days. Booth pointed out that the state was actually only $900,000 into the new system, proof that the agency's beefed-up oversight was effective. "Because of COSMOS," he said, "we caught ACES before the horse left the barn." Among those making hay was Sen. McDonald, a likely contender for the GOP nomination for governor in 1992. Whenever Gannett's Bob Partlow asked for an update on the computer projects, he'd begin with "You ran as someone who could manage…" Gardner would cut him off in mid-sentence, saying, "I know the diatribe." He was seriously rethinking whether he could take four more years of this. Nevertheless, a black-tie fundraiser organized by Ron Dotzauer raised $300,000 for the next campaign, be it a bid for a third term or the U.S. Senate.

Two former rivals suffered major setbacks that fall. John Spellman attempted to unseat Gardner's second Supreme Court appointee, Richard Guy, a former Spokane Superior Court judge who had strong bipartisan support. Bob Williams, thought to be in a tight race with Congresswoman Jolene Unsoeld in Southwest Washington's 3rd District, was also soundly defeated.

Gardner's last two years as governor were dominated by extraordinarily eventful legislative sessions and broader responsibilities. He was chairman of the National Governors Association and a national leader in education reform. As he weighed where he would be in 1993, he told Jill Severn he was thinking about the challenges of governing in "a global, historical, human context." The governor and his young speechwriter were in Washington, D.C., for a meeting of the Governors Association on the eve of the first Gulf war, which Gardner opposed. Protocol called for the chairman to give a toast to the president. Booth wanted it to be both thoughtful and respectful. "We finally came up with a line that suited him," Severn remembers. "He toasted the president as someone who 'had to make the most difficult decisions on earth.' "

January of 1991 found America in a state of war and the Legislature in a state of uncertainty. Operation Desert Storm, launched with an aerial blitzkrieg on the 16th, booted Saddam Hussein's troops out of Kuwait in nothing flat, which was a relief to the budget writers. They'd been warned that a protracted war could cause a spike in the price of oil and reduce state revenues by as much as $400 million. All was not quiet on the home front, however, and the Legislature's battle with the Washington Education Association was still raging when spring rolled around. The teachers, way better organized than the Iraqi army, warned repeatedly that they would strike if all they got was another "chintzy" cost-of-living raise. They were roundly miffed when an unbiased study found they were considerably better compensated than they claimed—twelfth in the nation and $4,000 higher than the average. On the other hand, the student-teacher ratio ranked 40th. Sen. McDonald and Rep. Gary Locke, the up-and-coming chairman of the House budget committee, agreed with Gardner that a 10 percent raise over the 1991-93 biennium wasn't in the cards.

Teachers in districts all around the state walked out. The governor's daughter, Gail, an English and social studies teacher at a Tacoma middle school, called at 7 a.m. on the first day to give him a ribbing. "Dad, if the president

Iowa Governor Terry Branstad speaks outside the White House in the wake of a Governors' Conference on education in 1989. From left, Arkansas Governor Bill Clinton, Booth and South Carolina Governor Carroll Campbell. *Gardner family album.*

can solve the railroad strike in one day, why can't you solve the teachers' strike?" Dad said President Bush passed the buck to Congress to negotiate a back-to-work package for the railroaders, while he and the Legislature had already offered the teachers the best they could do, given the state of the budget. Gail made herself scarce when 13,000 teachers descended on Olympia on April 19. Their ranks swelled to 21,000 eight days later, only to be outflanked by the governor. He was tired of being booed and reasoned that a six-week cooling off period would be good for everyone. Booth found an ally in Clyde Ballard, the tough but gentlemanly GOP leader in the House. Ballard blocked a legislative move to do an end-around on the governor and call itself into an immediate special session. The teachers had to go back to school, although they ended up with more than Gardner was willing to spend when Senate Republicans boosted his K-12 budget. However, raises for teachers and most other state employees would amount to about 8 percent over the biennium, slightly less than what the governor had proposed at the outset.

Gardner appointed a special commission of business, community and school leaders to address education reform, which had bogged down over merit pay, masters degrees and tests for teachers and students. The governor strongly favored student testing, but he warned again that one size wouldn't fit all. "You can't just raise the bar and say every child must reach it." The dropout rates will soar if the stakes are too high, he said, and teachers could end up "just teaching to the test." (In the years to come, as the controversial Washington Assessment of Student Learning—the WASL— was instituted, he regretted not making that point even more forcefully in the 1980s. "I'm willing to admit I was wrong," he said in 2005. "I was naïve…and time has shown me there's a better way.")

Dan Evans, Mike Lowry and Jim Ellis, Seattle's visionary civic activist, lent their support to Gardner's proposal to lift the state's statutory debt ceiling by one percent to allow a billion-dollar general obligation bond issue. The money would be earmarked for new schools and university buildings as well as low-income housing. Another chunk would be invested in preserving recreational land and wildlife habitat.

Evans and Ellis reminded a House committee that the state borrowed millions of dollars to expand public facilities as the population boomed in the wake of World War II and issued more bonds in 1971 to keep pace with changing needs. "I think it's time again for Washingtonians to take stock of their future," Evans said. Gardner added that it was vital to protect more land from development "before it's gone forever," while Lowry emphasized that rising property values and decreasing federal aid were leaving increasing numbers of poor folks out in the cold. Evans, Gardner and Lowry, so dramatically different in temperament,

Courtesy David Horsey

would frequently find common cause on progressive issues in the years to come. This time, they struck out. McDonald and Locke were worried about what would happen when the bills came due.

~

Chang Mook Sohn's revenue forecasts were hotly debated from January to June of 1991. Some called him "Dr. Doom." Others maintained he was Dr. Feelgood, succumbing to political pressure to gin up more optimistic numbers so everyone could declare victory after two tedious special sessions and head home. Bristling at that suggestion, the chief economist nevertheless found another $73 million and Gardner's staff announced a $55 million windfall in federal Medicaid assistance.

In September, when the Forecast Council next met, Sohn had bad news: Consumer confidence was tanking. The national recession had caught up with Washington. Boeing was selling fewer planes, Weyerhaeuser a lot less lumber. The demand for services—welfare, jobless benefits, smaller class sizes—was escalating as revenues declined. The bottom line, Sohn said, was that by New Year's Day there could be a $200 million deficit.

President Bush, riding high in March after smashing Saddam, was now watching his poll numbers plummet like a Scud missile. In Little Rock, James Carville was telling Governor Bill Clinton he could be president of the United States. It was as easy as 1, 2, 3, the campaign strategist said. He hung a sign on the wall. It said:

1. Change vs. more of the same.

2. The economy, stupid.

3. Don't forget health care.

Despite the malaise, Booth's poll numbers in the fall of 1991 were as good as ever. In a *Newsweek*-Gallup poll, his peers ranked him among the nation's top three governors. Clinton was No. 1; Roy Romer of Colorado No. 2.

Gardner was about to make a stunning announcement.

CHAPTER 16:

Out of gas

It was October 22, 1991. As they filed in for an unexpected press conference, the press corps knew something big was up. With his wife at his side and cabinet members and other supporters rimming the room, Booth announced he was "out of gas." He would not seek a third term. His eyes were dull. A month earlier, he had told the AP's David Ammons that despite a deteriorating economy and the possibility that voters would approve the term-limits initiative on the November ballot he was strongly inclined to run for re-election.

Jean Gardner looked resolute and relieved. It was no secret, at least in Olympia and Pierce County, that their marriage had long been bumpy. Being governor was stressful in the best of times, and she too was tired. He was just so exasperating. His deep-seated insecurities collided with his ambition and competitiveness. All that was amplified by exhaustion and eating habits that pushed his cholesterol level to 300. Looking back, he believes he was exhibiting some of the telltale early symptoms of Parkinson's disease, including fatigue, depression and indecisiveness. Sometimes his speech was slurred, which left some members of his staff wondering if he was drinking on the job. "I was ambivalent about things that I used to handle in stride, and I delegated more than I normally did. I knew

Booth announces he will not seek a third term. Jean is very pleased.
Photo courtesy Louie Balukoff.

something was wrong but I couldn't put my finger on it."

Jean put him on notice that they needed "some solitude," not another campaign. Her recollection is that they "talked it over and it was very non-emotional....Basically he had had a good run. You know, enough is enough, and it's time to do something else." However, Ammons says, "You could tell there was a lot going on beneath the surface." It was written all over Booth's face. He fielded their questions, then asked himself one: "Has it been a tough decision?" "*Yes.* I feel like I've lost an arm. It's very excruciating....But we've got young people to motivate, cultures to explore, books to read, languages to learn and other challenges ahead of us, whatever they may be." He heatedly denied that the term limits proposal on the November ballot, which he denounced as a terrible idea, had anything to do with his decision. (The initiative was soundly defeated 12 days later.) Booth said he wouldn't rule out running for the Senate if fellow Democrat Brock Adams bowed out. He might challenge Republican Senator Slade Gorton in 1994—even run for governor again if his successor "comes in behind me and trashes the office."

Booth was indifferent about another controversial issue on the 1991 ballot—"Death with Dignity," which would have allowed a terminally ill person to request and receive a lethal dose of drugs from a physician. "My instincts tell me people ought to have the choice as it relates to themselves," he said in an interview. "Then I made the mistake of starting to think about it. The more I think about it, the more I think it needs to have a good open debate and discussion, and I need to get involved in some of that. It takes two doctors to declare a terminal illness. Then you get into what's 'terminal,' because we're always talking probabilities." Another thing that gave him pause was the possibility that weary caregivers could pressure terminally ill people "to make a decision that it would be best for them to terminate their lives, when in reality maybe they don't want to do so at all. But having said all that, my instinct is that it ought to be a personal choice."

The issue was rejected by the voters, with nearly 54 percent opposed. The Roman Catholic Church spent nearly $500,000 and waged a full-pulpit-press against physician-assisted suicide and an initiative to reaffirm abortion rights, narrowly losing on the latter issue. Seventeen years later, a revised Death with Dignity issue would be Booth Gardner's "last campaign."

The governor invited an unsuspecting Denny Heck to a private lunch at the mansion about a week before his announcement. His chief of staff had barely unfolded his napkin when the governor leaned forward and said there would be no third term. "You could have knocked me over," Heck says. "It was a real gut-shot. It was so far ahead of time. He didn't have to make a decision for months." Earlier that year, Heck says, Booth seriously considered running for the Senate. Adams had been wounded by allegations he had drugged and sexually molested a former congressional aide. Booth would have been the instant frontrunner even if Adams had run. He caught hell from the Adams people and other Democrats when he worried out loud about the party's prospects for keeping the seat if Adams or Mike

Lowry won the nomination. Dick Larsen charged that Gardner's candor was fresh evidence that he was "imperious, tactless and politically dumb." He posited that it was the handiwork of Heck, "the Ayatollah of the governor's strategy shop, to give Gardner some new spark by floating the notion of him as a U.S. Senator." For Heck, this was a veritable badge of honor and better by far, in any case, than a "Blame Governor Heck" button.

Gardner and Heck had even practiced putting their tray tables in the upright position. "We were in D.C. for a meeting," Booth remembers, "and I said to Denny, 'Let's simulate a trip I'd typically make if I was a senator. We'll take the red-eye Friday night, and we'll get back in Seattle early Saturday morning.' We got to Seattle, made a speech, then went from there to an afternoon Democratic gathering. Sunday morning I had to myself, but that afternoon was filled with more campaign stuff. Then we got back on the plane and flew back to D.C. When I got there the second time I talked with the 15 members of the Senate who were former governors. Fourteen of them said the best job in the world was governor. Only Jay Rockefeller was happier being in the Senate. Dan Evans never loved the U.S. Senate like Slade did. Dan said, 'Why don't you get another four years as governor?' I didn't know what to do. I was really conflicted."

With Gardner out of the way, a host of hopefuls began jockeying for governor and Adams' Senate seat. The Republican field for governor featured Attorney General Ken Eikenberry, Congressman Sid Morrison and Senator McDonald. Speaker Joe King was the leading Democrat, with Lowry as the wild card. Would the old-shoe liberal rather be governor than a U.S. senator? And which office offered better prospects for victory? King and McDonald would occupy center stage in the 1992 legislative session, giving them the advantage of bully pulpits and the disadvantage of being cooped up in Olympia while the others were busy raising money.

Booth was one of four candidates for headmaster of his high-school alma mater, the Lakeside School in Seattle. He spent Christmas playing lame-duck Scrooge and his last year in office dealing with the largest budget deficit in state history, $900 million. "Very much at peace" with his decision to not seek re-election, he seemed reinvigorated by the challenge. For starters, he ordered all state agencies to cut spending by 2.5 percent. Next, he proposed canceling the raises set for 1993 for teachers, college faculty and other state workers. He also advocated deeper cuts in health care and social services programs and called for dramatically higher college tuition, rather than pruning faculty. He was even willing to siphon $200 million from reserves, depleting the rainy day account to $60 million. That was anathema to his instincts as a businessman, but he saw no alternative. A recession is a "deadly time" for a general tax increase, he said.

Securing prime-time for his State of the State Address, Booth told the Legislature its biggest challenge was health care reform, not the budget deficit, although the problems—then as now—were intertwined. Pointing to polls that found health care to be the voters' No. 1 issue, the governor noted that state-paid health benefits alone were $850 million higher in the last budget year, while health insurance costs for most employers were increasing by 20 percent annually. "Anyone who says we can't afford health care reform has got it exactly backwards," he said. "We can't afford not to do it....Health care is a right." His plan would extend coverage to the estimated 550,000 Washingtonians who had none. Its centerpiece —"play or pay"— was the most controversial part. Businesses that didn't provide employees with health insurance would be assessed $138 per month per worker to create a fund to cover the uninsured. To his disadvantage, Gardner's own 17-member Health Care Commission was still undecided about "play or pay" after 12 months of study. Its report wasn't due until year's end.

Speaker King's Democrats delivered a plan the governor could live with. McDonald's Republicans stonewalled it in the Senate. Booth was furious, particularly with Jim West, the tight-fisted senator from Spokane who headed the Health Care Committee. West brusquely denied his request for a bipartisan negotiating team from both houses. "The public needs to keep the heat on the Republicans," the governor said. "The people must

Booth at the legendary annual Pacific County Democrats Crab Feed in 1991.
State Senator Sid Snyder is at right, Congresswoman Jolene Unsoeld at left.
Claude Iosso © The Daily World, Aberdeen.

make sure their voices are heard over those of the insurance companies
and the medical industry..."

The 1992 session marked the rise of a new star for the Democrats, Gary
Locke of Seattle, who headed the House Appropriations Committee. Hard
to peg, then and in the years to come when he became a two-term governor, Locke's supplemental budget proposal cut 1,800 state jobs but restored
3 percent raises for the teachers and the other survivors. Booth was peeved.
No one had asked him for advice or consent. If they had, he would have
said the Locke plan was calculated to make things even worse come 1993.

McDonald upped the ante by proposing to cut 3,600 state employees.
At the same time, he wanted to give the teachers a 3.6 percent raise. The
others would get zero. The new Growth Management plan lost much of
its funding. The rainy day fund was unmolested. It's "fiscal chaos," the
governor fumed. On this Locke agreed, pronouncing McDonald's plan
"heartless, unfair and unwise."

They adjourned in March with a weary whimper. The teachers and other state employees emerged with a 3 percent raise. Some 2,000 jobs were to be cut, most by attrition. The rainy day fund was reduced by $160 million. (Locke wryly observed that it wasn't raining.) Health care remained unhealthy. Booth used his veto to restore funding for growth management planning and programs to benefit low-income mothers and their children.

With Heck as his tail-twister, Gardner's second term was far more successful than the first. Still, "the legislative process frustrated me," Booth says ruefully. If only he had been able to push through tax reform and health care reform, he says "it would have improved the quality of life in this state immeasurably and allowed us to fund the best educational system in the world."

In March of 1992, Senator Adams withdrew from the race in the wake of a *Seattle Times* article that said he'd victimized seven other women. Booth was under enormous pressure to capitalize on his popularity and keep the seat for the party. Jean held him to his promise to take a break from politics. She made no bones about it: A Senate campaign could jeopardize their marriage.

On the campaign trail that summer, all five politicians who wanted his job promised to create world-class schools, health care for all and a bumper crop of new family-wage jobs. There was a giant pothole in the road to Shangri-La: Another billion-dollar deficit for the 1993-95 biennium.

For the Democratic nomination, Lowry swamped King, taking 29 percent of the vote overall, to the speaker's 8.35 percent. Eikenberry edged Morrison to become the GOP standard bearer. McDonald was a distant third. Intelligent and handsome, the senator suffered from the same charisma deficit that was Maleng's undoing.

Booth helped Mike beat "Eik." His protégé, Chris Gregoire, was elected attorney general, trouncing Maleng. The upset special was Patty Murray, the tiny "mom in tennis shoes," who moved from the Shoreline School Board to the U.S. Senate in the space of four years. Murray was the underdog until her opponent, Congressman Rod Chandler, ended one of their debates with a chauvinistic rendition of the refrain from a popular Roger Miller ditty: *"Dang me, dang me/They oughta take a rope and hang me/High from the highest tree/Woman would you weep for me!"* Having supplied the noose, he did the weeping. Murray took 54 percent of the vote.

Bill Clinton ousted George H.W. Bush, and Booth began lobbying to become ambassador to Japan. Some 1,200 friends and admirers threw him a goodbye party at the Seattle Trade Center, the site of his 1984 victory party. Many wore replicas of the original "Booth Who?" campaign button.

Gardner's farewell address on January 12, 1993, was brief, but his emotion was palpable. Many said it was the best speech he'd ever given. He started with the story about that logger in Hoquiam who'd asked "What about me?" and ended with a plea for his successor and the lawmakers to set aside partisan differences and "have the courage to change even when change is uncomfortable. In a democratic society," he said, "the status quo is the enemy of stability, not its friend."

The consensus in the chamber was that he would be remembered more as a CEO-like leader than a politician. "I don't think anybody ever doubted Booth Gardner was doing this for any other reason than that he wanted to serve the state," said Brian Ebersole of Tacoma, the new speaker of the House. "People didn't question his motives."

Booth's last act was a letter to state employees: "As I leave office this week, I want to thank you for the hard work you've performed for the past eight years. I think we all know that the contributions of state employees often aren't fully understood or appreciated by the general public. I want you to know that I have learned firsthand how dedicated you truly are.... and rest assured that I'll speak highly of your efforts in the years ahead.

"We've all learned how to do more with less these past eight years, and I'm confident that you'll continue to pursue excellence in your respective fields and make me as proud of you tomorrow as I am today.

"Sincerely, Booth"

CHAPTER 17:

The Tin Man

Walter Mondale, the former vice president, got the job in Japan. Booth's consolation prize was Geneva as the U.S. ambassador to the General Agreement on Tariffs & Trade, which was poised to become the World Trade Organization. Before long, Booth would say GATT really stood for the "Gentlemen's Agreement to Talk and Talk." Since its inception in the wake of World War II, they'd been talking and talking for round after round in mind-numbing multilateral minutiae. It was an important job, or so they said, but one calculated to make Gardner's brain bounce. He couldn't claim he wasn't warned. Slade Gorton and Patty Murray gave him a rousing bipartisan endorsement when he appeared before a Senate committee weighing his confirmation. "His work in our state was distinguished," Gorton testified. "He retired undefeated, untied and unscored upon as governor and this is not only a wonderful reward for him as a capstone of his career...I am convinced he will serve the United States in a distinguished and highly successful fashion." Daniel Patrick Moynihan, the erudite committee chairman from New York, quipped, "May I suggest that sending a person to those 90-hour sessions in Geneva is not necessarily a reward. We have to find out what he did wrong in some previous life."

"When I got there they were talking about bananas," Booth says. "And when I left they were talking about bananas." When he got there he was also alone. Geneva is a beautiful, cosmopolitan city in the heart of central Europe but Jean was the newly elected president of the Seattle Symphony Board. "That was very important to me," she says, "and I felt I needed to be doing something that was important to me." Seattle and Vashon Island, coupled with their grandchildren's school activities and sports, held more

Ambassador Gardner meets the press.
Gardner family album.

attractions than an apartment with a view of Lake Geneva and the Alps. "So we agreed that I would go over there every so often and he would come here every so often." Their marriage was inexorably winding down. Booth began seeing other women. In fact, he met someone on the plane trip to Europe. Women had always been attracted to him.

He arrived in Switzerland in the winter of 1993. The Uruguay Round of talks, ongoing since 1986, was giving birth to the World Trade Organization. His boss back at the White House was U.S. Trade Representative Mickey Kantor, a crafty political strategist who was fascinated by the machinations of the global economy. Gardner was no neophyte. He had traveled widely, especially along the Pacific Rim, pursuing trade alliances for the state. In 1987, Washington had entered into a joint-venture with Hyogo Prefecture in Japan to jump-start demand for value-added forest products and introduce Western housing technology. "The Washington Village," a subdivision of American-style 2X4 frame-construction homes was constructed near Kobe.

Across the Rue de Lausanne from the sprawling GATT headquarters, in a nondescript office building a mile from the center of the city, Ambassador

Gardner immersed himself in the arcane details of tariffs and treaties. He quickly became fluent in trade jargon, a chore only a wonk could relish. Through the haze of bureaucratese, he saw one thing clearly: It was a pivotal moment for relations between the U.S. and China, which was demanding to become a founding member of the WTO. Now was the time for the U.S. to extract concessions from the emerging economic giant, Booth said. Yet his role remained undefined. "It's a tough feeling to be sitting out here with no specific objectives," he told a visitor in the summer of 1994.

He was also unusually tired. He found it hard to focus on those mounds of paperwork. It was "a nagging malaise," disquietingly different from the Attention Deficit Disorder he'd long since learned to work around. He was stiff all over. Sometimes he was jolted by a sharp shiver that radiated from between his often-repaired shoulders. When he went skiing, he was disconcerted to discover he couldn't make right turns. He was bewildered and afraid. "What's wrong with me?" he asked himself. He tried to walk it off. Up and down the halls he'd go. Even though he'd had trouble with his shoulders since his youth, he'd always had an athlete's coordination. Now he felt "like the Tin Man" in *The Wizard of Oz.*

Rosalie Gittings, his personal assistant during most of his years as governor, was hiking in Europe with a friend in the fall of 1995. He greeted them with hugs at the train station and they spent the afternoon at his lovely apartment, chatting about old times and the attractions of Europe. "I noticed there was something different about him," Gittings remembers, "but I wasn't sure what it was. He walked back to the train with us, and when we said goodbye I realized his eyes were wide open in a strange way. He had the most beautiful, intense eyes. Now they were different."

Booth caught a cold he couldn't shake and decided it was time to go to the doctor. The one recommended to him also spoke English. That made him feel better because he knew it would be hard to describe how he felt. They reviewed his medical history and recent symptoms and talked amiably about America and Europe. Then the doctor said, "Would you mind walking down the hall and back?"

"I thought it was a strange request, but he was the doctor. Then he sat me down and said, 'I think you have Parkinson's.' I was stunned. I vaguely knew what it was—tremors in the hands. I asked him how he could tell, and he said, 'We've been together for 10 minutes and you haven't blinked or changed your facial expression.' " His wooden gait was another giveaway.

"Utterly depressed and scared," Booth went home and pulled the covers up to his chin. The more he learned about Parkinson's the worse his anxiety grew. It was the ultimate curve ball. He was no longer in control. Dopamine, the naturally occurring drug that had seldom let him down, was being depleted by a maliciously degenerative disease. Parkinson's struck him as a living nightmare—worse than cancer. "I was afraid I'd be a stumbling, stuttering, blank-eyed, stiff-legged human train wreck—someone who couldn't tie his own shoes and needed a road map to find the bathroom," bouncing off the walls en route.

Two neurologists in Geneva confirmed the diagnosis and prescribed medication. They told him it was a disease with many manifestations. Maybe he'd be lucky. Researchers were exploring new treatments.

Through a mutual friend, he met an attractive young woman from Texas who was vacationing in Europe. Cynthia Perkins was 23 years his junior, slender and vivacious. She worked in public relations and marketing. "He was very charming, and very humble, given his accomplishments," Cynthia says. "I was struck by his humility and his interest in other people." They exchanged e-mails and phone calls. They got together when he made a trip back to the states, and she made another trip to Geneva. "When they got him on the correct medications, the symptoms of Parkinson's were pretty well controlled," she recalls, and he was feeling upbeat. They just clicked. The miles that divided Jean and Booth grew longer. He says Cynthia was so caring, so full of life and funny that it boosted his spirits. "She was amazing." He told himself that he would learn everything there was to know about Parkinson's and fight it with all his emotional and financial resources. In helping himself, he could help thousands of others—maybe even find a cure. What a legacy that would be, he thought.

~⁀

In the spring of 1996, however, it was clear to Gardner that he was no longer up to being trade ambassador. Others noticed, too. Word filtered back to Kantor that something was wrong with Booth. In Washington State, a seemingly farfetched rumor surfaced: Gardner's hat was in the ring to become superintendent of the 2,000-student Eatonville School District, 30 miles southeast of Tacoma in the foothills of Mount Rainier. Two weeks later he jetted in from Geneva to interview for the job. "This is something I've always wanted to do," he told reporters. "If I hadn't been in politics, I would have been in school work, either as a coach or teacher. . . .I think it would be a lot of fun. I like working with kids in their formative years."

A survey found that the former governor was the first choice of 72 percent of the district's teachers. If they didn't hire him, "we will be the laughingstock of the state for having missed this once-in-a-lifetime opportunity," said one. Eatonville's weekly newspaper added pages to handle the deluge of letters to the editor. The community hotly debated whether Gardner was a rich-guy dilettante—and a liberal one at that, pro-choice and a supporter of gay rights—or a high-profile innovator with the potential to transform the district "like a breath of fresh air." In the flesh, however, he seemed tired and "appeared stiff, frequently biting his lip and rarely moving his eyes" as he addressed a crowd of 125 in the high school library. "He spoke slowly, often taking long pauses before answering questions, but was frequently funny and always articulate," Michael Paulson of *the Post-Intelligencer* added in an insightful story. He was the first reporter to document the impact of Parkinson's on Washington's formerly effervescent ex-governor, although the patient was a long way from being ready to reveal his condition. "It may not seem like I have a lot of energy now," Booth told the crowd, "but it's 5 a.m. where I come from." He always was "a great masker," Gittings notes.

Adele Ferguson warned Eatonville that he was all talk and no action. "As a man of his word," the *Bremerton Sun's* syndicated flamethrower counseled, Booth Gardner "makes Bill Clinton look like Thomas Jefferson."

Perhaps spooked by the spotlight, the School Board played it safe. It voted 3-0 to give the job to a superintendent from Eastern Washington. The crowd that night spilled into the hallway. The fourth board member, who would have voted for Gardner, couldn't even make it to her seat.

Ralph Munro, the former secretary of state, heard him give a speech on world trade and was shocked. "He was pausing for long moments, slurring his words and he looked beat. It was awful. I was real scared for him." Ron Dotzauer, Booth's former campaign manager, and Pete Taggares, the potato king who had loaned him his plane for the 1984 governor's race, rented a hotel room in downtown Seattle to confront him about his health.

~

Gardner came home in January of 1997 and settled into a condo on the west side of Lake Washington. The symptoms of Parkinson's were accelerating, particularly muscle rigidity. His handwriting began to look like hieroglyphics; his speech was frequently slurred. It was like he was seeing himself in slow-motion. Sometimes an arm would jerk or a leg would kick. His limbs seemed to have a mind of their own. They'd wake him up in the middle of the night. The man with the exceptional memory was now forgetful. He'd lose his keys, misplace a book, miss an appointment. His expressive face—the one that could produce hilarious Johnny Carson double takes, feigned grimaces and boyish grins—was changing. A good neurologist could spot it as Parkinson's from across the room.

Burton peninsula on Vashon Island, where the Gardners have had a getaway since the 1890s, was just a few miles downwind from the notorious Asarco smelter at Ruston. Booth has no proof, but he's convinced the smelter is the culprit. Its 562-foot smokestack spewed a periodic table of environmental toxins into the air, soil and water for nearly a century. Uncle Edwin Booth—Aunt Lou's husband—had Parkinson's, but he grew up in Seattle with Booth's mother. About 10 percent of those diagnosed with the disease have what is called familial Parkinson's. In those cases, the disease frequently has been rampant for generations. For the other 90 percent, many researchers say genetics loads the gun but the environment pulls the trigger. They didn't talk much about what ailed Uncle Edwin back then. It was embarrassing when his hands shook.

Bill Clapp, Booth's half-brother, let him work on some real-estate projects. It was a sweet gesture that didn't come to much because his attention span was spotty. When Booth learned that depression and anxiety were common symptoms of Parkinson's, he was glad he wasn't just losing his mind. The chemistry of his brain was under attack. "I was bouncing along at the bottom," he recalls. "I was dysfunctional. I went four to six weeks one time without being able to sleep." The first time he visited a neurologist in Seattle, he complained that he couldn't imagine feeling more terrible. "If I keep feeling this way," he said, "I don't think I want to keep on living." The doctor immediately called a Parkinson's specialist who said he could see the former governor immediately. "Can I trust you to walk over there, or do you want me to take you?" the doctor asked intently. Relieved that someone understood how desperate he was, Booth said he could make it on his own.

They adjusted his meds. A new drug called Mirapex quickly made him feel dramatically better for a quite a while. About three weeks after first taking it, he felt "reborn"—"It was a reawakening," he said. He took up golf, which was physically and emotionally therapeutic. Parkinson's tremors often decrease, even disappear, when major muscles contract under strenuous movement, so his chip shots had some extra oomph. He became president of the board of Seattle's Municipal Golf Association and joined the board of the Seattle/King County YMCA. He tried to learn to cook, which "didn't take," and learned woodworking, which did. He loved sawing and hammering "because I can see the results of what I do." Working with power saws, he joked, also required concentration. His sister Joan was the recipient of one of his first projects, a handsome table. Other relatives and friends received rockers and clocks. He began splitting his time between the condo in Seattle and his new basement workshop on Vashon Island. His loved going to his grandchildren's games. Gardner also returned to the Central

Area to help revitalize its athletic programs and tutor kids. He joined his old friend Emory Bundy in opposing Sound Transit's light-rail expansion plan, asserting that the money would be better spent on arterial improvements.

On May 22, 2000, sporting a gray beard and his old impish grin, the 63-year-old former governor gave his first major interview in four years. It was with Denny Heck on TVW, the public affairs network his former chief of staff had helped found. Looking healthy and sounding relaxed, he revealed for the first time that he was fighting Parkinson's and announced that he planned to launch a clinic bearing his name.

Booth during his TVW interview in 2000. *Courtesy TVW.*

Next, he sat for an interview with Bob Partlow for *The Olympian* and the other Gannett papers. He talked about Parkinson's and revealed that his marriage to Jean was headed for divorce. He regretted that, but said he'd met someone new and special in Europe. "I've never been happier," Gardner said. "I don't have to do a damn thing I don't want to any more."

When he had goals he felt alive. The Booth Gardner Parkinson's Care Center opened on July 3, 2000, at Evergreen Hospital Medical Center in Kirkland. Key allies in the project were Dan and Nancy Evans and Nancy's nephew, Bill Bell III. Bell's mother and stepmother—Nancy's sisters in law—and godfather suffered from Parkinson's, as did Dan's brother. They had become increasingly frustrated by the lack of specialty care for Parkinson's in the Puget Sound area. "What we needed," Bell says, "was a holistic, one-stop shop for Parkinson's care, including a Movement Disorder specialist and a myriad of therapists—neurologists, nutritionists, social workers and counselors—all working together, to ensure people with Parkinson's can have an optimum quality of life." Bell became the foundation's executive director, Booth chairman of the board. The center now sees more than 10,000 patients per year.

On January 5, 2001, the Gardners' 40-year marriage ended in divorce. Eight days later Booth married Cynthia Robin Perkins in Las Vegas in a quiet ceremony attended by a few family members and friends. His ex-wife got the news from the media.

⌒

Booth and Dan Evans were back on the campaign trail in 2003, seeking more money for higher education. They had attended a luncheon that spotlighted the growing technology gap at Washington's universities. The Evergreen state was losing limbs and its edge. Boeing moved its corporate headquarters to Chicago. Someone asked Microsoft's Bill Gates to cite the most important single thing a concerned citizen could do to promote a better economic future for the state. "Support your local university," he said. Afterward, Gardner called Evans, asking, "Did you hear what I heard—and are you as concerned as I am?" Evans had and he was. "Booth is the one who lit the fire under me," Evans says. "The message at that luncheon was that we were in trouble. The key to our future is how good we are, and

Nancy Evans greets Booth. Dan Evans looks on. *Photo courtesy Dick Baldwin.*

how good we are depends on how well educated we are. Brains are now our most important natural resource. Higher education—particularly our research universities—is all about our future." Still, Evans says he had no idea what Gardner was getting him into. They went on to draft an ambitious plan to provide additional debt capacity to fund capital construction projects at the universities, then hit the road to sell it. They lobbied the Legislature, visited editorial boards and did the service-club circuit—"all of that all over again."

By then, the cocktail of new drugs that had given Booth such a boost was no longer potent. He had trouble buttoning his shirt. His voice was frequently reduced to a whisper. The man with the perpetual spring in his step was now a lurcher. He called it the "Muhammad Ali Shuffle," in honor of a fellow sufferer. "I'll never forget the day when we were walking across the capital campus," Evans says. "I had two bad knees, and I was kind of hobbling along. Booth was alongside me, having a little trouble moving himself. Finally he turned to me with that inimitable wry smile and said, 'What the hell are a couple of old punks like us doing down here?' "

What they were doing, Evans says, was helping create "a legacy to leave for my grandchildren and Booth's grandchildren and the grandchildren of all of us." The Washington Legislature in 2003 adopted the Building Washington's Future Act, better known as the Gardner-Evans Plan. It authorized $750 million in general obligation bonds to fund new buildings and improve facilities on college campuses statewide over the next six years.

They couldn't have done it without another old Olympia hand, Bob Edie. Edie worked for the State Senate for 10 years and was staff director for the Senate Ways & Means Committee in the mid-1980s when Jim McDermott was the chairman. Edie became director of government relations for the University of Washington and a vice president at Western Washington University. With their bipartisan political moxie and experience as academics, Evans and Gardner became what Edie views as the most formidable higher-ed tag team in state history. A progressive three-term governor who'd gone on to head a college and serve in the U.S. Senate,

Evans' bona fides gave anything he lent his name to instant credibility. Gardner, a former grad school director and CEO, had resuscitated higher education when "it was on its knees" in the 1980s, Edie says. "He's the only politician I've ever met who could go to the Rainier Club for lunch and the bowling alley on the way home and win votes at both places." Before revenues went south at the beginning of the end of his second term, Booth had succeeded in dramatically boosting faculty salaries. "That was huge," Edie says. "Competitiveness was the issue, and Booth hit it head on. With the support of great legislators like Helen Sommers and Dan McDonald, he got those raises. Next, they created the branch campuses, which expanded access to higher ed." Then, at a time in their lives when he and Evans could have been playing golf every afternoon, they were back at it. "They know a state can't be great without great universities."

When Edie suffered health problems of his own, Booth visited him in the hospital. They became good friends. Life is laced with ironies, Edie says with a laugh. "I tried like hell to beat him" in that bruising 1984 campaign for governor. It was Edie who helped prep McDermott for the Rotary Club debate where he ate Gardner's lunch.

⁓

At TVW's annual Gala on February 6, 2006, Booth was honored with the Founder's Award. He took the stage in a windbreaker and Dockers and commandeered the microphone from Ralph Munro. His voice had lost its buoyancy and he folded his arms across his chest in a wooden way, but the monologue was pure Booth. The crowd leaned forward, listening raptly.

He said he appreciated the award because he was proud of TVW and proud to have joined so many of them in public service. On the way over on the ferry from Vashon Island he said he'd struck up a conversation with a grizzled Army veteran:

"Where'd you serve?"

"Vietnam. 3½ years. How 'bout you?—Did *you* serve in combat?"

"Yeah. Eight years in Olympia!"

Everyone roared. Then he launched into a rambling story about how he loved to quiz the kids who visited his office. He'd ask if they knew his first name. If they didn't, he'd offer a clue: "Where do you go to use a phone?" As for his last name, when a girl seemed stumped, he said, "What's your mom do in the spring?" "Sleep!" she said. The audience howled.

He said a lot of people had heard he had Parkinson's. Someone was always asking how he was doing, so he offered an update: He'd been taking the most medicine the human body could tolerate for more than a decade. "Last year I hit the wall. I've been struggling since then, so I've made the decision that I'm going to have brain surgery." The crowd grew quiet. "They drill into your head, deep into the brain," he said, explaining that only about eight percent of his neurons were still firing on all cylinders. His brain was suffering from what he called a "leadership" deficit. "The operation will zap 'em, and I'm guaranteed five good years of life at half the medication if I survive it—*and I will survive it.*" The room erupted in applause.

He said he wanted those five good years because he had three goals. One was to create an alternative to the WASL test as a high school graduation requirement. "Every kid ought to be pushed to do the best they can," Booth emphasized. However, many children have learning disabilities or cultural challenges. Those kids need a chance to "become citizens of substance, too, because it has to be hard for a kid to go to bed at night knowing he hasn't passed the test…when all the scores are going to be in the paper and everybody seems to be celebrating but him. We need to allow kids more than one way of passing." They cheered.

Goal No. 2 was to write "a text book" filled with examples and case studies of all the things he'd learned as an educator and governor. The third goal was the biggest. He said he'd gone through 70 years of a complicated life being able to make "all the tough decisions"—how hard to study, which sports to play, where to go to college, who to marry and how many kids to have. "And I think I ought to have the right to make the last decision—when it's time for me to go and how I go. When I got back on my feet, I said to myself that I was going to make a sincere effort to do something more for the people of this state than I did as governor. So I'm going to head up an initiative and we're going to get that assisted-death law approved in our state." He said knew that would offend the religious beliefs of some people. He was sorry about that, but for him it was a matter of conscience and control—"control over *my* life."

He said it would be his last campaign. Most stood, applauding and cheering, for several minutes. But a few people walked out, deeply troubled over the idea of sanctioning suicide. The next morning, several reporters called. He told them he knew he could galvanize support for an assisted-death initiative. "It would be easier for me to say, 'I've done what needs to be done, you guys take over.' I don't mean to sound vain, but when I get involved in something, there's something about my personality....I'm very mediocre at everything else I do, but in politics I'm damn good. And I love it. It's really ironic. My body is telling me to slow down, and my mind is saying, 'Like Hell!' Right now, the mind's winning out over the body."

CHAPTER 18:

The Last Campaign

When Gardner told the audience at the TVW Gala he had "hit the wall" in 2005 it was literally true. He'd been bumping into things. His medications were doing little to alleviate his symptoms. They were worsening. He'd pop more pills, hoping for some relief, and become disoriented. He was an accident waiting to happen. One day, he drove alone to Portland to attend a family event. After dinner, he was tired and excused himself for a nap, adding that he had a board meeting to attend in Seattle the next day. He wasn't sure whether he would leave that night or first thing in the morning. He awoke after midnight and decided to head home. Hypnotized by the drugs and darkness, he went faster and faster. Longview's smokestacks went by in a blur. He zoomed on in a manic daze, sometimes hitting 120 mph. Luckily, there was little traffic on I-5 at that time of night. He made it to Tacoma in one piece, somehow managing to avoid the attention of the Washington State Patrol. After the board meeting, he went directly to his doctor's office. "I can't continue like this," he said. "I'm going to wind up killing somebody.…If this is what I'm going to be like, I don't want to keep on living." The doctor said there was an option, but it was risky—a procedure called Deep Brain Stimulation. Booth said he was up for anything.

245

Booth on Vashon Island in 2006. *Photo courtesy Brian Smale.*

During Deep Brain Stimulation, DBS for short, surgeons insert an electrode—the "lead"—into a carefully targeted area of the brain. Like an extension cord, the wire from the lead is threaded under the skin from the scalp to the neck and attached to a stopwatch-sized neurostimulator implanted near the collarbone. Like a Parkinson's "pacemaker," it delivers electrical impulses to areas of the brain impacted by the disease and blocks the bad signals. Unlike earlier surgical procedures to help Parkinson's patients, DBS spares healthy brain tissues. In April of 2006, at the University of California's San Francisco Medical Center, Booth underwent DBS on one hemisphere of his brain. He was anesthetized but conscious. When they drilled into his head, the sound reminded him of his workshop. The smell was reminiscent of dead fish.

The results were encouraging. Notably, he could walk with less stiffness. But he'd hoped for more. Maybe when they wired up the other half of his brain things would be a lot better. That summer, en route to his grandson Jack's baseball game, Gardner was driving so fast he soon had several police cars in tow. He had overdosed on one of his medications and for several miles was oblivious to the flashing lights in his rearview mirror. They booked him for reckless driving. Afterward, a cop drove him to the ball park. Jack, who had just turned 16, quickly sized up the situation. "Hi, Grandpa," he said. "Do you need a ride home?" Grandpa did. He was grounded for a while.

Booth says his marriage to Cynthia was "holding on by a thread" and it was his fault. His frustration and anxiety made him hard to live with. Friends say he seemed to be pushing her away, ostensibly for her own good because she was protective of him; because she was young and shouldn't be saddled with a disabled husband. Sometimes he was rude to her, several say.

"He was never rude to me," Cynthia says. "But he was struggling with his emotions. Before the deep-brain surgeries, there was a long period of increasing mania that exacerbated aspects of Booth's personality that did make him a challenge to live with." The increasing doses of medication, coupled with one of Parkinson's most insidious side effects—depression—took their toll.

"I never thought he was pushing me away. However, there was a huge age difference between us. In the beginning, the gap didn't seem so large. But as he aged those age differences became more pronounced. He was interested in *golf* and things like that that held no interest for me," she says with a gentle laugh. "So all that was causing strain. And I was hindering him, too, in some ways, from being comfortable with the age he was."

⁓

If Booth could write his own book, he says it would start like this: "It would be early on the morning of July 20, 2006. I'd be outside the hospital, getting ready to go in for the second deep-brain surgery. I'm sitting in the taxi, staring at the door to the hospital, hoping I can get my life back." From there, he'd take the reader on a flashback to his childhood "and all those curve balls."

Less than 24 hours after the second surgery, he was heading home. He felt incredibly better. "All the outward symptoms of Parkinson's had disappeared—magically, medically or miraculously. What did it matter? For the first time in 10 long years, I felt like a whole person again."

"It was a raging success," Gardner told Dave Ammons. "The doc said, 'I hit a home run with you.' " Having watched his decline with sadness, the longtime AP reporter was amazed by the results of the second surgery. "I'm on one-fifth the amount of medicine I was on before," Booth bragged. "You might see a couple of clues about the disease, but most of the time you wouldn't know I had Parkinson's. I am calm. My temperament is even. I'm not hammered with drugs." He said he'd been told he probably had "a good 10 years left" and he wanted to make the most them. Gardner turned 70 on August 21, 2006. It was a far happier birthday than the year before.

⁓

The morning after Booth announced his "last campaign" on TVW, he called Laird Harris, his former policy adviser. Harris had founded a public affairs consulting firm in Seattle after leaving the governor's office in 1987.

"I'd been working with him on education issues, so we talked often, but I had no idea he was thinking about a 'Death with Dignity' campaign until that call," Harris says. "It was typical Booth in many ways." He'd get an idea and run with it, recruiting old friends and making new ones. Soon, some of the Northwest's most successful Democratic campaign operatives joined the cause. Harris, an accomplished cat-herder, kept them on track.

The two national organizations lobbying for "physician-assisted dying" expressed immediate interest in joining the effort. Their cause had met with little success other than in Oregon, where voters had narrowly approved a "Death with Dignity" ballot issue in 1994. Three years later, they soundly rejected a move to repeal it, and in 2006 the U.S. Supreme Court, on a 6-3 vote, ruled that Attorney General John Ashcroft had overstepped his authority in seeking to punish Oregon physicians who prescribed drugs to help terminally ill patients end their lives. At the time of Gardner's announcement, a major effort was being made to get an Oregon-style aid-in-dying law through the California legislature. Having a popular ex-governor lead a campaign in Washington was a potential breakthrough.

One of the first questions Booth had to weigh was whether he wanted to run his own campaign or get involved with the already organized groups and their state affiliates. Booth, Cynthia and Harris attended a getting-to-know-you meeting with representatives of the groups in Seattle in late February. Robb Miller, the executive director of Compassion & Choices of Washington, was there, together with Dr. Tom Preston, a member of his board. Barbara Coombs Lee and Kathryn Tucker represented the group's national office, which sprang from the Washington State organization. Death with Dignity's national organization sent Eli Stutsman. Coombs Lee was a nurse, physician's assistant and attorney. Articulate and attractive, she had been the chief petitioner for Oregon's Death with Dignity Act. Stutsman, a Portland attorney, was its lead author. Preston, a handsome, gray-haired Seattle cardiologist, had been on the front lines of the 1991 campaign, emerging as a national activist for "aid in dying." Each of them would play key roles in the months to come, but Preston's Quaker roots, medical credentials and hard-won mastery of Politics 101 added up to what they needed most—a conciliator and sage.

They decided to meet regularly to share information and coordinate their efforts. Booth came away from the first meetings impressed with his new allies, Preston in particular, but deeply conflicted. What they were proposing didn't go as far as he wanted. Preston was emphatic that the Oregon law had to be their model. "The patient has to be terminally ill and self-administer" the lethal dose, the doctor said. "Otherwise there's too much opportunity for abuse. It won't pass the ethics test." Booth pushed for something he called "Oregon Plus"—a plan that would feature a panel of experts with the power to approve assistance in dying to people with Parkinson's and other debilitating but non-terminal afflictions. They all warned him that thousands of people passionately committed to Death with Dignity would drop out if he pursued that course.

Booth resolved to "keep on listening and learning." In April, at the Norton Building in Seattle, he convened a meeting attended by about 40 people, mostly family and friends. Dr. Preston was there, too. He played a pivotal role in "helping to weave together the various groups and to help Booth understand the subtleties of the issue," Harris recalls.

"I'd voted for him twice, but I'd never met Booth before we started getting together," Preston says. "He was bright and funny....His high regard for himself sometimes colors things he says, but a lot of successful people are like that, and he was struggling to come to grips with Parkinson's. I liked his spirit. I liked Cynthia, too. She was young and bright. I will always remember how she was attempting to counter his headstrong desire to let anyone die who wanted to. She seemed to understand my concerns about the approach Booth was taking."

Kelly Evans, a marketing and advertising specialist highly recommended by Denny Heck, agreed to join the team. She helped with research, including focus groups and polling. All of the feedback was very encouraging. (Evans became Governor Gregoire's re-election campaign manager late in 2007. By then the key organizational work had been done by the team.)

During the legislative session, State Senator Pat Thibaudeau, a Democrat from Seattle, introduced the Washington Death with Dignity Act. It failed to emerge from the Health & Long-term Care Committee before the 2006 session ended in March. Gardner, Harris and Evans met with a number of political people around the state to get a sense of whether there was any hope of passing aid-in-dying legislation in 2007 or 2008 or whether prospects were better for an initiative. Most counseled that passing legislation would be difficult under any circumstances and harder by far in an election year. The governor was facing a bruising rematch with former state senator Dino Rossi. Both were practicing Roman Catholics.

After listening to a series of focus groups, Booth realized that Preston was right. Going beyond the Oregon-style law was a prescription for failure. If they restricted "Death with Dignity" to the terminally ill and incorporated several other safeguards, the pollsters said they were going to win. "I was always optimistic about our chances in 2008," Preston says. "Since 1991, a whole new generation of people had watched their parents and grandparents die. The Baby Boomers were not tied down by ideology....Booth's great contribution was being Booth. From the moment he announced his desire for a law, public attention and opinion was mobilized—and galvanized—and it was largely favorable. Fundraising was also a lot easier. Then Dan Evans endorsed us—another huge boost." Former governor Gary Locke would also lend his support to the campaign.

Christian Sinderman, a campaign consultant, came on board as Death with Dignity's part-time project manager in the spring of 2007. Sinderman led the team through the process of deciding on a campaign structure. Everyone agreed that an initiative stood the best chance of succeeding, particularly in 2008, a presidential election year sure to produce a big turnout. By fall, they were ready to launch.

Blair Butterworth, an old pro who was tight with Jim McDermott, became chief campaign strategist for Death with Dignity. Katherine Bragdon, a veteran of the initiative wars, was hired to manage what became a highly successful signature-gathering campaign. The gatherers were volunteers, but the consultants were well paid, a fact that did not escape the attention of Death with Dignity's detractors. They said the proponents had a masterful command of euphemisms.

Booth crisscrossed the state in 2007, helping recruit volunteers, addressing newspaper editorial boards and appearing on public affairs programs. By fall, however, his inexorable disease was already finding new ways to short-circuit the surgeons' handiwork. He and Cynthia had separated. Their marriage was another victim of Parkinson's. Still good friends, they talk every few weeks.

〰

Sometimes Booth would go blank in the middle of his presentation. It was embarrassing to him but he was a trouper, and with few exceptions "his audiences were more than understanding," Harris recalls. The former governor drew impressive coverage wherever he went, with the "last campaign" hook ever present. To a convention of mostly sympathetic social workers he declared, "I feel that God gave me a mission in life, and he also gave me the ability to think. That includes thinking about when I want to leave early. Under no circumstances should my fate be put in the hands of a pinhead politician who can't pass ninth-grade biology." Most chuckled and several gave him a standing ovation. However, three African American social workers "left the room visibly upset." One said that inequalities in health care left minorities and poor people particularly vulnerable to proponents of euthanasia. Booth said he knew it would be a rough ride to Election Day. Abortion and euthanasia are two of the most emotionally divisive issues in American politics. One man's "Death with Dignity"—like one woman's "choice"—is another's blasphemy. Who was Booth Gardner to play God? He said he'd heard it all. He was unprepared, however, for what happened next. It got very personal, and he felt as if he'd been "blindsided by a blitzing linebacker, or actually two," because he learned not only the breadth of opposition to the initiative but the depth of a schism in his own family.

Daniel Bergner, a former Seattleite who contributed stories to the *New York Times Magazine*, called in the summer of 2007, asking for an interview. The magazine had some four-million Sunday readers. Booth took Bergner to Vashon Island and spoke with unusual candor during two lengthy interviews. They walked and talked along the lane between the beach and the Gardner family compound, watching his grandchildren navigate the driftwood. "His walk was a vigorous lurch. One foot twisted inward, one knee buckled," Bergner wrote. "His torso keeled slightly with each step. He has Parkinson's....He is 71, and his last campaign is driven by his desire to kill himself. 'I can't see where anybody benefits by my hanging around,' he told me, while his blond grandchildren, sticks prodding, explored the water's edge."

"His leprechaun eyes lost their glint; his fleshy cheeks seemed to harden, his lips to thin, his face to reshape itself almost into a square," Bergner observed, as Gardner explained why he was taking on what he called "the biggest fight" of his career: "I want to be involved in public life. I was looking for an issue, and this one fell in my lap. One advantage I have in this thing is that people like me. The other is that my logic is impeccable. *My* life, *my* death, *my* control." But the plan Gardner was backing wouldn't give him that control, Bergner added, because Parkinson's isn't a terminal disease. What the former governor really wanted was "a law that would permit lethal prescriptions for people whose suffering is unbearable,...a standard that elevates subjective experience over objective appraisal and that could engage the government and the medical profession in the administration of widespread suicide....Would physicians be writing suicide prescriptions for the depressed? Gardner's campaign is a compromise; he sees it as a first step. If he can sway Washington to embrace a restrictive law, then other states will follow. And gradually, he says, the nation's resistance will subside, the culture will shift and laws with more latitude will be passed...."

Published on December 2, 2007, the piece was headlined "Death in the Family." The family part was what hurt. Booth Gardner was portrayed as not only a self-absorbed, suicidal shadow of his former leprechaun self, his son testified that he had been a terrible father. "He provided for us, but he wasn't there for us," Doug Gardner, who was 45, told Bergner. A born-again Christian, Doug said he was lost before he found his Lord and Savior, thanks to his tennis coach at Pacific Lutheran University. "Dad has done all these things. Success in business. Owning sports teams. State senator. County executive. Governor. How? He cut corners. He lost his wife. He didn't spend enough time with his kids. Kids equate love with time, with being there. Not with 'Dad bought me a great tennis racket.' My dad missed it. Where was he when I needed help?" Then the governor's son lowered his voice and winced, Bergner wrote. It "seemed part of a strenuous attempt to restrain a lancing anger." Finally, he said, "We don't need Booth and Dr. Kevorkian pushing death on us. Dad's lost. He's playing God, trying to usurp God's authority....I fear the day when he meets his maker."

In 2004, however, after he was elected as an alternate delegate to the Republican National Convention, Doug told a reporter that Booth had been "a great dad and a great granddad." He said their political differences took a back seat to their family life. Booth had never suggested he'd been anything approaching a great dad. In fact, to being an absentee father he had frequently pleaded guilty as charged. He thought those public mea culpas helped. What he didn't grasp until Bergner's article was the extent of his son's bitterness about his failings as a father and perceived shortcomings as a Christian.

Booth maintains he never told Bergner his campaign was driven by a desire to kill himself. He says the writer jumped to that conclusion from his musings about how anyone could benefit from him "hanging around." Moreover, he says that by emphasizing his alleged ulterior motive to wear down resistance to Netherlands-style mercy killing Bergner skewed the story toward the slippery slope. He also believes the writer was biased by the fact that his own father suffered from Parkinson's. Bergner readily admitted in the story that Gardner's plight had "a particular resonance" for him. Just before he left for Seattle, Bergner wrote, he told his father about his assignment, emphasizing, "This isn't a message." Bergner "had been scared that the mere fact of the subject being broached between us would lower barriers—within him, within me; against suicide, against a quiet kind of patricide ..."

On balance, the story Bergner found tangled in the driftwood was poignantly compelling: A rich and famous fading father at odds with his deeply religious son over a life-or-death issue of interest to everyone in America. A great storyteller, he wrote it with arresting pace and a keen eye for detail. Some of the wounds Booth suffered from it were clearly self-inflicted. What the piece most lacked was a second articulate voice favoring assisted suicide—someone like Dr. Preston. When Bergner introduced his mixed emotions about his own father's struggle with Parkinson's, it gave the story a thought-provoking personal perspective. It also lowered a barrier and called into question his objectivity.

Jean Gardner says a number of her friends viewed it as a cautionary tale. "I was disappointed that he dwelt so much on the relationship of Doug and Booth and how Doug was taking all of this. I felt that the focus of the article should have been the issue of death by choice. But, on the other hand, I had many, many calls from friends saying that they loved the article and that they were giving it to their husbands to read, and to their sons to read so that the husbands and the sons could know the importance of a relationship, of a father and a son, and how important it is to communicate and to respect each other."

Booth feared the story would derail the Death with Dignity initiative and create a permanent fissure between him and Doug. He intimated to old friends that he was considering dropping out of the campaign if Doug would, too. "After a week of wandering the beach and a few conversations with Doug," he decided to stay the course. "He came within a whisker of dropping the whole campaign," Doug affirms. "He was at the line—I mean one inch more and he would have just said, 'It's not worth it.'"

The article caused a stir in Washington State, but it was mostly about the depth of Doug's feelings, not the merits of the initiative. Many of Booth's friends felt his son was being hypocritical. "The essence of Christianity is forgiveness," one said. The feedback from focus groups and polling remained positive. They needed 224,880 valid signatures by July 3, 2008, to win a place on the General Election ballot in November.

⌒

With a phalanx of supporters, Booth filed the paperwork for Initiative 1000 in the office of Secretary of State Sam Reed on January 9, 2008. Opponents, including Doug Gardner, were also out in force. Everyone was polite, but the battle lines were drawn. The first skirmish was over semantics. The Death with Dignity campaign was armed with an "It's Not Suicide" handout for reporters. "Suicide in our culture has a negative connotation," said Arline Hinckley, a social worker who would become one of I-1000's leading voices. "It conjures up images of terrorists or severely depressed people, or even teenagers whose romance has gone awry. Suicide is an irrational act of an otherwise healthy person," while "controlling your own dying process is a well-thought-out, rational decision by a person who would want to live if their physical circumstances were otherwise." Hinckley said the campaign hoped reporters and editors henceforth would use "Death with Dignity" or "aid in dying." Austin Jenkins, Public Radio's State Capitol reporter, wryly observed afterward that Hinckley did not address whether a terminally ill Middle Eastern suicide bomber "should thus be called a 'hastening-death bomber.' "

Booth said suicide was "blowing your brains out in the garage," and there was "nothing dignified about that." Other proponents pointed out that the American Academy of Hospice & Palliative Medicine was on record against the term "physician-assisted suicide." Further, the 9th U.S. Circuit Court of Appeals had ruled in 1996 that "to hasten by medical means a death that is already in process should not be classified as suicide."

To Duane French, a quadriplegic who directs a disability program in Washington's Department of Social & Health Services, it sounded like a cross between George Orwell and Joseph Goebbels. " 'Suicide,' if you look up the definition in Webster's, is someone taking their own life," he said, "and when you ingest a lethal dose of medication, that is taking your own life." Unwaveringly civil, French would emerge as the most effective spokesperson for the Coalition Against Assisted Suicide. At every opportunity, he testified to his deep respect for Booth Gardner. He thought he had been "a wonderful governor" and understood his pain. "I love him," French said. "As a person with a disability, he is a brother, but in this he is misguided." The affection was mutual.

French had been in a wheelchair for 40 years. On a hot August day in 1968, he went swimming with his pals. With the sun on his back and joy in his 14-year-old heart, he dove off a 13-foot bridge into a portion of the river he didn't realize was only three feet deep. Like many "quads," French has relied on laughter—and a healthy sense of the absurd—to stay sane in a capricious world. The founder of the Washington chapter of a national disabilities group called Not Dead Yet, he is, of course, a Monty Python fan. "Bring out yer dead," cries the collector of corpses in *Monty Python & the Holy Grail* as he trails a handcart heaped with victims of the plague. But "I'm not dead!" protests one hapless chap slung over someone's shoulder. "Oh, don't be such a baby!" he's told. When his yelping persists, the dead collector whacks him over the head with his club.

⌐⌐

The same day he filed the initiative, Booth arrived at a meeting of the Tacoma School Board to express his interest in becoming the district's next superintendent. The board was conducting a public hearing on what qualities the new leader should have. Before the meeting got under way, however, Gardner stumbled, fell to the floor and slid into a wall, sustaining a two-inch laceration over his left eye. Paramedics took him to the hospital. He left his written comments with the meeting facilitator, who shared them with the board and the audience. Gardner said Tacoma schools needed a superintendent who understood the community; someone with a track record of working with unions, community groups and families; someone with a strong background in assessment and instruction and "someone who recognizes that schools continue to 'lose or fail' too many students of color or poverty and knows that standardized tests alone are not the answer to improving academic success."

Noting that Gardner was suffering from Parkinson's, *The Tacoma News Tribune* included his mishap in its report on the meeting. "Shame on you," one reader wrote. "The details regarding the incident added nothing to the story and probably did damage to this very prestigious individual." Others disagreed. "As a result of your article," one said, "I was 'challenged' personally to seek out an understanding of this disease… Isn't this the purpose of good journalism?" Another wrote, "The man is fighting a tough battle. The disease makes many who suffer from it retreat from public view. Gardner impresses me because he doesn't retreat. How many political leaders are there that truly demonstrate toughness, courage and a total lack of self pity? In my experience the answer is damn few. By reporting the facts you have only made him look better in my view."

Gardner was frustrated by the fall, one of several that would leave him bruised and depressed. He realized no one was going to appoint him school superintendent but he wasn't ready to retreat. He hoped he could inspire others with Parkinson's to persevere. "And I realized the initiative needed all my attention."

～

Despite I-1000's momentum and money, neither French nor his allies were going away quietly. On April 26, Gardner and French debated the initiative at the University of Washington's Evans School of Public Affairs. The event was broadcast around the state by TVW and covered by most Seattle TV stations.

A handsome man with a voice that radiates sincerity, French employs his partially paralyzed arms with remarkable dexterity. He is so alive and engaging that discomfort over his disability quickly evaporates.

French began by pointing to the raging national debate over the cost of health care. He worried that if assisted suicide became law in Washington, picked up steam and accelerated across America it wouldn't be long before "they won't have to use direct coercion" to prompt the terminally ill to check out early and reduce the bill for end-of-life care. French added that doctors frequently underestimate the amount of time a person has left to live. His dad was given a prognosis of three to six months, he said, "and he lived seven years after that—seven of the richest years of his life."

French warned that enactment of the law Gardner was championing could open the state to litigation and the possibility of paying substantial damages to a family member left out of the loop when a loved one committed suicide. Moreover, assisted suicide disproportionately hits those with disabilities, minorities, the poor and other disadvantaged people, French said. "At the onset of any disability, chronic illness or terminal illness people are very depressed. They feel helpless and hopeless and are more inclined to consider assisted suicide at that point," yet depression is an illness that can be treated with great success. French said he got involved in Not Dead Yet because four quadriplegics "died at the hands of Jack Kevorkian." One was 21, another 26, and two were in their forties. "I have to be honest," he said. "If

Duane French talks with well-wishers after I-1000 is filed. Thomas James Hurst
© *The Seattle Times*, 2008. Reprinted with permission.

assisted suicide had been legal, at many points in my life I probably would have chosen it and I would have missed the full wonder and joy that I live now—that is my life—and I wouldn't have met Kelly, the love of my life and I wouldn't enjoy the immense pleasure I have found in our relationship."

Gardner moved woodenly to the podium. What happened next was vintage Booth. "Is your wife here?" he asked French, who nodded toward her in the audience. He spotted Kelly Boston's pretty face, flashed one of his most charming old Booth smiles and pronounced her "a good-looking lady." French agreed. "I'm a lucky guy." Though disabled himself, Booth had seized the moment. "I respect your values," he told French. "I only ask that you respect mine—and I thought you did a great job with your speech."

"One of the values we have as Americans is compassion," Booth said slowly, asking for their patience if he fumbled for words. He told the story of Nancy and Randy Niedzielski. Suffering from a vicious brain tumor, Randy "was ready to die—a highly intelligent man." With about 30 percent of the people in hospice "you can't cross that pain barrier," he said, adding that Niedzielski asked for more morphine when he had six more months of agony to endure "but they wouldn't give it to him." Again showing flashes of his old self, his face grew more animated, his voice steadier. "If there had been a problem in Oregon, don't you think we'd have heard of it? Don't you think someone would have stepped up in the past 10 years and said, 'Wait, this isn't working'?"

Booth insisted that the safeguards embraced by the initiative were more than ample to prevent abuses. Two doctors had to say you were terminally ill, with less than six months to live. The patient had to repeat the request twice, then again in writing. If either doctor believed the person was not competent to make the request, a mental health evaluation would be required. The patient had to be given information about pain relief and hospice care, and it would be a crime—"a felony crime"—to coerce a terminally ill person to seek assistance in dying. Finally and crucially, he said, physicians were not being asked to violate their Hippocratic Oath to "not play at God." "A patient must be able to self-administer the medication."

He said that "80 percent of the people who use it in Oregon are in hospice before they die."

He couldn't catch his next thought. He stared blank-faced at his notes, then turned to Arline Hinckley with a bashful smile. "Give me a cue," he asked the campaign spokesman. "Pardon me, folks, this is part of dealing with Parkinson's." Cued, he concluded by saying that the Coalition Against Assisted Suicide had issued a statement asserting that "it's not a matter of choice," it's about suicide. "This bill isn't about suicide," Booth said emphatically. "It's about death with dignity. Look at the title. It's 'Death with Dignity.' There's nothing dignified about suicide in any fashion."

Hinckley said she had worked with the terminally ill for 35 years. "When quality of life is outweighed by suffering—by intractable pain, intractable nausea and a humiliating loss of dignity," she said aid in dying was the mark of a compassionate society.

⌒

On July 2, 2008, I-1000 supporters, led by the former governor, presented the Secretary of State with 320,000 initiative signatures, nearly 100,000 more than required. They assembled on the steps of the Capitol for a news conference. Arrayed on the steps below were about 60 opponents, including Doug Gardner. They recited the Lord's Prayer, said Hail Marys and distributed "No Assisted Suicide" cards. But "they hushed when the elder Gardner asked them to respect his right to speak," Carol M. Ostrom wrote in *The Seattle Times*. "We've passed the first hurdle with room to spare. I think we're going to go all the way," Gardner said. "I'll bet on it."

Nancy Niedzielski spoke next: "Two years ago this month, my husband died of brain cancer. He became incontinent, had double vision, couldn't close his eyes, lost his hearing, couldn't control his arms and legs, had painful muscle contractions and lived daily with the fear and anxiety of knowing his suffering would only get worse. Randy was very intelligent and was fully aware of what his death would be like. He was outspoken that he wanted aid in dying, He asked me to promise him that I would change the law in Washington State. Please help me fulfill the final promise I made to my husband." She signed the last petition and held it to the sky. "This is for you, Randy!" she declared, tears streaming down her face.

Carefully measuring his steps on the smooth marble, Booth made his way down to the sidewalk and greeted French, who again told him "you're one of us." French said he was deeply concerned about how an assisted suicide law would be monitored, since the disabled were already "disenfranchised and secluded." Booth vowed to use his influence—"if there is any left"—to make sure the safeguards were enforced. French asked why the law was needed. "You and I could do it on our own, and nobody would be harmed," he said. "I don't see it that way," Booth said. They parted amicably. Over the final four months the gloves came off, but their friendship survived.

～

With I-1000 handily winning the fundraising race, opponents branded Death with Dignity "a dangerous deception" and framed the issue as an affront to all thoughtful people. "It's a monstrously selfish act," said the Rev. Paul R. Smith of Seattle's West Side Presbyterian Church. "It says my own will and my desire and my comfort are the only thing that's important to me. The effect on people who love me and or even the impact on the whole of society—whether measurable or not—is of no consequence. ... It devalues our sense of human community."

Physicians said they had seen "some absolutely phenomenal" recoveries that defied dispassionate clinical verdicts that a patient had only a few months to live. In any case, given modern palliative care and hospice, they said there was no need for anyone to die in relentless, excruciating pain. One commercial featured a senior citizen who kept "remembering what that governor in Colorado said about the elderly with terminal illness have a duty to die" and save the system billions of dollars in end-of-life health care. Others said aid in dying, if approved by the voters, was sure to emerge as a cost-containment issue. "Any number of warm and fuzzy and vague euphemisms are used to hide the ugly truth that this is suicide—physician-assisted suicide," said Shane Macaulay, a Bellevue radiologist.

"It will not stop here," warned Sharon Quick, the Washington state co-ordinator for the American Academy of Medical Ethics. "We've seen what happened in the Netherlands…And what about the person who is paralyzed" and unable to place the lethal pills in his or her mouth? "Isn't that discrimination not to let them take their own life?" Quick, an anesthesiologist was an assistant clinical professor at the University of Washington Medical School.

An Elway Research study commissioned by the Washington State Medical Association in 2007 found physicians equally conflicted by the issue. About half of the respondents supported an I-1000 aid-in-dying option for their patients; 42 percent were opposed. While the poll sampled only 502 of the Medical Association's nearly 7,000 members, Stuart Elway, a respected pollster, said he was confident of its accuracy.

Robert Spitzer, the Jesuit priest who headed Gonzaga University, argued passionately against the initiative. "I'm very much against it because one person's option can become another person's duty—the duty to die." Vulnerable people could be sucked into the trap, Spitzer said—the depressed, those with low self-esteem, even "good, strong, stoic people." Well-meaning relatives could undermine a person's will to live. And the law could also provide an opening for evil, greedy ones "who really do wish a person ill. …Whatever it may be, the duty to die looms large and it will touch the vast majority of our population."

After an early-September Elway poll found 57 percent favoring the initiative, the opponents called on Hollywood for help and launched a $750,000 TV and radio campaign. In a compelling 30-second spot, Martin Sheen warned against the initiative. The award-winning actor was a staunch opponent who volunteered his time. "We have a health care system where the more money you have, the better medical care you receive," he said. With a voice steeped in gravitas, Sheen took off his dark-framed glasses and leaned forward to look the viewer in the eye. "It's a dangerous law that could be imposed on the poor, the disabled and most vulnerable in our society. Initiative

1000 tells doctors it's OK to give a lethal drug overdose to a seriously ill person even if they're suffering from depression. Additionally your spouse could die by assisted suicide and you wouldn't have to be told. People who are ill need real medical care and compassion, not lethal drugs."

The rebuttal was swiftly on the air. Called "Lies about I-1000," it replayed Sheen's comments, interrupting him in mid-sentence and stamping "LIE!" across his face. "Disability, ethnicity and economic class are irrelevant under I-1000," it said. As for depression, "The patient must be mentally competent. If there's any question about depression, the patient must be referred for a mental health evaluation."

Another ad charged that a "small group" of "out-of-state religious leaders" were trying to impose their will on the electorate and defeat "Washington's Death with Dignity law." That was the final poke over the line for Joel Connelly, the veteran *Seattle Post-Intelligencer* columnist and political reporter, who bestowed on I-1000's backers the 2008 "Sheer Gall Award." Washington had no such law, Connelly said. The issue was whether there should be such a law. The "religious leaders" line was a slam at the Catholic Church, he said, adding that I-1000 backers had "openly bashed" Catholics "in missives to liberal bloggers" and used "code phrases" in the Voters Pamphlet. Never a fence-sitter, Connelly was usually reviled by

Martin Sheen warns that I-1000 is the slippery slope.
Courtesy No On 1-1000 campaign.

the right, which didn't notice how often he enjoyed his declarations of independence. At the outset of the campaign, Connelly had concluded that Gardner, once an optimistic people person, was now a singularly "self-absorbed guy." For a reality check, he turned to 61-year-old Chris Carlson, a hiking buddy who had known Gardner for years. Carlson, a leader of the Coalition Against Assisted Suicide, was fighting Parkinson's as well as a rare form of neuro-endocrine cancer. In 2005, he was told he had only six months. It's still "a matter of time," Carlson conceded, but just look what the past two years had brought him: "He has hiked in Hell's Canyon, welcomed a new granddaughter into the world, rejoiced as a son returned safely from Iraq …," Connelly wrote. "Will our society accept killing as compassionate when it has the world's most advanced medical treatment, has made leaps in controlling pain and developed legal devices such as living wills that set limits on treatment?"

The columnist kept the heat on Gardner and the I-1000 campaign, quipping that with Gardner's deep pockets they had "a financial advantage that most campaigns would die for." Blair Butterworth, an I-1000 consultant, jabbed back, telling Connelly, "I respect your faith, but in terms of public policies that reach beyond it, I'd feel better if you kept it to yourself." Connelly said that was "a weird thing to say to an Episcopalian."

Knute Berger, writing on *Crosscut.com*, observed that if Booth "thought he was going to be a poignant poster child for difficult end-of-life issues, he was mistaken. Instead of being praised for empathy and self-sacrifice, he stood accused of being on an ego trip and plotting to bring back the glory days of the Third Reich. …Despite the accusations of selfishness, Gardner would not be able to benefit from the law" because Parkinson's is not considered a terminal disease. The crux of the matter, Berger continued, is that the Oregon law "restores the promise of choice, and sometimes that is comfort enough.…Gardner's law wouldn't mandate anything. It's not euthanasia; it doesn't legalize suicide; it doesn't ask doctors to do the killing. It strings safety ropes across the slippery slope to prevent abuse. It permits a type of self-administered care that gives dying patients a choice in how and when they 'go gentle into that good night.' Rather than a narcissistic act," Berger wrote, "the chronically ill Gardner is spending his remaining political capital on what he calls his 'last campaign,' one that restores the right of adults to choose how they live right up to the end."

The battle over I-1000 also raged in cyberspace, a far different atmosphere than in 1991. But if the blogs and Web pages intensified and illuminated the debate, TV was still the medium for the messages that meant the most. And TV is expensive. This time, the Catholic Church and the Knights of Columbus, the leading donors against the earlier Washington initiative and the landmark 1994 Oregon initiative, were outspent by more than $3 million. I-1000's supporters raised about $4.9 million, its opponents some $1.6 million. Booth put his money where his heart was, writing checks totaling $470,000. Other family members, notably Stephen and James Norton Clapp, and the Booth Gardner Legacy Committee, contributed $300,000. Nevada multimillionaire Loren Parks donated $275,000, while Compassion & Choices of Washington and its political action committee contributed about $775,000. The Oregon Death with Dignity PAC donated nearly $1 million. The opposition's major donors were Roman Catholic dioceses and the Knights of Columbus.

Many observers believe the ad that sealed the victory was the one that featured former Oregon governor Barbara Roberts. It emphasized that I-1000 was modeled after the Oregon law. "The same exaggerations were made in Oregon as we passed a Death with Dignity law here," Roberts said. "None of those worst-case scenarios happened—*none of them.*"

On November 4, 2008, Washington voted to become the second state in the nation to allow aid in dying. It was a landslide: 57.82 percent in favor. Initiative 1000 was approved by voters in 30 of the state's 39 counties, including every population center. The dissenting counties were all in Eastern Washington, with Yakima and Benton as the most populous opponents—and in Benton opponents carried the day by only 50.70 percent.

"This is a very special day for me," Booth told cheering supporters at a downtown Seattle restaurant. "And it is a very special day for all of us. This is a day that will be remembered by history." His voice was stronger than it had been for months. He said it was a bittersweet moment. "This has been

called 'my final cam-
paign.' I have been an active participant in politics
for most of my adult life.
I don't believe politicians
can ever truly retire. The
political itch simply runs
too deep. At the same
time, I have come to
recognize the limitations
that Parkinson's disease

Former Oregon governor Barbara Roberts endorses
I-1000. *Courtesy YesOn1000.org.*

places upon me. I no longer have the capacity to fully engage in the political process going full speed ahead, and that is the only way I know how to
do it. So this truly is my final campaign....I trust that our achievement today
will be a catalyst for similar actions in other states across our country.

"On election night I do not allow myself to get too happy. For every
high there is a corresponding low, and when elected governor twice I knew
much work lay ahead. But I am exceptionally happy tonight. The difference? We the people have made law together in a shared undertaking, and
on this at least our work is done....But know that each of you can make a
difference. So while this is my final campaign, you have many more campaigns in you. So thank you again, each of you, and thanks to our blessed
democratic process and the wondrous will of the people."

The opponents said they found nothing the least bit wondrous about
"institutionalizing suicide" in another ostensibly enlightened American
state. The best they could salvage from the outcome was the hope that the
campaign would be "a wake-up call for the State of Washington" that more
must be done to provide high-quality end-of-life care for all, said Eileen
Geller, who coordinated the opposition's efforts.

On March 5, 2009, "Death with Dignity" became law in Washington State. Eleven weeks later, Linda Fleming of Sequim became the first person to use it. Diagnosed with a ruthless Stage 4 pancreatic cancer the month before, the 66-year-old resolved to check out before pain-killers glazed her brain. When she died, she was surrounded by family members, including Seri, her beloved Chihuahua. She left behind a statement. "I am a very spiritual person, and it was very important to me to be conscious, clear-minded and alert at the time of my death," she wrote. "The powerful pain medications were making it difficult to maintain the state of mind I wanted to have at my death. And I knew I would have to increase them." She said she was grateful for the new law, which provided her "the choice of a death that fits my own personal beliefs." Her two children and former husband "were involved and supported her choice," according to Compassion & Choices of Washington.

By the law's first anniversary, 63 prescriptions for aid-in-dying drugs had been dispensed, according to the Washington State Department of Health. At least 36 people took their own lives under provisions of the law in its first nine months. In Oregon, an average of just over 36 terminally ill people have used the law each year since it took effect in 1997, 401 in all. There were 60 assisted deaths there in 2008, the highest number to date.

At year's end, the Montana Supreme Court ruled that nothing in state law prevents its residents from seeking aid in dying. A year earlier, a lower court held that constitutional rights to privacy and dignity protect the right to die. The high court's ruling on statutory grounds gives Montana doctors the freedom to prescribe lethal doses of barbiturates to mentally competent, terminally ill patients without fear of prosecution, Compassion & Choices said. However, Montana's attorney general said the issue still needs to be resolved by the Legislature.

In Washington State, Chris Carlson was Exhibit A for the opponents. On New Year's Day, at the dawn of new decade and some five years after he'd been given six months, he was enjoying the bowl games, still "not dead yet."

CHAPTER 19

Soul searching

It's bad enough that Parkinson's attacks your ability to walk and talk, even smile. Adding insult to those injuries, Booth says it dulls your mind and "ravages your soul." Doug Gardner empathizes with his father's infirmities, but worries most about his soul. Coming to terms with his son is one of Booth's major pieces of unfinished business. "It's growing better and better," Jean Gardner says, adding that their son is "deep, very sensitive and reads a lot. *He's a good guy*. Both he and Gail are understanding Booth a lot better, and they're seeing what some of us would say is the real Booth."

Who is the real Booth? "Well, I'm not going to say that to you. But Doug in particular, he's seeing all that now. The good thing is he's accepting it: 'This is who my dad is. I love him but I don't necessarily admire him like I want to.'"

If you're picturing Doug Gardner as a dour Bible-thumper, think again. He has an irreverent sense of humor and an infectious laugh. When his father's biographer pitched him a tough question roughly 10 seconds into their interview, he quipped, "And of course you'll want to know all about my sex life, too." Surprisingly, in light of what has been written about him, he also sees some shades of gray in the debate over aid in dying. "My take

Booth in 2009 with a photo of the moment in 1984 when he learned
he had been elected governor. *John Hughes for The Legacy Project.*

is that they don't really know with 90 percent plus surety that someone is
going to die until the final few weeks of life. That's where I wish the debate
would have been. But they brought in this six-month window and that just
bugged me to the end. People can live 10 or 15 years past that six-month
diagnosis."

Doug says he also regrets that "a father-and-son rift" played into "what
sells" in popular culture and amplified his disagreement with his dad. "You
go on the Internet and it's all about who broke up today." Still, he felt
compelled to speak out against the initiative because "there was a slippery slope that Dad hadn't examined. Dad says, 'We've put in all these
safeguards. Yada, yada, yada.' Well, we'll see. There are a lot of disabled
people like Duane French who are concerned that the value of life is going to be based on someone's perception of their value—that people are
expendable and the disabled might be the first to go....Dad put hundreds
of thousands of dollars of his own money into that campaign. Anybody
who stood in his way turned into an enemy, and you just can't do that
without repercussions."

Is it only fair to attribute some of his father's failings to his own fractured childhood? "Oh, absolutely," says Doug. "It had to be hard." But instead of turning to God for help, "I think he just said, 'Nope. It's all about me.' To me, it all boils down to life with God or without God. I can't believe Dad doesn't see that in me. People don't even recognize me now, I've been so transformed....But Dad was working all over the place and coaching. He was just too busy for family. Family is a lot of work."

They talk more often now and can laugh together. The tension is beginning to dissipate, but the wick of Doug's disappointment over his father's failure to see the light keeps flickering.

Booth loves his son and believes "he'll come around." He once gave him a homemade coupon "good for one free lunch a month with your old man." He regrets not being the kind of father and husband he "really wanted to be" but says he was dealing with a lot of curve balls.

His daughter Gail, a chipper, confident woman with the Booth clan's striking eyes, stayed out of the Death with Dignity debate. She wouldn't talk to reporters, even if they were from *The New York Times*. For the record, she says her mother was "the solid one," but she loves her father, warts and all. She's now his personal assistant, a job she handles with efficiency and aplomb. She banters with him, but never humors him. When a documentary film, "The Last Campaign of Governor Booth Gardner," was up for an Academy Award in 2010, they flew to Hollywood to attend the ceremony. It didn't win, but Booth enjoyed the outing. He was feeling friskier than he had in months, thanks to some new meds and working out with a trainer three times a week. Old friends were dropping by for lunch more often. "I don't think about dying anymore," he told one of the reporters who arrived to interview him about the Oscars, basking in the attention. "But I always go to the base that people ought to have the right to choose."

Sitting at the dining room table in his condo, which is comfortable but nothing showy, he takes a bite of his Frisko Freeze burger, sips the last ounce of his Coke and looks out over Tacoma's great gray Commencement Bay.

How does he want to be remembered? He thinks about that for several minutes. "I tried to help people," he says finally. "I got out of the office and talked with real people, and I think I made a difference." He believes his legacy is one that his eight grandchildren can be proud of. His friends and admirers, including Chris Gregoire, Denny Heck, Laird Harris and many others who were inspired by his example to pursue public service, say he was an innovative and intelligent leader—a man who cared passionately about education, from early childhood to the university campus, and ended his career in public life the way it began—fully engaged. To them, that's the "real" Booth Gardner. Cynthia Perkins says her former husband "is a person with a huge heart, a person with incredible tolerance and compassion for everyone."

"He's extremely bright and complex, but also kind and generous," says Joan Blethen, the stepsister whose first impression all those years ago was that he was a brat who wouldn't eat his peas. "People have no idea how many people he has helped. He could have become a reclusive nut." He saw human weakness up close, she adds, survived it and resolved to be "someone better."

"There's something I've seen him do a million times that tells you a lot," Joan says. "On the ferry or from down the block, a kid will come by with a basketball and he'll stop him and say, 'How was your game?' And the kid will just light up. Booth *loves* doing that. To me, it's the essential Booth Gardner. He really cares outside of himself."

Maybe he sees himself in every kid with a ball or bat.

APPENDIX:

"Who's for a divide?"

Robert Moore, Booth Gardner's great-great-great-grandfather, was a re-markable character. When he decided to go West with the Peoria Party out of Illinois in 1839, he was "gray-haired and portly." His wife, Margaret, was in poor health and they decided she should stay behind for the time being. Their 10 children were mostly grown. Several would make the trek to Oregon in the next few years, including the governor's great-great-grandfather, James Marshall Moore. James arrived in 1847, together with his 10-year-old daughter, Elizabeth Jane, Booth Gardner's future great-grandmother. The pioneers of '47 were particularly hard hit by sickness and mishaps that orphaned a number of children along the trail. Margaret Moore never made it west, dying in Missouri in 1848.

Fractured by tribulations and squabbling en route, the Peoria Party was organized to "raise the American flag" and run the Hudson's Bay Company out of Oregon. The earliest emigrants faced many tribulations. Gardner's great-grandfather, Ronald C. Crawford, came to the Willamette Valley with the 1847 group. Crawford's older brother, Captain Medorem Crawford, arrived in 1842. Medorem's detail-rich diaries have proven invalu-able to Northwest historians. "From Walla Walla to the Willamette Falls occupied about 20 days and, all things considered, was the hardest part of the journey," he wrote. "What with the drifting sands, rocky cliffs and rapid streams along the Columbia River, and the gorges, torrents and thickets of the Cascade Mountains, it seems incredible how, with our worn-out and emaciated animals, we ever reached our destination. On the 5th of October, our little party, tired, ragged, sun-burnt and hungry, arrived at the falls, now Oregon City, where we found the first habitations west of the Cascade Mountains."

Their Northwest boundary dispute unresolved, Great Britain and the United States nominally held joint control over the Oregon Country. But for those with their boots and ploughs on the ground, the source of law was often ambiguous. Order, likewise, was haphazard in the face of the inevitable "quarrels and crimes which called for community action."

The cast of this complicated frontier drama featured Methodist and Catholic missionaries; former Hudson's Bay Company operatives; the nationalistic American emigrants; mountain men grudgingly attempting to recycle themselves as farmers and assorted stragglers. The settlers soon discovered that with no codified laws practical problems arose. For instance, how to exercise probate when someone died without heirs or a will? Further, their livestock were falling victim to marauding wolves and cougars. Some sort of bounty program was urgently needed. The "Wolf Meetings" that took place in the winter of 1843 were also a subterfuge by the Americans to promote political organization. The Canadians suspected as much but lacked wiggle room. "A good part of the Canadian element" agreed to consider the merits of organizing a civil government.

The French-Canadians who came to the meeting at the Champoeg warehouse on May 2, 1843, knew they were being rapidly outnumbered but stood their ground. The proposal to form a provisional government and authorize a militia was rejected on a voice vote. The Americans protested that many were confused over what acceptance of the report would mean. The secretary called for a division of the house, a parliamentary procedure requiring factions to physically divide into groups. It was then that a larger-than-life character—Joseph Lafayette Meek—plopped himself in the middle of Northwest history. At 6-2 and a lithe 200 pounds, Meek cut an intrepid figure in his beard, buckskins and white vest. Leaving Virginia as a teenager, he became a Rocky Mountain fur trapper. Meek engaged in hand-to-paw combat with more than one big bear and had mixed relations with the Indians, literally and figuratively. He married the daughter of a Nez Perce chief and had several mixed-race children whom he loved dearly, fuming when they were ostracized. Tales of his exploits sound too good to be true. Happily, most of them are.

Joe Meek when he was Oregon's U.S. Marshall.
Courtesy Oregon Historical Society.

At Champoeg that fateful day, Meek bellowed, "Who's for a divide? All for the report of the committee and an organization follow me!" Robert Moore strode to his side, together with Medorem Crawford. When they counted noses, the Americans had narrowly prevailed. Meek reportedly waved his hat and gave a shout, "Three cheers for our side!" The Americans roared. Meek, Moore and Crawford went on to serve in the Oregon Legislature.

Often romanticized, the events at Champoeg hold their own in objective accounts. They "symbolize the entire movement to establish a provisional government" for what was to become the Oregon Territory, historian John A. Hussey concludes. Champoeg State Park near Newberg, a lovely diversion midway between Portland and Salem, is one of the Northwest's most important historic sites. As the breeze rustles in the trees along the ridge above the river, you get the feeling you're not alone. (Champoeg is, and was, pronounced *chuhm-POIeek* by Native Americans. The settlers said *cham-POH-eg*, while the common pronunciation today is *sham-POO-ee*.)

⁓

"Uncle Joe" Meek, 33 years old, was chosen sheriff. A nine-member legislative committee was elected to draft a code of laws until the sovereignty questions could be resolved. The committee lacked a lawyer, but Booth Gardner's great-great-great grandfather served ably as its chairman. Robert Moore had acquired some 1,000 acres on the west side of Willamette Falls, opposite Oregon City. Most settlers simply took whatever land they wanted, but Moore purchased his property from an Indian chief. He platted a town site he dubbed Robin's Nest. Two years later it was renamed Linn City in honor of the late U.S. Senator Lewis Fields Linn, a neighbor and family friend of the Moores in Missouri. (Linn City was washed away years later in a flood, but West Linn is now a suburb of Portland.) Senator Linn was a proponent of "Manifest Destiny," the belief that the U.S. was destined, verily divinely ordained, to control the continent from sea to shining sea. Linn saw the American emigration to the Oregon Country as crucial to countering Great Britain's claims.

Robert Moore published one of Oregon's first newspapers. In 1849, he argued indignantly against "thinly-veiled" attempts to confiscate the Oregon City holdings of his friend, Dr. John McLoughlin, the former chief factor (regional manager) for the Hudson's Bay Company. Robert Moore, his son James and Medorem Crawford denounced the move as "a vile injustice" to McLoughlin, who had assisted thousands of Oregon emigrants. Standing 6-4, "with a dramatic mop of white hair and imperious eyes," McLoughlin was called "the white-headed eagle" by the Indians. In their later years, he and Robert Moore often savored a glass of wine from Moore's aerie overlooking the meandering Willamette. They died a few days apart in 1857.

⁓

In 1846 Joe Meek was elected to the provisional Oregon legislature. With Congress still dragging its heels, the lawmakers dispatched the mountain man to Washington, D.C., to press Oregon's case for territoryhood. Meek had the wilderness know-how to make it there in one piece, as well as boundless chutzpah and promising connections. President James K. Polk's wife, Sarah Childress Polk, was his cousin. Arriving in tattered trapper's regalia, including a wolfskin cap and jaunty red sash, and cheekily billing himself as "Envoy Extraordinary and Minister Plenipotentiary from the Republic of Oregon to the Court of the United States," Meek headed straight to the White House. The president greeted him warmly and insisted that he stay at the mansion. Meek demurred, but the president sent for the First Lady to persuade him. "When I heard the silks rustling in the passage," Meek remembered years later, "I felt more frightened than if a hundred Blackfeet had whopped in my ear. A mist came over my eyes, and when Mrs. Polk spoke to me I couldn't think of anything to say in return." The mountain man soon was the talk of the town.

Great Britain and the U.S. finally compromised on a boundary at the 49th parallel and Oregon became a territory in 1848, with Joe Meek as its first U.S. marshal. In 1853 its northern half became "Washington."

Booth Gardner's maternal grandfather, Laurence S. Booth, a history buff, told a Works Progress Administration historian in the 1930s that Robert Moore and Joe Meek were related. Proof has proven elusive, but if a dash of whimsy doesn't hurt history, Booth Gardner could make a case that he's a shirt-tail relative to President Polk. It is no stretch, however, for him to boast that he is a direct descendant of pioneers who helped put in motion the forces that in due course created the very state he was elected to lead 141 years later.

Some sources, including Governor Gardner's maternal grandfather, the otherwise fastidious Laurence S. Booth, list Robert Moore of Champoeg fame as Elizabeth Jane Moore's father. Professor Edmond S. Meany, a distinguished pioneer historian, says in two places that Moore was her *grandfather*. It is well documented that Elizabeth Jane arrived in Oregon in 1847 at the age of 10 as part of a wagon train that included James Marshall Moore. She was listed in Census records as part of his household in Illinois. At least one good source lists James as her father. There is no doubt that Booth Gardner is either the great-great-great or great-great-grandson of the Champoeg pioneer. Adding credence to Professor Meany's account is the fact that Robert and Margaret Moore would have been in their mid-50s when Elizabeth Jane was born. While not impossible, it's highly unlikely that they were her parents. We conclude she was their granddaughter and refer to her as such here and in Chapter One.

Also for the record, Robert Moore was nothing if not stubborn. When the church he attended at Oregon City switched from Presbyterian to Congregational, he organized a Presbyterian Church "in his own house and employed a minister to preach to him each Sunday."

⌒

Ronald C. Crawford, Booth Gardner's maternal great-grandfather, served in the Washington Territorial Legislature (1875-77), then was named superintendent of the federal penitentiary on McNeil Island. Two years later, the family moved to Seattle, where he became a securities broker. In the 1880s he handled circulation for the fledgling Seattle *Post-Intelligencer*. His son, Samuel Leroy Crawford, "who never knows what it is to be tired," had been assistant clerk of the Territorial House and an apprentice printer on the pioneer *Washington Standard* at Olympia. Sam, who was Booth Gardner's great-uncle, joined *The Daily Intelligencer* as a 21-year-old pressman three weeks after its first issue in the summer of 1876 and also covered sports. Sam's passionate pastime was baseball. He organized Seattle's first amateur team, the Alkis, and was hailed as "one of the best amateur players on the sound." Booth Gardner's grandfather, Laurence Booth, was a teammate. They were to become brothers-in-law.

Sam Crawford and Thomas Prosch, another pioneer newspaperman, bought *The Daily Intelligencer* in 1879, and in 1881 merged it with the faltering *Post* to create the *Post-Intelligencer,* which was quickly dubbed "the *P-I*" by staff and readers alike. Crawford shortly thereafter sold his interest in the paper but stayed on as city editor.

Booth Gardner's Great-Uncle Sam left newspapering in 1888 and made a fortune in real estate. Together with another hustling former *P-I* employee, Charles T. Conover, he launched Crawford & Conover, whose first-year property sales amounted to $1.25 million. The firm platted much of northwest King County and also sold fire insurance. Spending heavily and creatively on regional and national advertising, Crawford & Conover in 1890 published and distributed 50,000 copies of a handsome 60-page booklet, "Washington the Evergreen State and Seattle, its Metropolis." Their preface noted, "In the title we have sought to give the new commonwealth its most appropriate soubriquet—'The Evergreen State.' " It stuck, and two former printer's devils soon found themselves with one hell of a lot of money. They split $50,000 in commissions that year. Sam Crawford promptly financed "the first real (professional) baseball club in Seattle," the Reds.

As a boy, Sam Crawford had learned Chinook Jargon, a pidgin trade language, and later picked up key phrases in the Lushootseed language. Chief Seattle's eldest daughter, "Princess Angeline," who took in laundry and sold baskets on the streets of Seattle, counted Crawford as one of her advisers—a "tillicum." After she died in 1896, Crawford campaigned for Seattle schoolchildren to donate their pennies to erect a monument over her grave. "He appealed to children rather than adults in the hope that contributing to this fund would make them feel linked in some measure to the early history of their city." In 1911, pioneer historian Clinton A. Snowden concluded that Sam Crawford's life "has reflected honor upon his sturdy ancestors who braved all the dangers and suffered all the privations of the remote West to make possible the rich inheritance of their posterity."

~⸏

Laurence Stephen Booth, the governor's maternal grandfather, was the son of Manville Stephen and Mary Roe Booth. He was born in Battle Creek, Michigan, on March 26, 1861, just before his father's departure for Washington Territory. Mary Booth "was born in England in 1833 of English and Irish parentage." She followed the same route to the Northwest that Manville had taken—by merchant ship from New York, down the Atlantic Coast and around to Panama. Now, however, the Civil War was raging. The ship that had departed just prior was waylaid by the famous Confederate sloop of war *Alabama*. It bagged dozens of Union merchant ships and sank or burned all but a few. Mary Booth's ship somehow eluded the blockade. At Panama, Mary and the children crossed the Isthmus by rail and boarded another vessel for the trip up the Pacific Coast and into the Strait of Juan de Fuca. She was the only woman on board and grateful that the men helped her care for the children.

As a young man, Laurence Booth had been a Democrat. Disgusted by William Jennings Bryan's "Free Silver" presidential campaign in 1896, he "shifted his allegiance to the Republican standard" and became an admirer of Theodore Roosevelt. A reformer, Booth was active in the successful 1911 campaign to recall Seattle Mayor Hiram C. Gill, whose "open town" administration was soft on vice. Brothels, gambling dens, dance halls and saloons—shades of the days when Seattle was the gateway to the Klondike gold rush—thrived in the "restricted district" south of Yesler Way. Booth believed Seattle needed to shed its lusty image to become a truly great city. He was active with the Chamber of Commerce for 45 years. Booth recalled Seattle's freewheeling days with no fondness in 1933. *American Mercury* magazine published his blistering rebuttal to an article by James Stevens, the popular Northwest writer. Entitled "The Natural History of Seattle," Stevens' piece said a brothel had played a role in the rivalry between Seattle and Tacoma. Mixing boosterism with his first-hand knowledge of Seattle history, Booth wrote, "That brothel had no more effect on" the "forces leading to the development of Seattle into a world city and the creation of the Seattle Spirit…than the wart on the hand of a boy has on the character of the mature man. …Seattle was never known as Madame Damnable's town."

"Like all rapidly growing cities," Booth added, "Seattle has had its trouble with the elements of vice and disorder, but it settles them in stride. In 1882, toughs sought to terrorize the city. A vigilante committee in a night and day hanged three and drove the others out. In 1910, gambling houses and houses of ill-fame were being openly and brazenly run under the protection of a too complacent city administration. The administration was recalled....In 1909, the reds thought to take over the government of the city. They were quickly and effectively squelched as will be modern gangsters if the occasion arises.

"Seattle, today, fronts the western ocean, undismayed by the Depression, alert, resourceful, self-reliant, ready to avail itself of every helpful influence and to take advantage of every opportunity, confident, however, that it is the master of its own destiny. Mr. Stevens as a writer of entertaining fiction outdoes himself when he gives to his creations the garb of history."

The bit about Seattle being undismayed by the Depression was a combination of wishful thinking and whistling past a graveyard. Washington was one of the hardest hit states in the nation. A conservative investor, Booth appears to have weathered the 1930s far better than many of his fellow movers and shakers in Seattle. He was "well known in club circles," holding membership in the Seattle Athletic Club, the Arctic Club and three country clubs, as well The '89ers, an exclusive group of pioneer Seattleites. Booth was a fourth-degree member of the Knights of Columbus. He also served on the executive committee of the Seattle Community Fund. His suffragist spouse was a club woman and deeply involved in the Catholic Diocese of Seattle.

In 1937, Spencer & Pollard's boosterish *History of the State of Washington* noted Laurence Booth's leadership of the Washington Title Insurance Co. It saluted "his active connection with a business which has occupied his principal attention for almost half a century. ...By virtue of his many other interests in business and civic affairs (he) exercises an important influence in the general life of this city. His standing among men similarly engaged is indicated in the fact that he has been honored with the presidency of the Washington Association of Title Men and is now the president of the American Association of Title Men. He possesses an intimate knowledge of abstracts and property titles in King County which is probably excelled by no other figure ..."

ACKNOWLEDGMENTS

Phil Graham, publisher of *The Washington Post*, famously observed in 1963 that journalism is a "first rough draft of history." From his debut as a state senator in 1970 to his "last campaign," the Death with Dignity initiative in 2008, Booth Gardner's career was chronicled by some of the most talented journalists the state has ever seen. They have left us a first draft that's rich in detail, remarkably accurate and rarely rough. Before becoming a fulltime historian, I spent 42 years as a newspaperman—writing the second and third drafts on the side—so I admit to some bias. There's an old saying in journalism that I first heard from the great Northwest historian Murray Morgan, who cut his teeth in newspapers: "The best way to ruin a good story is to check it out." But very few of the "first rough drafts" I read didn't hold up to further scrutiny. From dozens of reporters working on deadline I was gratified to find only a handful of substantive errors, all relatively benign in the bigger picture—the wrong date, a misspelled name or two. Notably, if David Ammons, Peter Callaghan, Walter Hatch, Bob Partlow, Joe Turner or Carol Ostrom wrote it, you can take it to the bank. From various soapboxes, the legacy of the Gardner years is also enriched by some inimitable voices, including Richard W. Larsen, Adele Ferguson, Joel Connelly, Rebecca Boren, Shelby Scates and Henry Gay.

Booth in his prime. *Gardner family album.*

During the 1980s, the "new journalism," with its emphasis on lively description and dialogue, melded with the best of the old—accuracy and attention to detail. When Gardner was governor, there were three times as many reporters covering Olympia. Seattle had two vigorously competitive dailies. Ed Seeberger, who wrote a definitive guide to the Washington State legislative process, and legislative historians George W. Scott and Don Brazier can also attest to the quality and quantity of the "daily clips" of articles about government in Washington State. It was the golden age of Washington journalism. I doubt we will ever see its like again. The Internet may be *vox populi* personified, but it's scary to grasp just how many people believe that everything they read on line is the gospel truth—every half-baked urban legend, rumor and rant.

I thank all those hard-working, underpaid reporters, columnists, editorial writers, photographers and cartoonists for helping me tell Booth Gardner's life story. Booth also had a platoon of volunteers—"The Clippers"—who employed scissors and paste every day to assemble huge scrapbooks for him. Thanks to them, the Washington State Archives contain microfilm featuring virtually every story ever written about Gardner from the time he announced for governor in 1983 until he left office 10 years later. Conscientious historians know how important it is to corroborate oral histories and interviews. Those clippings, together with the work of some outstanding Northwest historians, were invaluable to this biography. Special thanks to David Zeeck of *The Tacoma News Tribune*; Frank Blethen and David Boardman of *The Seattle Times* and Chris Rush and Doug Barker of *The Daily World* at Aberdeen for generously sharing their photo files. Thanks also to the late Walt Crowley and his wife, Marie McCaffrey, for an indispensable source of accurate and illuminating Washington history, HistoryLink.org.

Sources

Interviews and conversations with: Booth Gardner, Jean Gardner, Doug Gardner, Gail Gardner Gant, Cynthia Perkins, Joan Blethen, Laird Harris, Denny Heck, Dean Foster, Rosalie Gittings, Chris Gregoire, Dan Evans, Al Rosellini, Ron Dotzauer, Steve Excell, Larry Faulk, Ralph Munro, Terry Sebring, Dick Milne, Duane French, David Ammons, Peter Callaghan, Walter Hatch, Stephen Merrill, Mari Clack, Norman "Bud" Branchflower Jr., Shirley Winsley, Joe Staton, Jim Griffin, Robert G. Edie, William Gerberding, Emory Bundy, Reese and Cecile Lindquist, Duane Dolan, Nick Handy, Sam Reed, Margi Pratt, Dr. Tom Preston, Chris Carlson, Chase Riveland, Mary Faulk Riveland, Don Brazier, Bill Bell III, Mike Murphy, Jill Severn, Joe Daniels, Charles Z. Smith, Robert F. Utter, Brad Owen, Sid Snyder, Adele Ferguson, Bob Partlow, Joe Turner, Orin Smith, Sheryl Hutchison and Charles R. Cross.

Historians, archivists, librarians, colleagues, journalists and other sources whose advice and work proved invaluable: Trova Heffernan, Lori Larson, Dick Allen, Robert Johnson, Rick Anderson, Constantine Angelos, Louis Balukoff, Doug Barker, Karen Barkstrom, Mike Bay, Knute Berger, Daniel Bergner, Shannon Besoyan, Les Blumenthal, Don Brazier, David Brewster, Charles E. Brown, Marty Brown, Nicolette Bromberg, Jack Broom, Lyle Burt, Susan Brynes, John Cahill, Jim Coates, Teresa

Cronin, Robert Cummings, John De Yonge, John Dodge, Sandi Doughton, Don Duncan, Stephen H. Dunphy, Kathie Durbin, Stuart Elway, Dick Ferguson, Marcia Friedman, Nick Gallo, Al Gibbs, Susan Gilmore, Jean Godden, Susan Gordon, Arthur Gorlick, Jody Gripp, Dave Hastings, Worth Hedrick, Ben Helle, Sandy Hofferber, Vance Horne, Dave Horsey, Claude Iosso, Kristin Jackson, Austin Jenkins, Pat Jenkins, Greg Johnston, Dean Katz, Jim Kershner, Steve Kink, John Komen, Rachel La Corte, Greg Lane, Larry Lange, Chris Lautz, John Lawrence, Mike Layton, Gordon Lee, Mark Matassa, Pete McConnell, John McCoy, Robert McDaniel, Pete McConnell, Mike Merritt, Bill Mertena, Neil Modie, Lee Moriwaki, John S. Murray, Rich Nafziger, Eric Nalder, Robert T. Nelson, David Nicandri, Scott North, Dee Norton, Mike Oakland, Kit Oldham, Kevin B. O'Reilly, Virginia Painter, Michael Paulson, Laura Parker, Ed Penhale, Emmet Pierce, David Postman, Eric Pryne, Jerry Pugnetti, Kathy Quigg, Dan Raley, Carla Rickerson, Pete Rinearson, Elizabeth Rhodes, Herb Robinson, Mary Rothschild, Claudia Rowe, S.L. Sanger, David Schaefer, Gordon Schultz, George W. Scott, Edward D. Seeberger, Rick Seifert, Barbara Serrano, Kim Severson, Dee Anne Shaw, Linda Shaw, Kris Sherman, Bruce Sherman, Jim Simon, Brian Smale, Hal Spencer, Richard Stansfield, Eric Stevick, Jack Swanson, Cassandra Tate, Roger Thias, George Tibbitts, Ralph Thomas, Solveig Torvik, Joe Turner, Roberta Ulrich, Doug Underwood, Jeff De Vere, Sam Howe Verhovek, Kenneth P. Vogel, Dan Voelpel, Emily Walker, Jeff Weathersby, Robert Marshall Wells, John White, Scott Wilson, Marcia Wolf, Dave Workman, William Yardley and Caroline Young.

Watch out for curve balls.

—*John C. Hughes, 2010*

Four old pros: John Spellman, Booth Gardner, former Lieutenant Governor John Cherberg and Al Rosellini. *Gardner family album.*

Donors

With gratitude to the following donors, whose generous gifts
to the Washington State Heritage Center Trust made the
publication of this book possible. Special thanks to Laird Harris
and Mari Clack, who spearheaded the fundraising effort.

June, 2010

Anonymous

Anonymous

Joan Blethen

Bobbe Bridge

Artie and Sue Buerk

Mari and David Clack

Frank Countner

Robert Crittenden

Ann Daley

Ron Dotzauer and Eric Sorenson

Daniel J. Evans

Dean and Sharon Foster

Wendy Griffin

Laird Harris

Denny and Paula Heck

David McCraney

Michael K. Murphy

Dave Olsen and Anita Braker

Thomas Preston

H. Jon Runstad

Herb Simon

Orin Smith

SOURCE NOTES

Abbreviations: Associated Press, AP; United Press International, UPI; Seattle Times, Times; Seattle Post-Intelligencer, P-I; Tacoma News Tribune, TNT; Daily Olympian, Oly. For full information on books cited, see the Bibliography. Virtually every newspaper story from around the state during Gardner's two terms as governor was scrapbooked by volunteers and microfilmed by the Washington State Archives, Olympia. Reel No. 1 covers 1985 through 1987; Reel No. 2 covers 1988 through 1991.

Introduction

Interviews in 2009 with Booth Gardner, Chris Gregoire, Al Rosellini, Laird Harris, Joan Blethen, Dan Evans, William Gerberding, Harry Carthum, Sid Snyder, Adele Ferguson and Mari Clack. Dolliver's assessment of Gardner ("Booth was a charming young man...") is from his 1999 oral history with the Office of the Secretary of State: http://www.sos.wa.gov/legacyproject/collection/pdf/dolliver.pdf. Ferguson's oral history, featuring her views on the Gardner Administration, is also on-line: http://www.sos. wa.gov/legacyproject/oralhistories/AdeleFerguson/default.aspx. "He could step in dog shit...," Oly, March 13, 1986. "Health care is a right....," from "The crisis in health care," P-I, Dec. 9, 1991. "The Basic Health Care program is the first of its kind," from "State to begin dramatic new health care program," Times, June 10, 1987. "Gardner rated third most effective state chief executive in the nation," from Newsweek, June 24, 1991, and "Inside Politics," Times, July 1, 1991. Information on Parkinson's from the Parkinson's disease Foundation and the Booth Gardner Parkinson's Care Center, Kirkland, WA. (http://www.evergreenhospital.org/landing.cfm?id=577&fr=true)

Chapter One: Booth's Roots

Dozens of books deal with the Oregon Trail era and the historic Champoeg meeting. *Men of Champoeg* documents the role played by Robert Moore, Gardner's great-great-great-grandfather. "... irascible, opinionated and eccentric" is from that source. *History of Oregon, Vols. I and II*, is also authoritative on Moore, Joseph Meek and Medorem Crawford, as are *Willamette Landings* and *Outpost, John McLoughlin and the Far Northwest*. The observation that the events at Champoeg "symbolize the entire movement to establish a provisional government," is from *Champoeg: Place of Transition*. Oregon Trail historians confirm the arrival of Gardner's great-great-grandfather, James Marshall Moore; great-grandmother, Elizabeth Jane Moore, and great-grandfather, Ronald C. Crawford, in 1847. (Oregon Trail emigrants of 1847: Correspondence with Stephenie Flora, historian with http://www.oregonpioneers.com/ortrail.htm)

The exploits of Ronald C. Crawford are documented in *Living Pioneers of Washington*. Manville Booth is described as "a rather dashing figure" by C.T. Conover in his "Just Cogitating" column, *Times*, Nov. 10, 1947. An unpublished interview with Laurence S. Booth, Gardner's grandfather, was conducted on May 26, 1936, for the Washington Pioneer Project. It is in the Washington State Library Manuscript Collection, MS 31, Box 5, Tumwater. Laurence S. Booth's article *Seattle the Glorious*, appeared in *American Mercury*, January 1933. *Skid Road*, documents Booth's derring-do in Seattle's Great Fire in 1889. His membership in the Seattle Fire Department is documented in *Seattle Fire Department, 1889*. The *P-I's* interviews with the workers in the cabinet shop where the fire began were published on June 21 and 22, 1889. Further details about the Booth and Gardner families were gleaned from *Washington West of the Cascades, Volume III*, and *A Volume of Memoirs and Genealogy of Representative Citizens of the City of Seattle and County of King, Washington*. Also see *Sketches of Washington 1907*, Washington State Library, Tumwater, and *A History of the State of Washington, Vol. III*. Information on William Gardner is from *Tacoma—Its History and Its Builders*, Vol. lll, rare book collection, Washington State Library, Tumwater. Also, "Death Takes Wm. Gardner, Pioneer Plumber," *TNT*, Oct. 25, 1938. Information on the early Legislature from *State of Washington Members of the Legislature, 1889-2005*, with appendix on Territorial Assembly, 1854-1887. Samuel L. Crawford and Charles T. Conover's claim to originating "The Evergreen State" slogan is documented in *A Volume of Memoirs and Genealogy of Representative Citizens of the City of Seattle and County of King, Washington*, and in *Washington the Evergreen state, and Seattle: its metropolis*.

Chapter Two: The curve ball

Interviews in 2009 with Booth Gardner, Stephen Merrill, Jim Griffin, Joan Blethen, Nick Handy and Mari Clack. "Brick was the life of the party at 'uninhibited' dances," from "Summers at Burton were fun," *TNT*, April 7, 1985. Details of Booth's parents' wedding from *Booth-Gardner Nuptials*, June 2 and June 4, 1933, *Times*. King County Marriage Certificate No. 112, Bryson R. Gardner and Evelyn Booth, June 1, 1933. William Booth Gardner Birth Certificate, August 21, 1936, No. 146-1936-014241, Washington State Department of Health, together with microfilm of the original, document where his first name is changed to William. Gardner tells his "How I Got Here" and "Helicopter" stories during a Washington State Senate Civics Education program in Olympia on Feb. 21, 2007. It was recorded by TVW: http://www.tvw.org/media/mediaplayer.cfm?evid=2 007020185&TYPE=V&CFID=3245411&CFTOKEN=27106557&bhcp=1

Norton Clapp is profiled in *Washingtonians, a Biographical portrait of the state*, and in HistoryLink.org Essay 7295, 2005. Details of the Gardner and Clapp divorces are from "Tacomans Divorced," *TNT*, Jan. 15, 1941, "Clapp Wed in Montana," *TNT*, Jan. 16, 1941, and "Picturesque Colonial Mansion for sale," *TNT*, Nov. 2, 1941. Mary Clapp's demise is told in "Calif. Crash Kills Seattle Woman, Boy; 3 Sons Hurt," *Times*, July 20, 1945; the subsequent lawsuit is "Norton Clapp, individually and as executor of the estate of Evelyn Clapp, deceased vs. The United States," No. 463-60, United States Court of Claims, July 15, 1966. "That boy cried and cried on the train…," from "The Governor Who Loves to be Loved," *Seattle Times Magazine*, July 26, 1987. The Bryson Ross Gardner and Mildred McMahon Blethen marriage certificate is No. 84527, Pierce County, WA, May 26, 1944.

Chapter Three: Alone in the world

Interviews in 2009 with Booth Gardner, Stephen Merrill and Joan Blethen. Details on the crash that claimed Evelyn and Gail Gardner are from the Civil Aeronautics Board report on the crash of Southwest Airways Flight 7, April 6, 1951. http://aviation-safety.net/database/record.php?id=19510406-0 Also see *Times, P-I and TNT* stories, April 7, 8, 9, 1951. "All 22 on Coast Air Liner Killed," and "Mrs. Clapp of Prominent Seattle Family," *Times,* April 7, 1951. "Mrs. Norton Clapp Killed in Air Crash," *TNT,* April 9, 1951. Also "Tragedy in Clapp Family Third in Seven Years," ibid. "Seattle Woman One of 22 on Lost Plane," *P-I,* April 7, 1951, and "Good News, Then Tragedy, Mrs. Clapp Flew South to Accept Show Prize," *P-I,* April 8, 1951. "Final Mass for Gail Gardner, Mrs. Norton Clapp," *Bellevue American,* April 12, 1951. The divorce of Bryson R. and Mildred M. Gardner is documented in Pierce County Superior Court document No. 113265, Nov. 6, 1951.

Chapter Four: Running away

Interviews in 2009 with Booth Gardner, Laird Harris, Joan Blethen, Norman Branchflower Jr., Jim Griffin, Reese and Cecile Evans Lindquist, Joe Staton and Emory Bundy. Roberta O'Donnell, director of Alumni & Parent Relations for Vermont Academy, confirmed that Booth attended Vermont Academy during his sophomore year, 1951-52. The account of Booth moving in with his aunt after his fraternity brothers stole his non-allergenic pillow is from "The Governor Who Loves to be Loved," *Times.* Booth's encounter with Jimi Hendrix is also told in *Room Full of Mirrors, a biography of Jimi Hendrix.*

Chapter Five: Al's Helicopter

Interviews in 2009 with Al Rosellini, Jean Forstrom Gardner, Jim Griffin, Rosalie Gittings and Adele Ferguson. "The Helicopter Story" is documented in the Chapter Two source notes, but there are several variations. Booth's B.A., M.B.A. and attendance at the University of Washington Law School were confirmed with the registrars at the UW and Harvard University. The University of Washington *Tyee* yearbooks, 1955-61, document campus activities by Booth Gardner and Jean Forstrom Gardner. Gardner's wealth was estimated at some $38 million in 1984 when Jim McDermott and a supporter, Westport lawyer James Duree, were challenging him to reveal his holdings. "Pry into Gardner's wealth called 'dirty trick,' " *TNT* and AP, June 3, 1984, offers this: "According to the Associated Press, a 1980 proxy report shows Gardner controlling 1.4 million shares of Weyerhaeuser stock worth about $37 million today. Other 1980 reports showed Gardner in control of more than 55,000 individual and family shares in Puget Sound National Bank, worth about $1.2 million." "But he said estimates that his fortune exceeds $50 million are far too high...," from "Even Gardner doesn't know his complete financial worth," *TNT,* July 11, 1984. Jean Gardner's quote "He always felt uncomfortable...," from "The Governor Who Loves to be Loved," *Times.*

Chapter Six: Orphaned

Interviews in 2009 with Booth Gardner and Jean Gardner. Brick Gardner's purchase of Honolulu's KHON is documented in the *TNT* of Feb. 28, 1954, "Ex-Tacoman Buys Radio Station." Brick Gardner's demise is documented in Honolulu Police Department Report M47249 from January 25, 1966, and "Hotel fall kills Kahala man, 60," *Honolulu Star-Bulletin* Jan. 25, 1966. Also see *TNT* "Son of Pioneer Tacoma Family Dies in Honolulu," January 26, 1966. The story about Brick's "snippety" little dog is from "All Night on the Ala Wai," 1955, by Ron Jacobs. http://www.whodaguyhawaii.com/rj55.htm

Chapter Seven: Senator Gardner

Interviews in 2009 with Booth Gardner, Jean Gardner, Larry Faulk, and Cecile Lindquist. Additional insight into Norton Clapp's personality is from *Washingtonians, a Biographical portrait of the state*, and *HistoryLink.org* Essay 7295, 2005. "I have innate confidence in myself," from "Booth Gardner, New Bright Light in State Senate," Seattle *Argus*, Feb. 5, 1971. "He said he resigned because of business demands on his time...," "He currently does not reside in the district..." and "despite rumors he might wish to run for governor or other high office..." are from "Gardner quits legislature and MDC," *TNT*, Dec. 13, 1973. Katie Dolan's remarkable life is detailed in *We Lived in the Ghetto of Mental Retardation*. Also see "Katie Dolan, Mama Bear," *Times*, Nov. 14, 2006. Gardner's sale of 105,240 shares of Weyerhaeuser stock is documented in U.S. Securities & Exchange Commission records for 1976. "The state Public Disclosure Commission today agreed...," from "Gardner to open blind trust," *TNT*, June 26, 1984.

Chapter Eight: On-the-job training

Interviews in 2009 with Booth Gardner, Larry Faulk and Mary Faulk Riveland. Jean Gardner confirmed she and Booth had had a "stormy relationship" in "The Governor Who Loves to be Loved," *Times*. "I walked into the door jamb...," and "She and her friend, Connie Bacon, bought a Tacoma gift shop...," from "A very down-to-earth Jean Gardner learns to like life at the top," *P-I*, April 12, 1987. Details of the ham-handed Tacoma extortion ring from "Swept Away," the *Seattle Weekly, Sept. 30, 1998*. Doug Gardner's quote "He provided for us ...," from "Death in the Family," *New York Times Magazine*, Dec. 2, 2007.

Chapter Nine: "He's gonna get you next"

Interviews in 2009 with Booth Gardner and Larry Faulk. "The first must be the very best," from Gardner campaign ad, *TNT*, Dec. 16, 1980. "A chance for a fresh start," from "Gardner launches county executive bid," *Peninsula Gateway*, Dec. 17, 1980. "I don't think the election can be bought," from "Larry Faulk confident," *TNT*, Jan. 4, 1981. "They must be reading the same polls...," and "I'm just a runner," from "Executive race to be costly," *TNT*, January 5, 1981. "To send out an 'Urgentgram,' " and "Parker's actions were 'inexcusable,' " from "2 Democrats scramble for Pierce votes," *P-I*, Feb. 2, 1981. "Which man would you hire?" Gardner campaign ad, *TNT*, Feb. 1, 1981. "I'm stunned...," and "I think it was the best primary election Booth ever bought," from "Gardner trounces Parker," *TNT*, Feb. 4, 1981. "If Booth isn't thinking about it...," from "Gardner eyed as new Demo challenger, *TNT*, Feb. 8, 1981. "He is manna from heaven," from "Senators stump for executive candidates," *TNT*, Feb. 12, 1981. "I'd like to do this for eight years," from "Gardner looking only one office ahead," *TNT*, Feb. 20, 1981. "I won't have a conflict of interest," from "County executive hopefuls flail away," *TNT*, Feb. 20, 1981. "… through my efforts…," from "Candidate contributed $139,500 of his own," *Times*, Feb. 26, 1981. "He walked out on them," from Faulk campaign ad, *TNT*, March 1, 1981. "I strongly endorse his candidacy," from "Open letter to the Voters of Pierce County" by Spellman, March 3, 1981. "Booth Gardner offered the better of two good options," from "Gardner choice for county post," *TNT*, March 5, 1981. "Rich Man, Poor Man," from *P-I*, March 8, 1981. "I think Booth spent an awful lot of money…," from "Gardner beats Faulk," *TNT*, March 11, 1981. "He's one of the most efficient…," from "Gardner names Barlow top aide," *TNT*, March 12, 1981. "If he fails to take on the machinery…he will fail" and "That narrowness will eliminate him as a contender," from "Gardner must control Demos or fail—senator," *TNT*, March 13, 1981. Spellman's quote, "I suspect that he already knows that…," from "Be assertive, Spellman urges Gardner," *TNT*, March 12, 1981. "I'm not into material things…," and "then he drove his Volkswagen Dasher…," from "New Pierce Exec Booth Gardner savors," *P-I*, April 30, 1981.

Chapter 10: Earning his MBWA
Interviews in 2009 with Booth Gardner, Larry Faulk, Shirley Winsley, Terry Sebring, Adele Ferguson and Peter Callaghan. Gardner's quotes "Maybe the kings get along…" and "Now they use only one finger…," from "County 'kings' are dead," *TNT*, June 11, 1982. "Bujacich and Stortini opposed the new charter," from "With Gardner at helm," *TNT*, May 6, 1981. "Gardner considered the council members as 'his board of directors…;'" from "Booth Gardner reflects on his first year in office," *Peninsula Gateway*, Feb. 24, 1982. "He could become a Democratic Dan Evans…," from "An outstanding candidate and an education blueprint," *Seattle Argus*, May 27, 1983. "We have a high regard for Booth…," from "Gardner urged not to run for governor in '84," *TNT*, Dec. 30, 1983. "Booth Gardner. Remember the name," from "Democratic Party sees a rising star," Seattle *Argus*, April 30, 1982. "Like a cross between Bob Newhart and Tommy Smothers…," "Even his most vocal critics …" *and* "whomever is elected governor should hire Gardner…," from "Does Booth Gardner *Really* Want to be Governor?" *The Herald*, Everett, July 24, 1983. Barlow's quote, "I called them 'sidewalk decisions,'" from "The Governor Who Loves to be Loved," *Times*.

Chapter 11: Put on your crash helmets
Interviews in 2009 with Booth Gardner, Ron Dotzauer, Jean Gardner, Denny Heck, David Ammons, Joe Daniels, Emory Bundy, Peter Callaghan and Steve Excell. Dotzauer "One of the most successful political operatives in Washington history," *Times*, Sept. 4, 2006. "Amid chants of 'Booth! Booth! Booth!'" from "Gardner makes his race official," *TNT*, Feb. 13, 1984. "His voice was once likened to Elmer Fudd on helium," from "Gardner crusade…," *P-I*, Jan. 11, 2008. "Mexican bands. Tequila…," "His corporate jet is white….," from "Othello, tied intrinsically to Taggares," *Times*, Feb. 26, 1999. "Gardner is buying 3,000 campaign buttons," from " 'Booth Who?' Gets noticed now," *P-I*, March 29, 1984. "The Booth Gardner gubernatorial campaign apparently has proven it pays to

advertise," from "Gardner gets early jump on McDermott," *Oly*, May 8, 1984. "Gardner has spent nearly 14 times as much," from "Gardner far outspends McDermott," *P-I*, May 10, 1984. "The dual endorsement was a blow," from "State employees split support," *Times*, May 6, 1984. "Duree contends the so-called blind trust…," from "McDermott backer challenges ruling," *Times*, June 6, 1984. "Gardner was delighted to stop McDermott," from "Labor holds back," *P-I*, June 25, 1984. "It was not a good outing for Gardner," from "Gardner, McDermott open debate series," *Times*, June 21, 1984. "It was Booth Gardner's kind of audience…," from "McDermott comes out punching," *P-I*, June 21, 1984. "Gardner was showing more comfort as a debater," from "Gardner must pay price," *P-I*, June 27, 1984. "Nobody ever said Booth was a great campaigner," from "Gardner may not be the politician McDermott is," *Times*, Aug. 13, 1984. "Gardner aggressively held his own," from "Gardner knocks out notion he's a wimp," *P-I*, Aug. 25, 1984. "McDermott is a loser…," from "Democrats flail each other," *Times*, Sept. 3, 1984. "Gardner ignores McDermott attacks," *P-I*, September 3, 1984. "Booth went for a long walk…," from "Gardner energized," *TNT*, Sept. 12, 1984. "$400,000 on TV ads," from "Gardner has collected about $1.3 million for campaign," *P-I*, September 12, 1984. "One of the senator's 'last projects,' " and "I am personally voting for you," from "Lowry, Ex-Jackson aides give Gardner boost," *Times*, Sept. 15, 1984. "Never give in…," from "McDermott: Trying to project a mellower image," *Oly*, Sept. 15, 1984. "And the kid says, 'Bruce Gardner?' " also related by Partlow in "Gubernatorial race may turn on TV ads," *Oly*, Sept. 16, 1984. Callaghan told the author the kid actually said *"Bruce* Gardner." "2-1 victory margin," from "Rough race ahead," *Oly*, Sept. 19, 1984. "The finalists took to the air…," from "Gardner and Spellman take their shows on the road," *P-I*, Sept. 20, 1984. "John Spellman and Paul O'Connor better put on their crash helmets," from "Crash helmets readied," *Oly*, Sept. 23, 1984. "The dark secret lurking in Booth Gardner's past," from *P-I*, Sept. 26, 1984. "Agreed to three debates," from "Spellman hoped for more debates," *P-I*, Sept. 26, 1984. "Crashed the party," from "Candidates trade charges in sideshow," *Times*, and "Spellman and Gardner trade jabs," *P-I*, Oct. 2, 1984. "M. Lamont Bean," from "Donors hedge bets," *P-I*, Oct. 3, 1984. "Like a Ghostbuster fighting a phantom," and "shill for big labor," from "Spellman uses Gardner absence," *Times*, Oct. 4, 1984. "A meaningless mole hill," from "Gardner constructed a meaningless mole hill," *Times*, Oct. 3, 1984. "Ripped off the county road fund," from "It was a gentlemen's debate," *P-I*, Oct. 16, 1984. "Using the union label for the state seal," from "Spellman sharpens attacks," *Oly*, Oct. 10, 1984. "The governor owes an apology," from "Big labor takes the brunt," *P-I*, Oct. 11, 1984. "The volleys of press releases reached a dizzying pace," from "Spellman throwing barbs," *Times*, Oct. 11, 1984. "Good grief! Before our very eyes…," from "The Wimp vs. the Waffle?" *Times*, Oct. 14, 1984. "I'd like to teach the world to sing," from "non-issues questions," *Times*, Oct. 14, 1984. "Brothers and sisters of the labor movement…," from "Candidates came out swinging," *Times*, Oct. 16, 1984. "The biggest-spending Washington state governor's race of all time," from "Governor candidates amass $3.3 million," *Times*, Oct. 17, 1984. "Spellman continued slashing away," from "Spellman slinging mud, says Gardner," from *P-I*, Oct. 20, 1984. "The environmental movement has come of age," from "Governor race focusing on labor, environment," *Times*, Oct. 19, 1984. "I think you're run one of the dirtiest campaigns," from "Spellman and Gardner punches get rougher," *Oly*, Oct. 22, 1984. "Dotzauer…still expects an eight-point victory," from "Debate arms voters," *Oly*, Nov. 1, 1984. "We're on a roll," from "Evans takes stump for Spellman," *P-I*, Nov. 2, 1984. "Dotzauer…delivered a wheezing cough," and "Excell said, 'If we'd had another week or another couple of days….,' " from "Booth Gardner's historic victory," *Times*, Nov. 7, 1984.

Chapter 12: Transitions & Lessons
Interviews in 2009 with Booth Gardner, Dean Foster, Rosalie Gittings, Mary Faulk Riveland, Larry Faulk. Herman D. Lujan analyzes Gardner's new team in *The Gardner Transition: The Changing of the Guard in Washington*. "Most governors are legislators first…," from *A Majority of One: Legislative Life*. "In a survey conducted by *The Seattle Times*…" and "Women in the survey tended to rate Gardner…," from "Most expect Booth Gardner will be good manager of state," *Times*, Jan. 15, 1985. "The Triscuits and salami ran short," and "4,000 cheering revelers" from "In with a bang," *Times*, Jan. 17, 1985, and "No part of Capitol off limits," AP, *The Daily World*, Aberdeen, Jan. 17, 1985. "I just think it's going to work beautifully" and "Dean will be my alter ego," from "Gardner picks his chief of staff," ibid. Inaugural Address of Governor Booth Gardner, Jan. 16, 1985, Washington State Library, Tumwater. "The heart is there and I had questioned that…," from "Booth Gardner—Seattle Times Poll," *Times*, Jan. 23, 1985. "… honor a campaign pledge to spend at least one day a month in the state's public schools," *Times*, Jan. 27, 1985. "He's so cool," from "Governor goes to school for day," *P-I*, Jan. 31, 1985. "Gov. Gardner's honeymoon ends," *P-I* editorial, March 4, 1985. "Blood-and-guts warrior," from "Gardner buddy handed top job in National Guard," *Times*, March 6, 1985. "No other state agency director held a second full-time job," from "Telecommuting Guard General," *Times*, May 21, 1992. "Any talk of education excellence (is) a cruel joke," from "No room in school budget for raises," *P-I*, March 13, 1985. "Hey, Booth. You're doing a great job!" and "We've got a phenom in the statehouse" from "Gardner running ahead of expectations," *P-I*, March 26, 1985. "Macbooth's inner sanctum" from "Olympia Melodrama," *The Weekly*, April 3, 1985. "I'm very disappointed," from "Gardner, Lindquist find themselves at odds," *TNT*, April 21, 1985. "[T]hey just piss at each other," from "A revealing glimpse of Gardner," *P-I*, May 19, 1985. "OK, an A-minus…" from "Grade deflation," *TNT*, June 12, 1985. "An inexcusable failure," *Times*, June 12, 1985. "RCA-Sharp plant a coup," *P-I*, June 20, 1985. "Gardner's popularity climbs again," AP, *Oly*, June 24, 1985. "I'll vote for it," from "Income tax has his vote," *Times*, June 28, 1985. "Bud the Knife" from "Shinpoch: No split planned…," *Oly*, July 24, 1985. "Just an all-around decent, nice person" from "Patrol chief gets mostly high marks," AP, *Oly*, Aug. 1, 1985. "Gardner told to slow down on fast food," *TNT*, Sept. 13, 1985. "You're not supposed to be doing this, are you?" from "Fast-food clerk grills governor…," *Times*, April 30, 1986. He "more or less banged heads…," from "Gardner gets 'A' for strike role," *TNT* editorial, Sept. 30, 1985. "A babe in Christ," from "Gardner wants to help needy," AP, *Oly*, Oct. 3, 1985. "I run an organization that was designed to fail," from "Gardner on attack…," *P-I*, Nov. 26, 1985. "Depth Charge News," ibid.

Chapter 13: "Where are we going?"

Interviews with Booth Gardner, David Ammons, Bob Partlow, Rosalie Gittings, Chase Riveland, Mary Faulk Riveland and Chris Gregoire. "Goltz calls him 'The Cabbage Patch Governor'…," from "Gardner's first year reviewed," *Oly*, Dec. 2, 1985. "Declaring that taxpayers either will pay now or pay later…" and "Education is like no other box on the budget scorecard…," from "Education reforms," *TNT*, Dec. 15, 1986. "Turn the clock back to the era of pork barrel politics …," from "New GOP assault on plan to revamp bureaucracy," *TNT*, Dec. 21, 1986. "It will happen to this guy too …," from "Gardner wants to corral state's game department," *P-I*, Dec. 18, 1985. "People would say I must have married you for your money…," from "For 'Walkaround Booth,' " *Oly*, Dec. 22, 1985. "My administration will not tolerate discrimination," from "Gardner order allows state's hiring of gays," AP, *TNT*, Dec. 25, 1985. Gay rights stand costing him "any prospects of re-election in 1988," from "Gardner's bias ban draws fire," *Oly*, Dec. 25, 1985. "A cross-burning," from "Gardner calls for state campaign…," *Times*, Oct. 24, 1990. "I fully intend to go for two terms," from "Gardner says he'll seek a second term," UPI, *P-I*, Dec. 28, 1985. "Puget Sound, if left alone, will flush itself," from "Dixy says," *TNT*, Jan. 27. 1986. "It's time for me to retire and I've retired," from "Penal approach…," *P-I*, Jan. 22, 1986. "…he is showing signs of metamorphosis," from "Gov. Nice turning into Gov. Tough," *TNT*, Feb. 9, 1986. "…by God you'd think the world was coming to an end," from "Maxed out," *Oly*, Feb. 10, 1986. "The buck should stop …," from "Reorganization gets mixed reviews," AP, *Oly*, Feb. 11, 1986. "He has the ability to twist your arm without it hurting," from "They've done the big things," *Oly*, March 13, 1986. "I really think the tort system has gone too far," from "Gardner signs liability bill," AP, *Oly*, April 5, 1986. "…just meat and potatoes" and "It's the most massive reorganization…," from "DSHS shakeup," *Times*, May, 1986. "An income tax would require bipartisan support," from "Gardner rejects income tax," *Oly*, June 19, 1986. "Bob Williams would be able to fill two hours of the governor's time…," from "Gardner runs for cover," *P-I*, June 20, 1986. "Isn't going to set us back a lick," from "Economy state's most important issue," *P-I*, Aug. 14, 1986. "A 'Slim' majority," from "State Senate…" *TNT*, Nov. 5, 1986. "He really took the gloves off," from " 'Captain' Gardner is big winner," *Times*, Nov. 9, 1986. "If we don't win this one, we're incompetent," from "Booth Gardner among big winners," AP, *Oly*, Nov. 9, 1986. "…unalterably opposed" to Booth's salary plan, from "Pump $330 million more into schools," *TNT*, Nov. 19, 1986. "…a grinning, vacuous handshaker," from Larsen column, *Times*, Nov. 21, 1986.

Chapter 14: Taxing times

Interviews with Booth Gardner, Dean Foster, Denny Heck, Orin Smith, Walter Hatch, Adele Ferguson, Peter Callaghan, Mike Murphy, Cecile Lindquist, Charles Z. Smith, Gerry Alexander and Terry Sebring. "The future of the state is a lot more important…" from "Gardner to stake his all on education," UPI, *Oly*, Dec. 29, 1986. "He was so persistent that many considered him a pain in the neck," from "A Gardner critic," *P-I*, Jan. 29, 1987. "The staff still has a certain apprehension about Greg…," from "Gardner adds long-time adviser to staff," *TNT*, Feb. 19, 1987. "This isn't a career, it's an experience," from "Gardner shakes up administration," *Oly*, June 9, 1987. "Oliver North with a conscience…," from "Critics charge Gardner's management style, staff ineffective," *Oly*, March 15, 1987. "Well, here comes Rambo," from "Rambo back to rescue Gov.," *Olympia News*, March 5, 1987. "Republicans have a credible candidate," from "Governor's race lures prosecutor," *Oly*, May 21, 1987. "There has been tension between Smith and Barlow…," from "Orin Smith resigns," *P-I*, June 9, 1987. "Nothing in the Ray or Spellman administrations compares…," from "New budget boss…," *Times*, June 9, 1987. "If I were to pick the moment…," from "McDermott savors a political triumph," *Times*, June 11, 1987. "Loquacious Williams spices governor's race," AP, *Oly*, Sept. 14, 1987. "Governor Booth Gardner showed he can make a tough decision ….," from "Special legislative session is justified," *Times*, Oct. 5, 1987. "Pollsters hired by both parties," from "Polls agree: Gardner is popular," *P-I*, Dec. 4, 1987. "Skimpy revenues in a supplemental budget year," from "Gardner must be Scrooge," AP, *Oly*, Dec. 11, 1987. "I am committed to this job for eight years," from "Gardner: No plans to run for Senate…," UPI, *P-I*, Dec. 12, 1987. "It's the way I come off," from "Gardner's weak image," *Oly*, January 1988. "Vote for just a nice guy…," from "Maleng hopes to conquer Mount Gardner," AP, *Oly*, Jan. 18, 1988. "…the poor, homeless, hungry…," from "While they wined and dined," *Oly*, Jan. 18, 1988. "One of the first polls…" from "Gardner, Gorton head state poll," *TNT*, March 7, 1988. "What's this person doing in the Department of Ecology?" from "New state ecology chief's lack of track record…," *Times*, March 25, 1988. "Booth Gardner ranks right up there…," from "Gardner's petty, peevish campaign kickoff," *Times*, May 8, 1988. "…you can take a UBC diploma…," from "Governor's words insulted college…," letter to editor, *Times*, June 7, 1988. "We all have our character flaws…," from "Gardner requests an official pardon," *P-I*, June 21, 1988. "In short, the honeymoon's over…," from "The Guv is less loved by a less impressed press," *Seattle Weekly*, June 22, 1988. "Katie Dolan also encountered 'the tendency,' " from *We Lived in the Ghetto of Mental Retardation*. "Gardner made history" by appointing Smith, from Charles Z. Smith, oral history by The Legacy Project, and *Carl Maxey, A Fighting Life*. "Smokers howled …," from "Gardner imposes smoking ban," *Oly*, Aug. 29, 1988. "Dixy Lee Ray visited the Tri-Cities," from "Former Gov. Ray endorses Williams," AP, *TNT*, Oct. 15, 1988. "Last week, Williams staged an 'empty chair' debate…," from "Laughs counter the long odds in Williams campaign," *Times*, Oct. 17, 1988. "Like a flea boring in on a sleeping dog," from GOP challenger comes out snarling," *Times*, October, 1988.

Chapter 15: Tough choices

Interviews with Booth Gardner, Dean Foster, Denny Heck, Jill Severn, Peter Callaghan, Ralph Munro and Jean Gardner. "The Centennial Challenge," Governor Booth Gardner's Second Inaugural Address, Jan. 11, 1989, Washington State Library, Tumwater. "…the day the world turned upside down," from *On The Harbor, From Black Friday to Nirvana*. Also see "Gardner appeals to president on behalf of NW timber towns," *Times*, May 30, 1990. "Blame Governor Heck" buttons mentioned in "Gardner's men: images-builders—or busters?" *TNT*, April 30, 1989. "Booth shot down nearly 18 percent of the bills," and his overall veto, from *Sine Die, A Guide to the Washington State Legislative Process*. "Teachers demanded a 10 percent raise," from "All Eyes Focus on Surplus," *Times*, Jan. 8, 1990. "No more hot air!" from *Class Wars*. "Called for limitations on log exports," from "Gardner, Boyle take new stands," *Times*, May 1, 1990. "As the only African American in Gardner's cabinet…" and "saddened and heartsick," from "Gardner criticized over Turner," *Times*, Oct. 16, 1990. Turner "had misused at least $14,000 of state money for travel and telephone expenses," AP, *Times*, Oct. 23, 1990. "This state has lost the best employment-security director it has ever had," from "Gardner calls Turner a friend, mentor," *Times*, Nov. 4, 1990. "...Gardner pronounced Isiah Turner the greatest commissioner in the history of the agency," from "La Palm's firing official," *Times*, Dec. 29, 1990. "I think it's time again for Washingtonians to take stock of their future," from "$1 billion sought to finance growth," AP, *Oly*, Feb. 27, 1991. "Dad, if the president can solve...," from "State teachers strike hits close to home," AP, *Times*, April 20, 1991. "I know the diatribe...," from "Political Adventures, Chapter III, Prince Faintheart," *Times*, Feb. 3, 1991. "I'm fed up with the feds," from "Governor urges regional authority," *The Daily World*, Aberdeen, May 9, 1991. "Good ideas are at work out there in the state of Washington...," from "President Borrows School-reform plan," *Times*, July 9, 1991. "... to crack down on predatory sex offenders," from "Gardner halted an emotional stampede," *TNT*, June 11, 1989. "I'm willing to admit I was wrong. I was naïve...," from "Former governor now opposing WASL test for diploma," *Times*, Dec. 9, 2005. "The economy of our state is directly tied to quality of our institutions of higher education...," from "Ex-governors' higher-ed plan is a tough sell," *Times*, Dec. 11, 2002. "A great leader 'for Indians and non-Indians alike,' " from "State's tribes honor Gardner," AP, *Times*, Jan. 19, 1992.

Chapter 16: Out of gas
Interviews with Booth Gardner, Jean Gardner and Denny Heck. "I feel like I've lost an arm," from "Gardner won't seek third term," AP, *Spokesman-Review*, Oct. 23, 1991. "My instincts tell me people ought to have the choice as it relates to themselves," from "Gardner wants abortion, aid-in-dying votes," AP, *Times*, Jan. 23, 1991. "Booth was one of four candidates for headmaster," from "Governor as principal?" *Times*, Nov. 7, 1991. "Anyone who says we can't afford health care reform...," from "Gardner to emphasize health care reform," AP, *Oly*, Jan. 13, 1992. "A Senate campaign could jeopardize their marriage," from "Jean pulled Booth from the race," AP, *Longview Daily News*, published in *Ellensburg Daily Record*, June 20, 1992. "In short, Booth Gardner, for all his charm, is widely regarded as an airhead," from "Gardner would make a poor choice for Clinton Cabinet," *Valley Daily News*, Kent, July 23, 1992. "...Gardner has been lobbying for an ambassadorship" and "Dicks wryly told the crowd that Gardner has begun Japanese lessons," AP, Nov. 24, 1992. "Gardner's spokeswoman says he has shown little interest in a Cabinet post" and "Gardner's wife, Jean, doesn't want to live in Washington, D.C.," *Times*, Dec. 3, 1992. "Coal for Christmas: Cutbacks and tax increases," AP, *Times*, Dec. 13, 1992. "Many said it was the best speech he'd ever given" and "I don't think anybody doubted Booth Gardner," from "Gardner's farewell is a call to change," *Times*, Jan. 13, 1993.

Chapter 17: The Tin Man
Interviews with Booth Gardner, Bill Bell III, Denny Heck, Cynthia Perkins Gardner, Dan Evans, Bob Edie and William Gerberding. "We have to find out what he did wrong...." Statements by Daniel Patrick Moynihan, Slade Gorton and Patty Murray, U.S. Senate Committee on Finance March 16, 1994, "on the nominations of W. Booth Gardner and Lynn M. Bragg," U.S. Government Printing Office, ISBN 0-16-044328-8. "It's a tough feeling to be sitting out here with no specific objectives," from "Beyond

GATT—Ambassador Booth Gardner…," *Times*, July 31, 1994. Also sets scene in Geneva and describes Gardner's office building. "He's convinced the smelter is the culprit," amplified by "Asarco tried to shirk cleanup," *TNT*, Dec. 28, 2009. "The week's hottest rumor…," from "Back to school for ex-Gov. Booth Gardner?" *Political Notebook*, *Times*, March 31, 1996. "I think it would be a lot of fun…," from "Gardner jets in for school-job interview," AP, *Times*, April 15, 1996. "Last night, Gardner appeared stiff…" and "it's 5 a.m. where I come from…," from "Former governor wants to go to head of the classes," *P-I*, April 23, 1996. "We will be the laughingstock of the state…," "I guess he had a lot of jet lag or something…," and "A survey of 89 of the district's 115 teachers…," from "Town Gives Gardner Mixed Grades," *Times*, May 2, 1996. Same story quotes Adele Ferguson: "Booth Gardner, as a man of his word, makes Bill Clinton look like Thomas Jefferson." TVW interview of Booth Gardner by Denny Heck, May 22, 2000: http://www.tvw.org/media/mediaplayer.cfm?evid=2000050079&TYPE=V&CFID=3245411&CFTOKEN=27106557&bhcp=1

"I was bouncing along at the bottom…," from "Ex-governor crafts a new life," *Oly*, May 30, 2000. William Booth Gardner and Jean F. Gardner divorce, Jan. 5, 2001, Washington State Library Divorce Records Index 1968-2004, No. 717 1 027481. Marriage certificate for Booth Gardner and Cynthia Robin Perkins, Jan. 13, 2001, Nevada Marriage Index, Book 117, Page D269554. "In a quiet Las Vegas ceremony…," from "Ex-Gov. ties knot," *Times*, Feb. 21, 2001. "The Muhammad Ali shuffle…," "I literally bounce off the walls…," "I was real scared for him…" and "rented a room …for an intervention," from "Former governor wages active fight against disease," *P-I*, June 10, 2003.

Chapter 18: The Last Campaign
Interviews in 2009 with Booth Gardner, Doug Gardner, Jean Gardner, Duane French, Laird Harris, Cynthia Perkins, Denny Heck, Dr. Tom Preston and Chris Carlson. "He's been a great dad and a great granddad," from "Ex-governor's acorn fell far from the tree," *TNT*, Sept. 1, 2004. "It was a raging success…," "He had run out of gas…," "His marriage to Cynthia Gardner broke up…" and "He said he's been told he has 'a good 10 years left,' " from "Gardner mending after brain surgery," AP, *P-I*, Oct. 18, 2006. "He has hit the wall…," "I don't mean to sound vain…," and "My body is telling me to slow down…," all from "Gardner: I've thought about the end," *Times*, Feb. 10, 2006. "Death in the Family," *New York Times Magazine*, Dec. 2, 2007, is the source for important quotes in this chapter, including: "I can't see where anybody benefits by my hanging around," "I fear the day when he meets his maker," and "Dad's lost …" Parkinson's "ravages your soul" and "That's not dignity," from "Washington State Right-to-Die cause finds champion," *Oregonian*, March 26, 2006. Three African American social workers "left the room visibly upset," from "Seeking death with dignity," *P-I*, May 18, 2007. Gardner's stumble and fall just before the start of a Tacoma School Board meeting from "Ex-governor interested in school jobs," *TNT*, Jan. 10, 2008. Reader reactions to "Was our Booth Gardner story out of line?" from *thenewstribune.com*, Jan. 11, 2008. "Oh, my, what a self-absorbed guy," from "Gardner crusade is a selfish last act," *P-I*, Jan. 11, 2008. "…hastening-death bomber," from "Unlike father, unlike son…," *crosscut.com*, Jan. 11, 2008. "Despite the accusations of selfishness…," from "Booth Gardner's campaign is

selfless," *crosscut.com*, April 5, 2008. TVW coverage of the April 26, 2008, Death with Dignity debate between Booth Gardner and Duane French:http://www.tvw.org/media/mediaplayer.cfm?evid=2008040112&TYPE=V&CFID=3389892&CFTOKEN=81964608&bhcp=1. "A row of about 60 people…repeated the Lord's Prayer and Hail Mary's," and "I don't see it that way…," from "Death Initiative petitions filed," *Times*, July 3, 2008. "An Elway Research study," from "Doctors divided on assisted suicide," *Times*, Sept. 22, 2008. "An early-September Elway poll …," from "Polls show Washington voters favor physician-assisted suicide," *American Medical News*, Oct. 27, 2008. "There is no 'Washington's death-with-dignity law,' " from "I-1000 wins year's 'Sheer Gall Award,' " *P-I*, Nov. 2, 2008. Gardner's victory speech, "My feelings…are bittersweet," from "Political Buzz," *thenewstribune.com*, Nov. 5, 2008. Contributions to Initiative 1000 reported by *InternationalTaskForce.org* and the Washington State Public Disclosure Commission. "Initiative supporters raised about $4.9 million…," from "Assisted suicide measure passes," *Times*, Nov. 4, 2008. Results of the Nov. 4, 2008, General Election from the Washington Secretary of State http://www.sos.wa.gov/elections/ "I am a very spiritual person," from "First death for Washington assisted-suicide law," *The New York Times*, May 22, 2009, and "Choosing when to die…," *Times*, May 23, 2009.

Links to statements regarding Initiative 1000:

http://www.youtube.com/watch?v=EKXPBpGW2Fw http://www.youtube.com/watch?v=zGLaZmOZFxo&feature=related http://www.youtube.com/watch?v=1uTR_-abXnQ&feature=related

http://www.youtube.com/watch?v=B38MSTeJhSo&feature=related

http://www.youtube.com/watch?v=rycDlqAOGAM&feature=related

Chapter 19: Soul searching

Interviews in 2009 and 2010 with Booth Gardner, Jean Gardner, Doug Gardner, Cynthia Perkins Gardner, Joan Blethen, Chris Gregoire, Denny Heck and Laird Harris. "I don't think about dying anymore," from "The Last Campaign of Governor Booth Gardner," *TNT*, March 5, 2010.

Appendix: "Who's for a divide?"

Sources covered in Chapter One notes.

BIBLIOGRAPHY

Books, articles and manuscripts:

Andrews, Ralph W., *Historic Fires of the West*, Bonanza Books, New York, 1966

Bancroft, Hubert Howe, *History of Oregon, Vols. I and II*, The History Company, San Francisco, 1888

Barker, Doug, *The Spotted Owl*, from *On The Harbor, From Black Friday to Nirvana*, The Daily World, Aberdeen, 2001

Blankenship, Mrs. George E. (Georgiana), *Early History of Thurston County*, Olympia, 1914

Booth, Laurence S., *Unpublished Interview* conducted *on May 26, 1936*, by Adele Parker for the Washington Pioneer Project, Washington State Library Manuscript Collection, MS 31, Box 5, Tumwater, WA.

Booth, Laurence S., *Seattle the Glorious, American Mercury* magazine, January 1933

Boswell, Sharon A., and McConaghy, Lorraine, *Raise Hell and Sell Newspapers, Alden J. Blethen & The Seattle Times*, Washington State University Press, Pullman, 1996

Brazier, Don, *History of the Washington Legislature, 1854-1963*, and *1965-1982*, Washington State Senate, 2000 and 2007

Brewster, David, and Buerge, David M., (editors), *Washingtonians, a Biographical portrait of the state*, Sasquatch Books, Seattle, 1988

Clark, Malcolm Jr., *Eden Seekers, The Settlement of Oregon, 1818-1862*, Houghton Mifflin Co., Boston, 1981

Corning, Howard McKinley, *Willamette Landings*, third edition, Oregon Historical Society Press, Portland, 2004

Crawford, Samuel L., and Conover, Charles T., *Washington the Evergreen state, and Seattle: its metropolis*, Crawford & Conover Realtors, Seattle, 1890, Washington State Library Rare Book Collection, Tumwater, WA.

Cross, Charles R., *Room Full of Mirrors*, a biography of Jimi Hendrix, Hyperion, New York, 2005

Dobbs, Caroline C., *Men of Champoeg*, Metropolitan Press, Portland, 1932; reprinted 1993, Daughters of the American Revolution, Oregon Society.

Dodds, Gordon B., *Oregon, a Bicentennial History*, W.W. Norton & Co. Inc., New York, 1977

Dolan, Kathleen Adair, *We Lived in the Ghetto of Mental Retardation*, Oral history transcript, Washington State Department of Social & Health Services, Olympia, 1991

Duncan, Don, *Washington, The First 100 Years, 1889-1989*, The Seattle Times, 1989

Ficken, Robert E., and LeWarne, Charles P., *Washington, A Centennial History*, University of Washington Press, Seattle, 1989.

French, Hiram Taylor, *History of Idaho*, Lewis Publishing Co., Chicago & New York, 1914

Friedman, Ralph, *Tracking Down Oregon*, The Caxton Printers, Caldwell, Idaho, 1984

Gardner, William Booth, *Gubernatorial Scrapbooks* (microfilm), 1985-1991, Washington State Archives, Olympia.

Hodgins, Randy, and McLellan, Steve, *Wet and Wired, a pop culture encyclopedia of the Pacific Northwest*, Taylor Publishing Co., Dallas, 2000

Hunt, Herbert, *Tacoma—Its History and Its Builders*, Vol. lll , S.J. Clarke Publishing Co. Chicago, 1916, rare book collection, Washington State Library, Tumwater, WA

Hussey, John A., *Champoeg: Place of Transition*, Oregon Historical Society, Portland, 1967

Hutchison, Sheryl, *The Gardner Years*, Washington State Printer, 1993

Johansen, Dorothy O., and Gates, Charles M., *Empire of the Columbia*, second edition, Harper & Row, New York, 1967

Kershner, Jim, *Carl Maxey, A Fighting Life*; University of Washington Press, Seattle, 2008

Kink, Steve, and Cahill, John, Class *Wars, The story of the Washington Education Association, 1965-2001*; WEA and History Ink, Seattle, 2004.

Lewis Historical Publishing Co., *Washington Northwest Frontier Volume IV*, New York, 1957

Lujan, Herman D., *The Gardner Transition: The Changing of the Guard in Washington*, from *Gubernatorial Transitions: the 1983 and 1984 Elections*; Beyle, Thad L., editor, Duke University Press, 1989.

Meany, Edmond S., *Living Pioneers of Washington*, a collection of columns that first appeared in the *Seattle Post-Intelligencer*, 1915-1920, Seattle Genealogical Society, 1995

Morgan, Murray, *Skid Road*, Revised edition, The Viking Press, New York, 1960

Morrison, Dorothy Nafus, *Outpost, John McLoughlin & the Far Northwest*, Oregon Historical Society Press, Portland, 1999

Newell, Gordon, *Rogues, Buffoons & Statesmen*, Superior Publishing Co., Seattle, 1975

Newell, Gordon, and Sherwood, Don, *Totem Tales of Old Seattle*, Superior Publishing Co., Seattle, 1956

Oakley, Obadiah, *Expedition to Oregon*, Ye Galleon Press, Fairfield, WA, 1967

Sale, Roger, *Seattle Past to Present*, University of Washington Press, Seattle, 1978

Schwartzberg, Susan, *Becoming Citizens: Family Life and the Politics of Disability*, University of Washington Press, Seattle, 2005.

Scott, George W., *A Majority of One: Legislative Life*, Civitas Press, Seattle, 2002

Seattle Genealogical Society, *Seattle Fire Department*, 1889, Seattle, 1989

Seeberger, Edward D., *Sine Die, A Guide to the Washington State Legislative Process*, 1997 Edition, University of Washington Press, Seattle, 1997

Sensel, Joni, *Traditions Through the Trees, Weyerhaeuser's First 100 years*, Documentary Book Publishers, Seattle, 1999

Smith, Payton, Rosellini, Immigrants' Son and Progressive Governor, University of Washington Press, Seattle, 1997

Snowden, Clinton A., *History of Washington, The Rise and Progress of an American State*, Volumes II and IV, The Century History Co., New York, 1909, 1911

Spencer and Pollard, *A History of the State of Washington, Volume III*, American Historical Society, New York, 1937

State of Washington Members of the Legislature, *1889-2005*, with appendix on Territorial Assembly, 1854-1887, Legislative Information Center, Olympia, 2005

The Great Northwest, the Story of a Land and its People, by the editors of *American West*, American West Publishing Co., Palo Alto, CA, 1973

Tobie, Harvey E., *No Man Like Joe*, Binfords & Mort, for the Oregon Historical Society, Portland, 1949

Told by the Pioneers, Volumes II and III, Washington Pioneer Project, directed by the Office of the Secretary of State, 1938

Twining, Charles E., *Phil Weyerhaeuser Lumberman*, University of Washington Press, 1985

Vedder, O.F., and Lyman, H.S., *History of Seattle, Washington, with illustrations and biographical sketches of some of its Prominent Men and Pioneers*, American Publishing & Engraving Co., 1891, New York

Victor, Frances Fuller, *River of the West*, R.W. Bliss & Co., Hartford, CT,1870, reprinted by Long's College Book Co., Columbus Ohio, 1950

A Volume of Memoirs and Genealogy of Representative Citizens of the City of Seattle and County of King, Washington, Lewis Publishing Co., New York and Chicago, 1903

Warren, James R., *The Day Seattle Burned*, Lasergraphics, Seattle, 1989

Washington Northwest Frontier Volume IV, Lewis Historical Publishing Co., New York, 1957

Washington Pioneer Index, Washington State Genealogical Society, Washington State Library, Tumwater, WA.

Washington West of the Cascades, Volume III, S.J. Clarke Publishing Co., Chicago, Seattle, Tacoma, 1917

Wolfe, Wellington C., *Sketches of Washington 1907*, Washington State Library, Tumwater, WA.

Electronic sources:

Dolliver, James M., oral history by the Office of the Secretary of State. 1999 http://www.sos.wa.gov/legacyproject/collection/pdf/dolliver.pdf

Ferguson, Adele, oral history by The Legacy Project of the Office of the Secretary of State, 2009 http://www.sos.wa.gov/legacyproject/oralhistories/AdeleFerguson/default.aspx

Smith, Charles Z., oral history by The Legacy Project of the Office of the Secretary of State, 2009 http://www.sos.wa.gov/legacyproject/oralhistories/CharlesZSmith/default.aspx

HistoryLink.org essays:

Chesley, Frank, *Washington State Taxation* (Essay 5735), 2004 http://www.historylink.org/index.cfm?DisplayPage=output.cfm&file_id=5735

Crowley, Walt, *Seattle Burns Down* (Essay 5115), 2003 http://www.historylink.org/index.cfm?DisplayPage=output.cfm&file_id=5115

Lange, Greg, *Seattle's Great Fire* (Essay 715), 1999 http://www.historylink.org/index.cfm?DisplayPage=output.cfm&file_id=715

McClary, Daryl C., *McNeil Island and the Federal Penitentiary, 1841-1981* (Essay 5238), 2003 http://www.historylink.org/index.cfm?DisplayPage=output.cfm&file_id=5238

Oldham, Kit, *Washington Legislature Enacts Growth Management Act*, (Essay 7759), 2006 http://www.historylink.org/index.cfm?DisplayPage=output.cfm&File_Id=7759

Tallman, Tracy, *Woodway* (Essay 8572), 2008 http://www.historylink.org/index.cfm?DisplayPage=output.cfm&file_id=8572

Tate, Cassandra, *Norton Clapp* (Essay 7295), 2005 http://www.historylink.org/index.cfm?DisplayPage=output.cfm&file_id=7295

Wilma, David, *Mayor Hiram C. Gil* (Essay 2755), 2000 http://www.historylink.org/index.cfm?DisplayPage=output.cfm&file_id=2755

Other electronic:

The Great Seattle Fire, an essay in the University of Washington Digital Collections, http://content.lib.washington.edu/extras/seattle-fire.html

TVW interview of Booth Gardner by Denny Heck, May 22, 2000: http://www.tvw.org/media/mediaplayer.cfm?evid=2000050079&TYPE=V&CFID=3245411&CFTOKEN=27106557&bhcp=1

TVW presentation featuring some of Booth's favorite stories, Feb. 21, 2007: http://www.tvw.org/media/mediaplayer.cfm?evid=2007020185&TYPE=V&CFID=3245411&CFTOKEN=27106557&bhcp=1

TVW coverage of the April 26, 2008, Death with Dignity debate between Booth Gardner and Duane French: http://www.tvw.org/media/mediaplayer.cfm?evid=2008040112&TYPE=V&CFID=3389892&CFTOKEN=81964608&bhcp=1

Chronology on "assisted dying": http://www.deathwithdignity.org/historyfacts/chronology.asp

Washington Death with Dignity timeline: http://www.deathwithdignity.org/media/uploads/WashingtonDWDTimeline120408.pdf

Five former governors: Gary Locke welcomes Booth to Al Rosellini's 100th birthday party in January 2010 as Dan Evans, John Spellman, and Mike Lowry look on. *Photo courtesy Weldon Wilson.*

John C. Hughes joined the Office of the Secretary of State as chief oral historian in 2008 after a 42-year career in journalism, retiring as editor and publisher of *The Daily World* at Aberdeen. An award-winning investigative reporter, columnist and historian, he is a trustee of the Washington State Historical Society and a former president of Allied Daily Newspapers of Washington. He first met Booth Gardner in 1971 while covering the state Legislature.

INDEX